I0566937

"Don't only practice your art, but
force your way into its secrets."

- Ludwig van Beethoven

HERMANN
—PRESS—

Copyright © 2024 by Damian Hermann

All rights reserved.

First edition

ISBN 978-1-964383-16-3

Published by

www.HermannPress.com

All rights reserved. No part of this work may be reproduced in any form or by any means (electronic, mechanical, photocopying, recording, or other methods) without the prior written permission of the copyright holder. This work may not be processed, duplicated, or distributed using electronic systems.

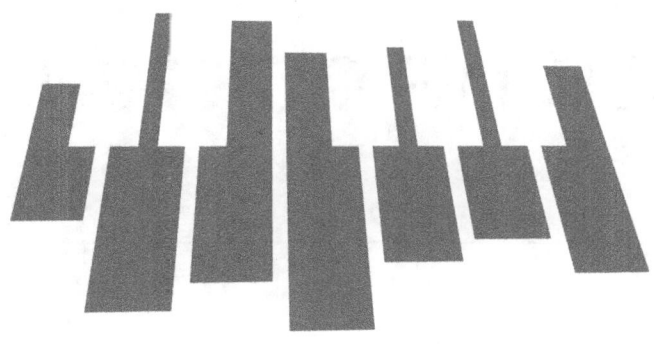

PIANO NOTE READING

WORKBOOK

Draw and Practice with 300+ Exercises

TABLE OF CONTENTS

Introduction

Chapter 1: Introduction to Reading Music

Chapter 2: Measures, Note Values & Rests

Chapter 3: Pitch & Key Signature

Chapter 4: Time Signature & Rhythm

Solutions

About This Book

Music is a language that anyone can learn, and you have already taken the first step by picking up this book.

In this book, you will be introduced to the basics of reading music in a clear and understandable way. With 75 practice sheets, each containing between 4 and 8 exercises, you will have access to well over 300 practical exercises in total. This will allow you to apply and deepen your newly acquired knowledge.

Although music theory is a vast field, and each topic could be explored in much greater depth, this book focuses on the four key areas that are especially important for beginners.

Our aim is to provide you with a solid foundation that enables you to learn wonderful pieces of music, write your own compositions, or further develop your skills in the world of music.

I wish you much joy, inspiration, and success on your musical journey!

Development of Music Notation

The origins of notation trace can be traced back to ancient Greece, but it was not until the Middle Ages that Western notation took shape, with the spread of writing in monasteries and educational institutions across Europe.

Guido of Arezzo revolutionized music notation in the 11th century with the line system, which more precisely defined pitches. Later, rhythmic symbols were added, and by the Baroque period (around 1750), notating music for orchestras and ensembles in scores became common, leading to the modern musical notation that is still used today.

The development of musical notation brought enormous benefits. It enabled the communication of musical pieces across space and time, allowing composers like Bach, Mozart, and Beethoven to record their works and pass them on to other musicians.

Without notation, many masterpieces of music history would have been lost. Moreover, the ability to read music opened new avenues for analyzing and interpreting musical structures and forms.

Today, written notes are a central element of music education. They are used to compose and document arrangements and compositions in classical music, popular music, and jazz.

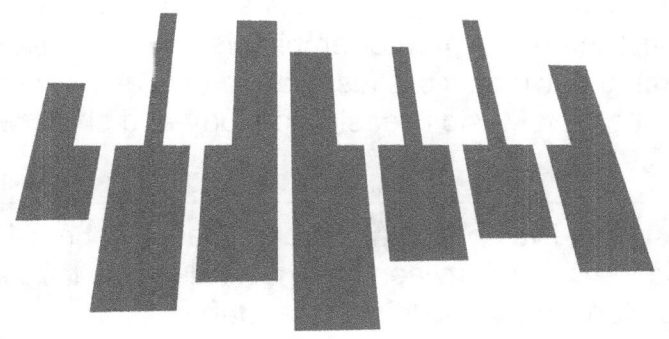

Chapter 1

Introduction to Reading Music

1. Grand Staff

2. Musical Clef

3. Exercises

Musical Staff

People spoke long before they invented writing. Similarly, people made music long before anyone wrote music down. Some musicians still play "by ear" (without notes), and in some musical traditions, there is a greater emphasis on improvisation and/or learning "by ear." Nonetheless, writing down music is also very practical for many of the same reasons that written words are helpful. Music is easier to study and share when it is written down.

The musical staff consists of five horizontal, parallel lines. Most musical notes are placed on one of these lines or in the space between the lines. Additional ledger lines can be added to represent a note that is too high or too low for the staff.

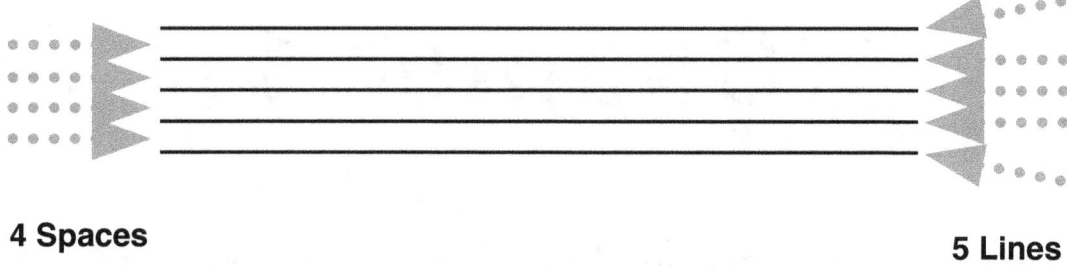

4 Spaces   **5 Lines**

Components of the Musical Staff

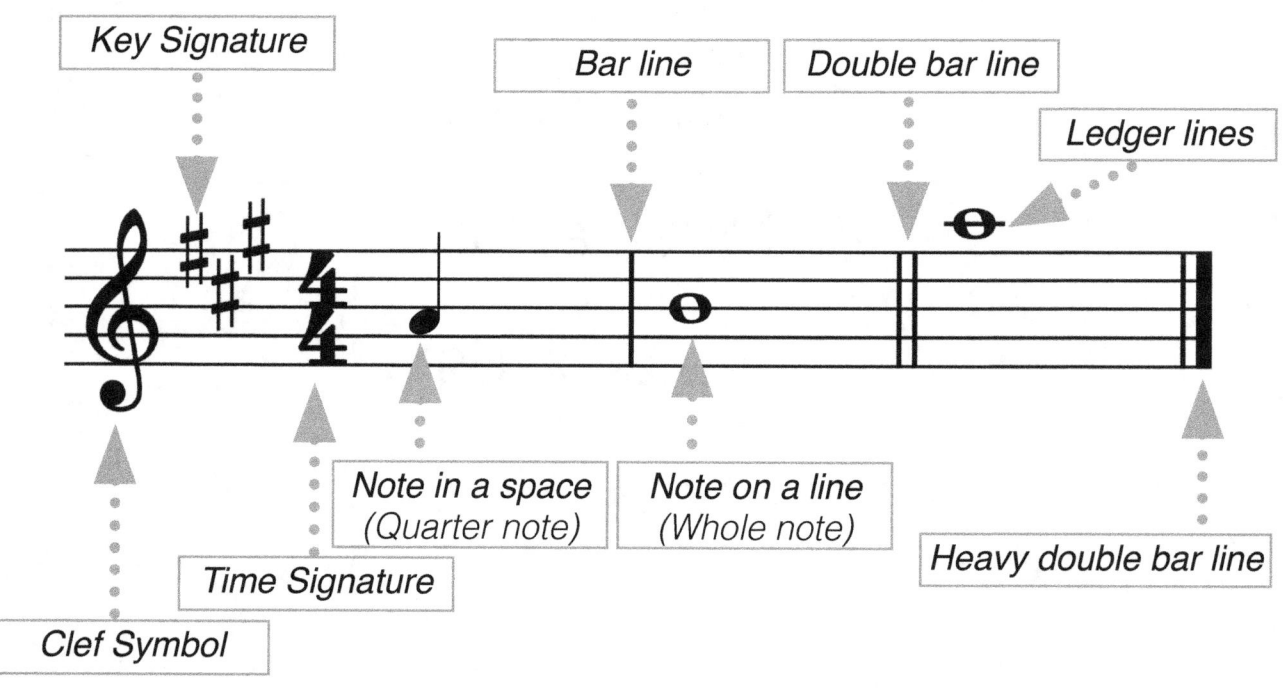

Vertical bar lines divide the staff into short sections called measures or bars. A double bar line, either heavy or light, is used to indicate the end of larger sections of music, including the end of a piece of music, which is marked by a heavy double bar.

Clefs

The first symbol that appears at the beginning of every staff is a clef. It is very important because it indicates which note (C, D, E, F, G, A, and B) is on which line or in which space.

The Treble Clef

For example, a treble clef indicates that the second line from the bottom (the line around which the symbol curls) is a "G." On every staff, the notes are always arranged such that the next letter is always on the next higher line or in the next higher space. After the letter G, the next letter is always an A.

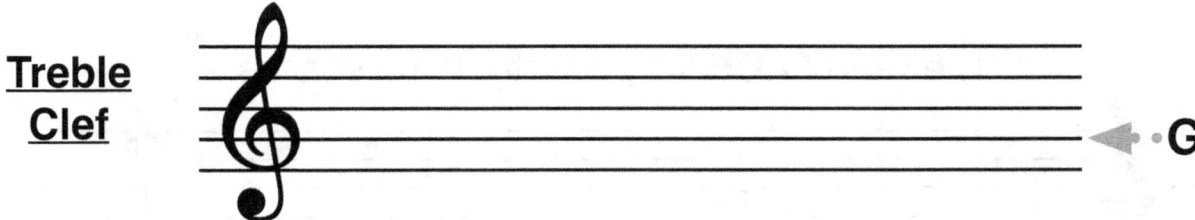

The Bass Clef

A bass clef shows that the second line from the top, marked by the symbol's dots, represents an "F." The notes are arranged in ascending order, but their positions differ from those in the treble clef.

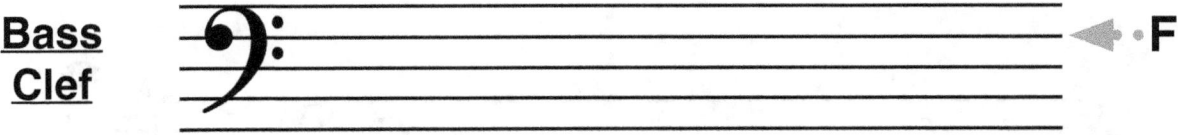

Movable Clefs

Most musical compositions today are written in either the bass clef or treble clef, so this book primarily focuses on these two clefs. However, some pieces are notated using the C clef.

The C clef is movable, with its central point indicating *middle C* (refer to page 9 for information on middle C). It's important to note that the same position on the staff represents different pitches across different clefs.

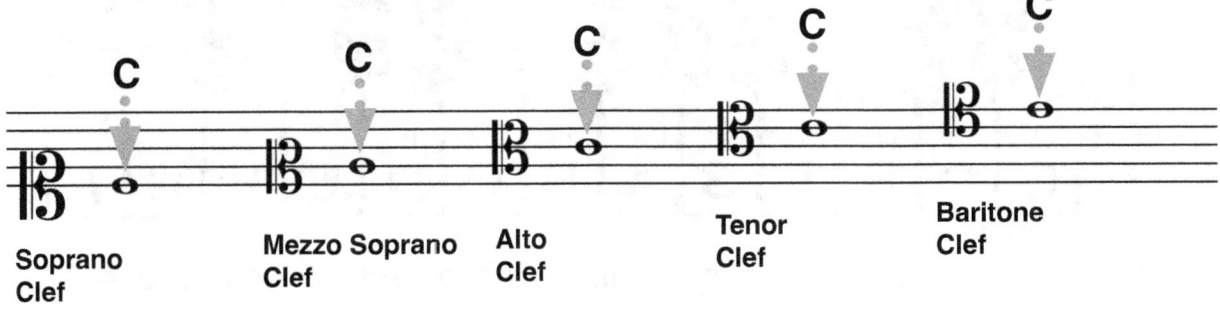

Notes in the Treble Clef (G Clef)

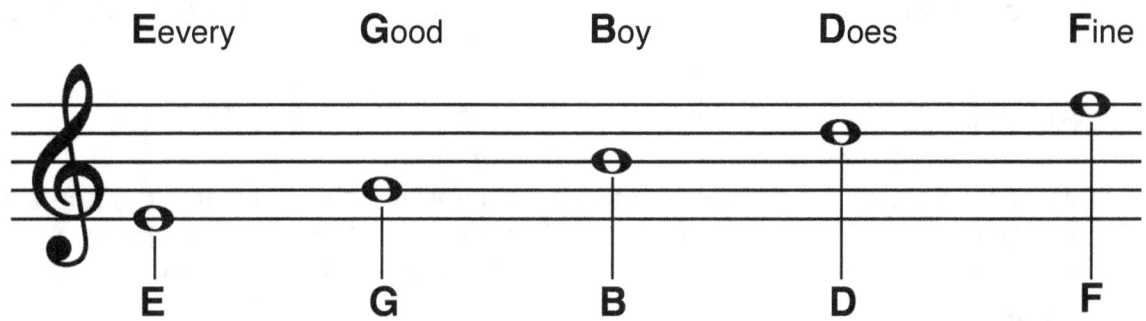

The word **FACE** fits perfectly in the spaces.

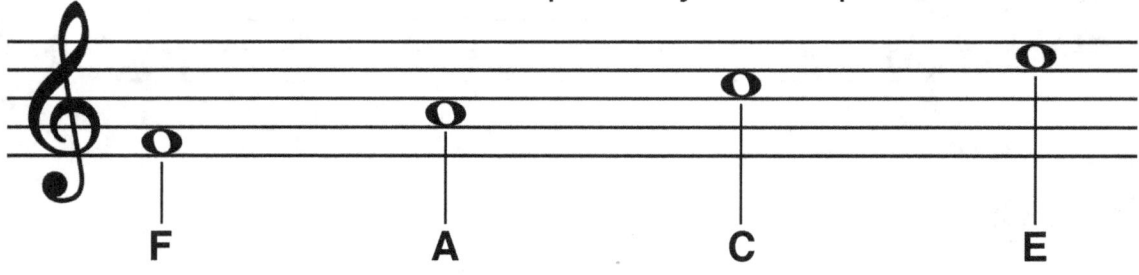

Although the traditional approach is helpful, it is easier to understand that the musical alphabet (A B C D E F G) ascends the lines and spaces on the staff.

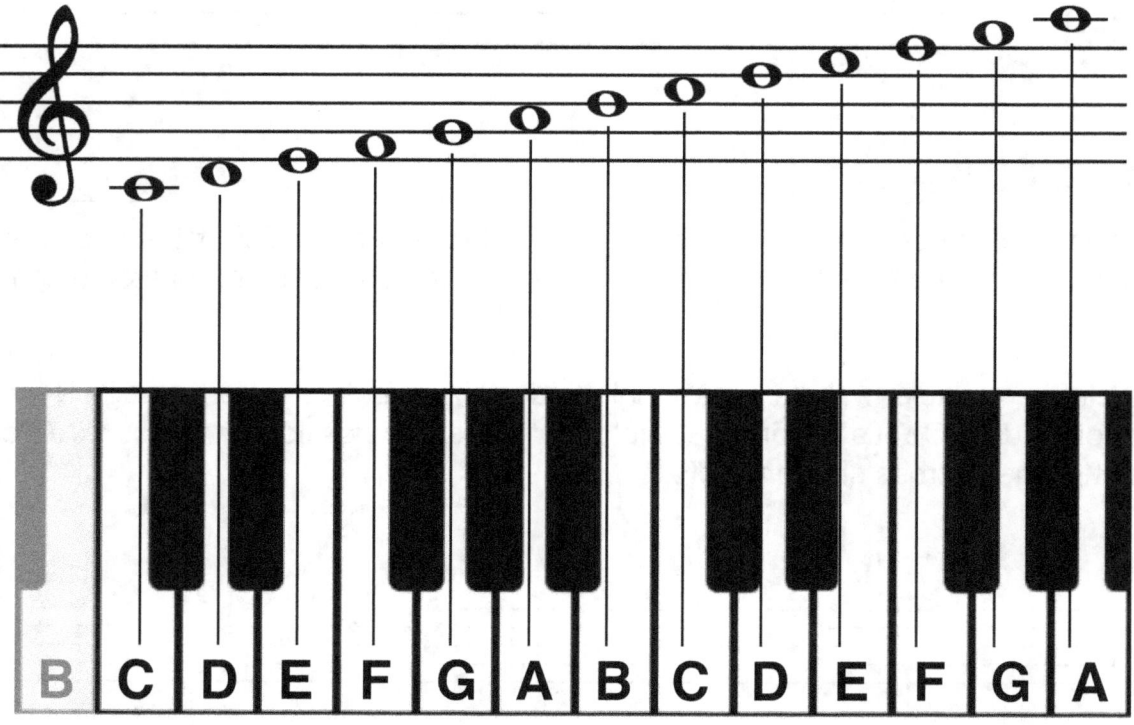

The natural notes correspond to all the white keys on the keyboard.

Notes in the Bass Clef (F Clef)

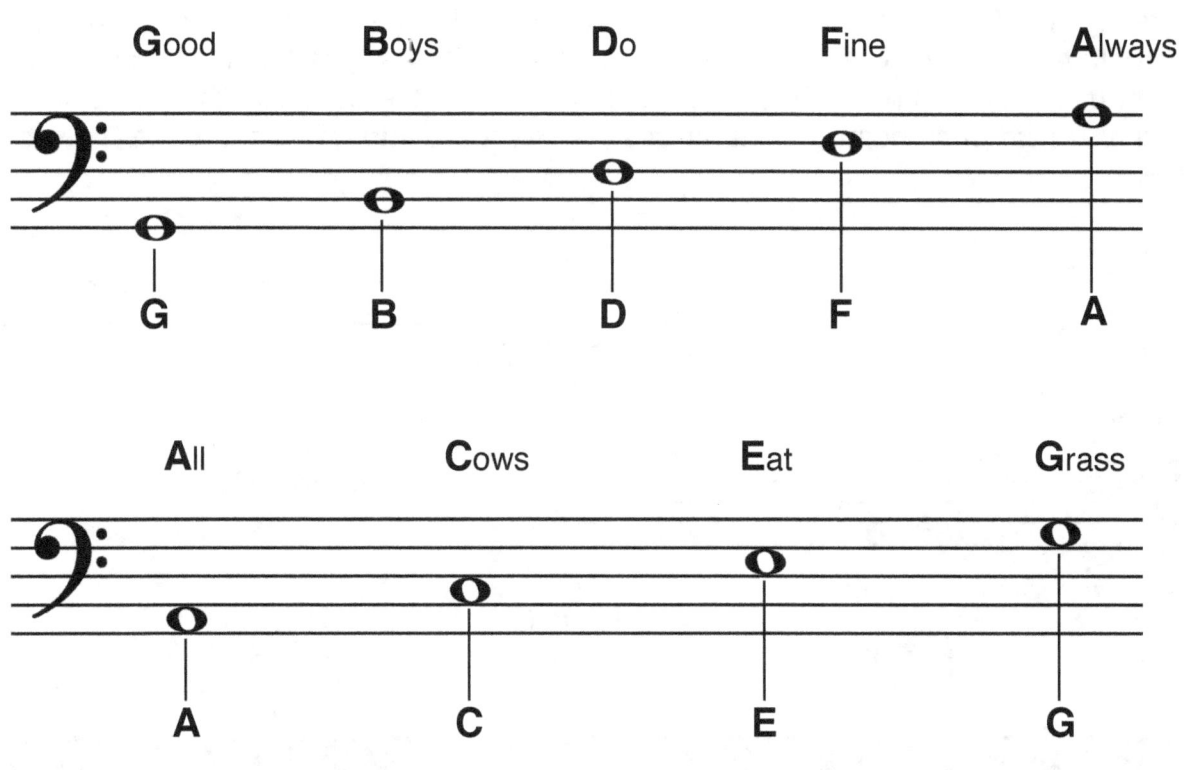

Good **B**oys **D**o **F**ine **A**lways

G B D F A

All **C**ows **E**at **G**rass

A C E G

Although the traditional approach is helpful, it is easier to understand that the musical alphabet (A B C D E F G) ascends the lines and spaces on the staff.

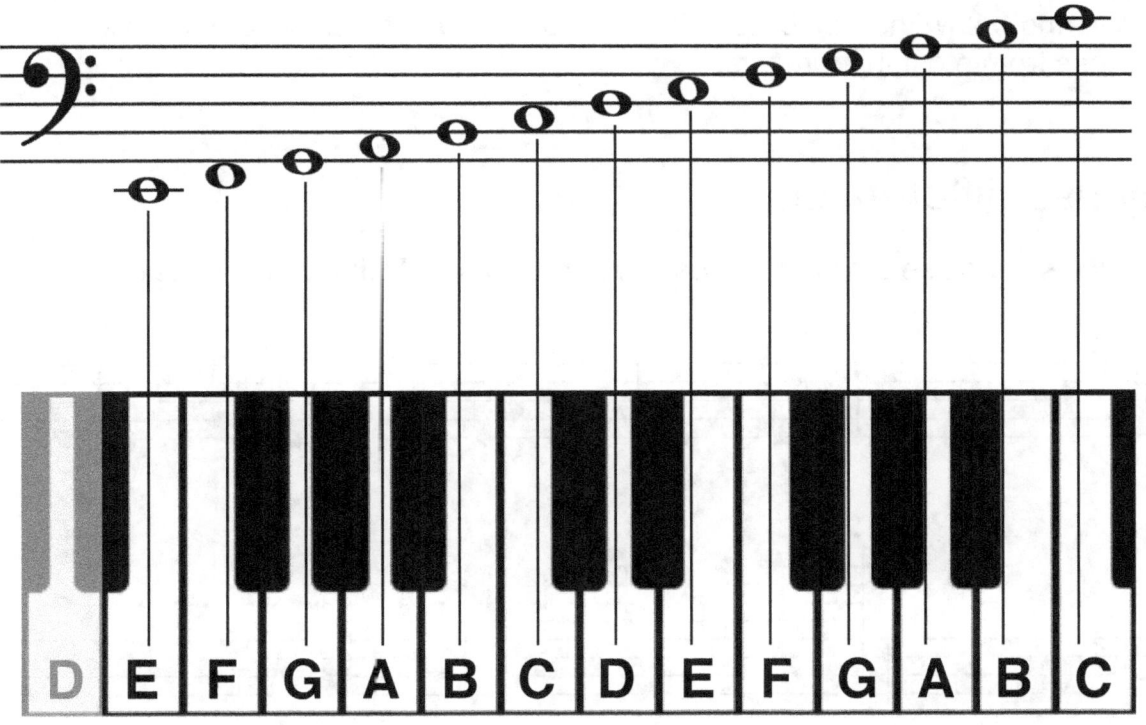

The natural notes correspond to all the white keys on the keyboard.

Grand Staff

A full keyboard has 88 keys, starting with the note 'A' and ending with the note 'C.' The letters are numbered with each successive octave, and the first A is thus A1, repeating in each octave up to A8. The same applies to all the C notes. The first is C1, and the last is C8. *Middle C* gets its name because it is located near the center of the piano keyboard, acting as a reference point that separates the keyboard into lower and upper halves.

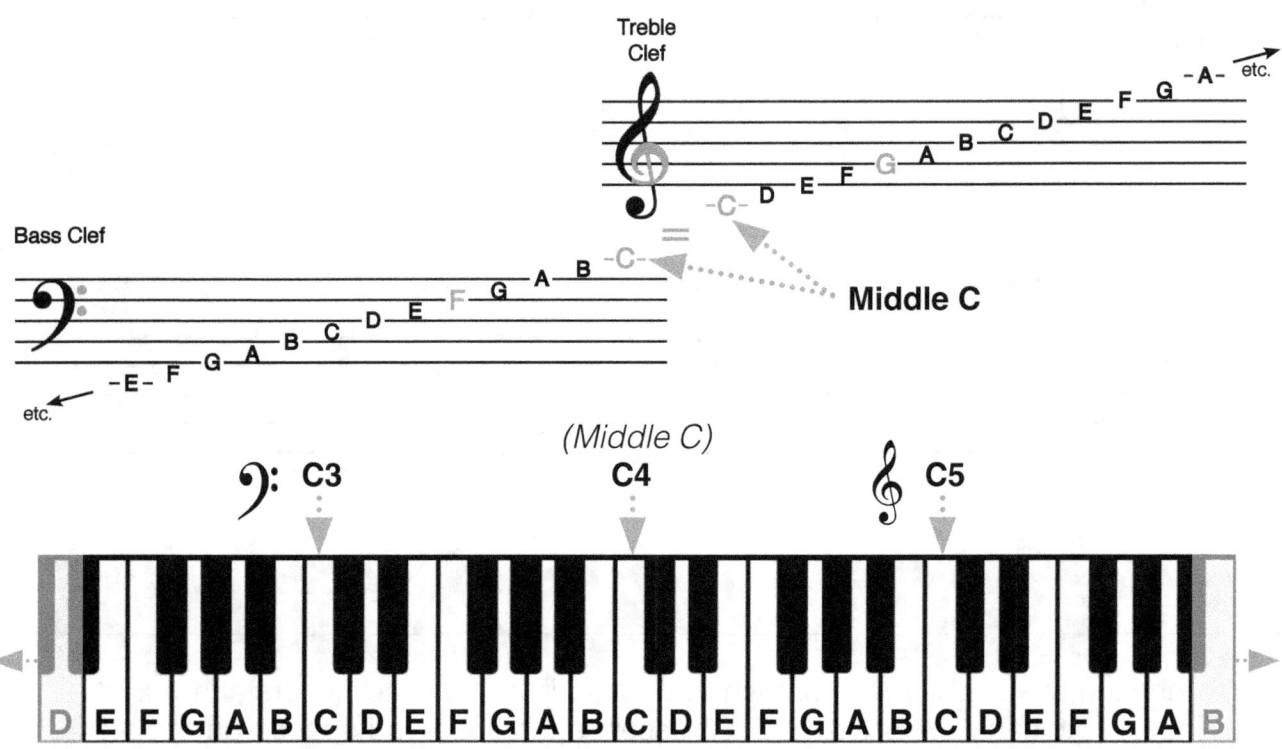

The illustration displays both clefs on the keyboard, with middle C positioned above the bass clef and below the treble clef. Together, these two staves cover the majority of notes and voices from most instruments.

Why use different clefs?

These two scores use the same notes in different clefs. (Treble clef & Bass clef)

In this example, the measures are easier to read and write in the treble clef because fewer ledger lines are used.

Exercise Treble Clef

Practice writing your treble clef symbol on this staff and write at least ten clef symbols.

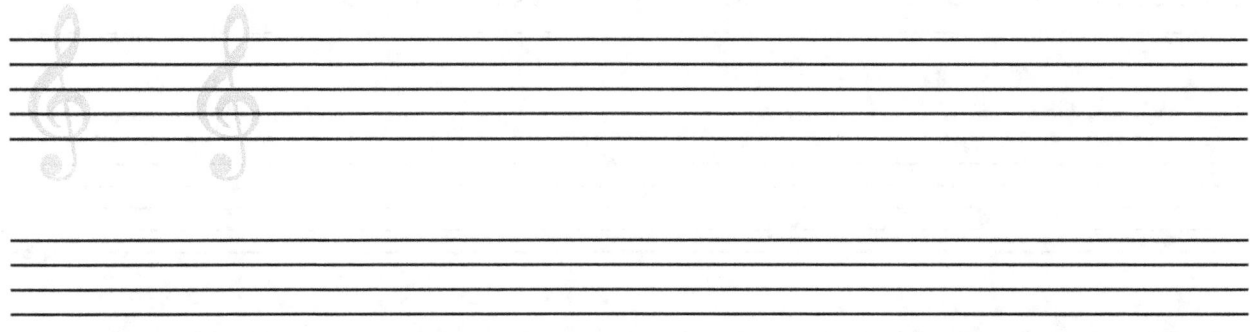

Name the notes of the lines, spaces, and ledger lines in the treble clef.

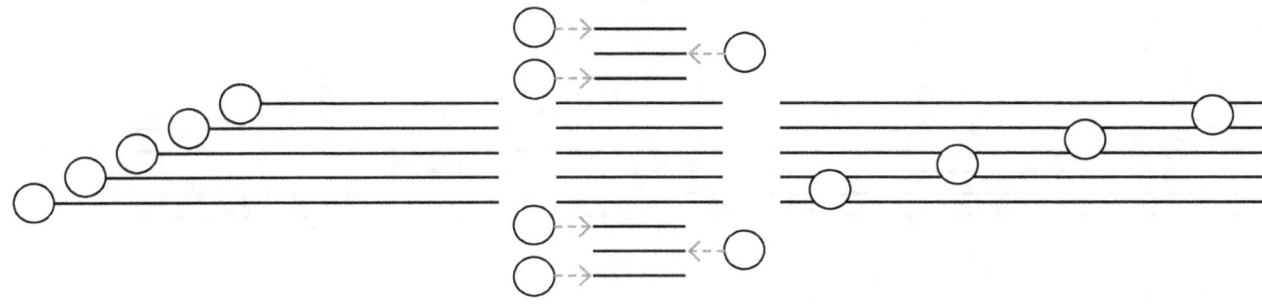

Exercise Bass Clef

Practice writing your bass clef symbol on this staff and write at least ten clef symbols.

Name the notes of the lines, spaces, and ledger lines in the bass clef.

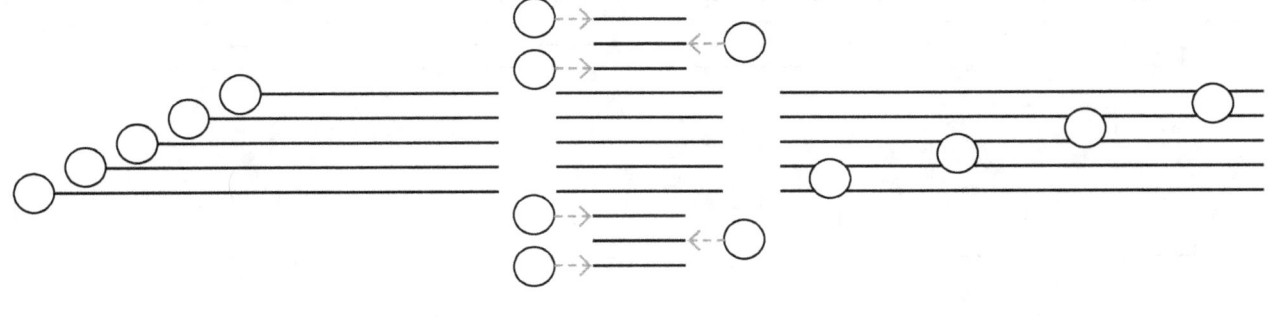

Write the correct **note names** in the boxes. Pay **attention** to the **clefs**.

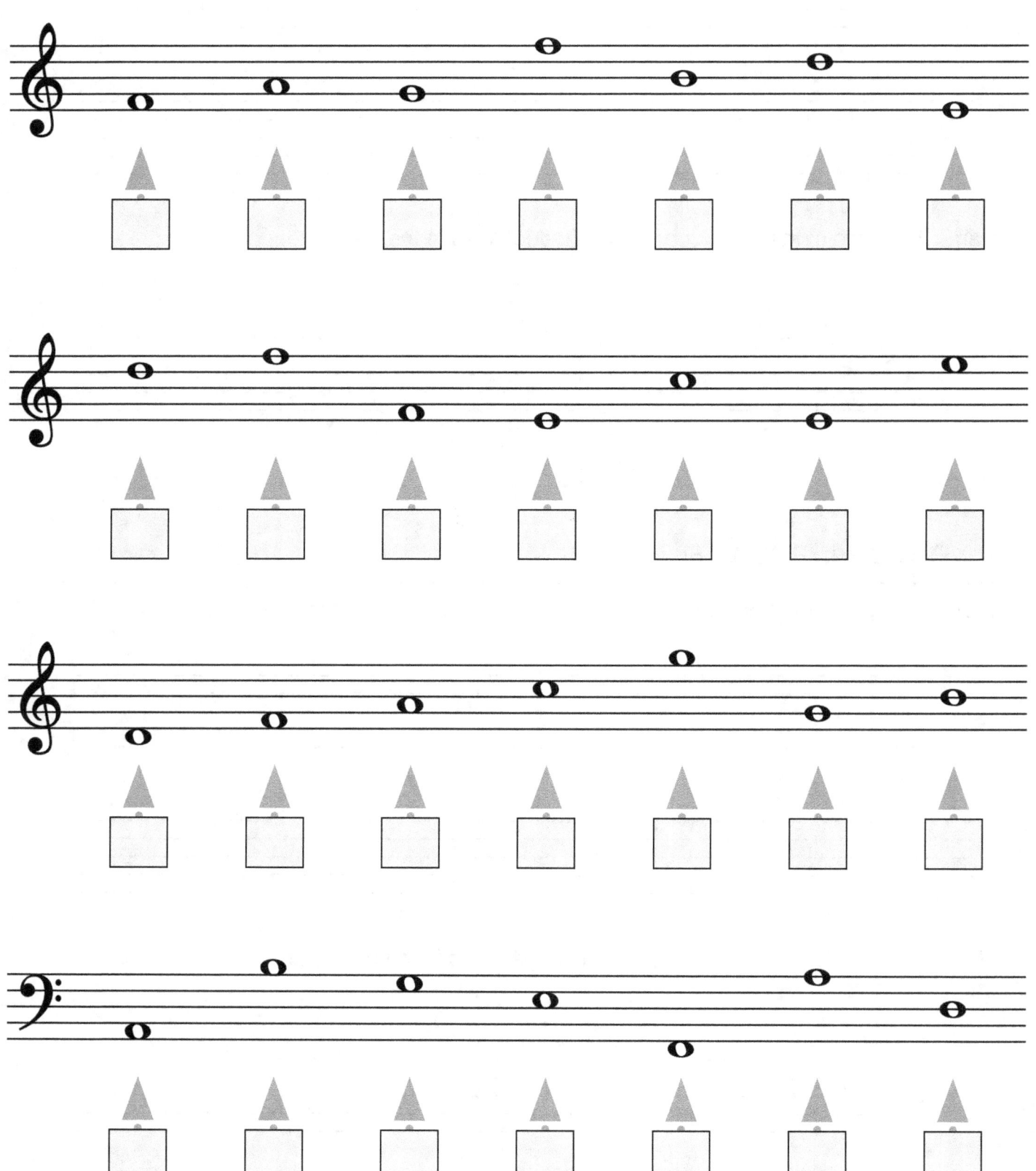

Write the correct **note names** in the boxes. Pay **attention** to / **draw** the **clefs**.

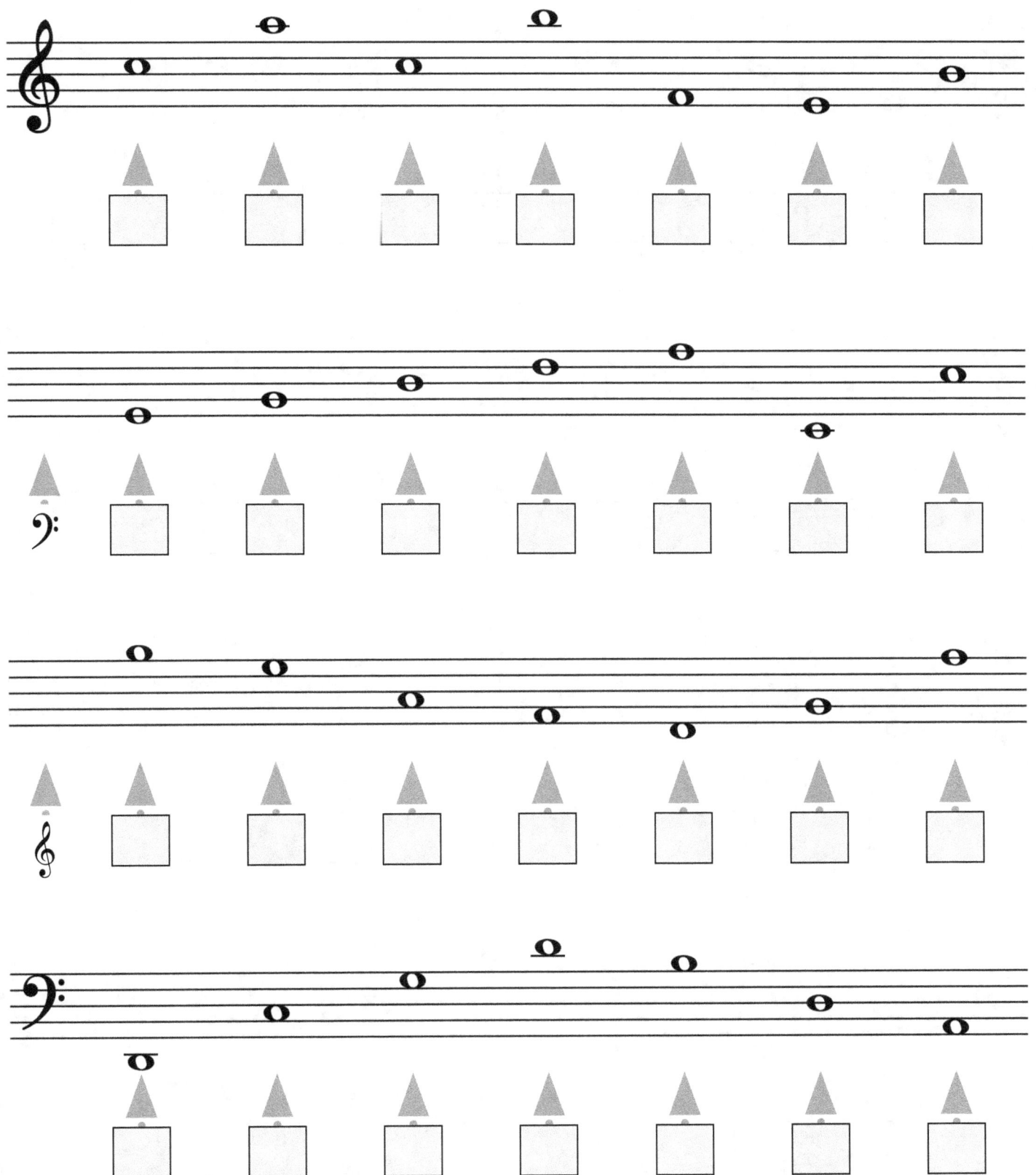

Exercise sheet 04

Write the correct **note names** in the boxes. Pay **attention** to the **clefs**.

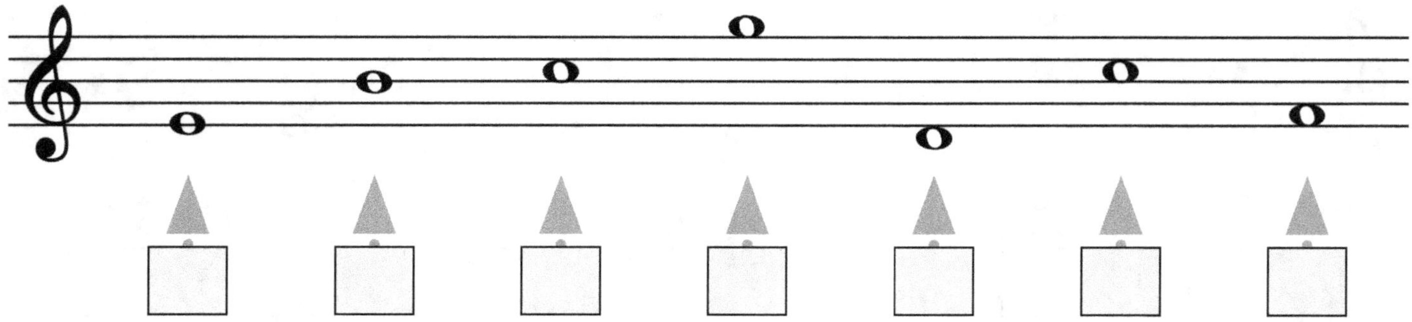

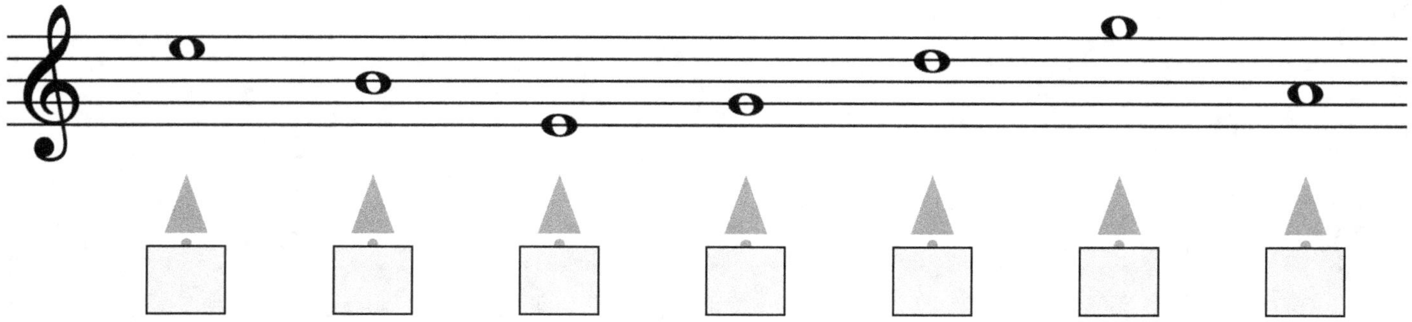

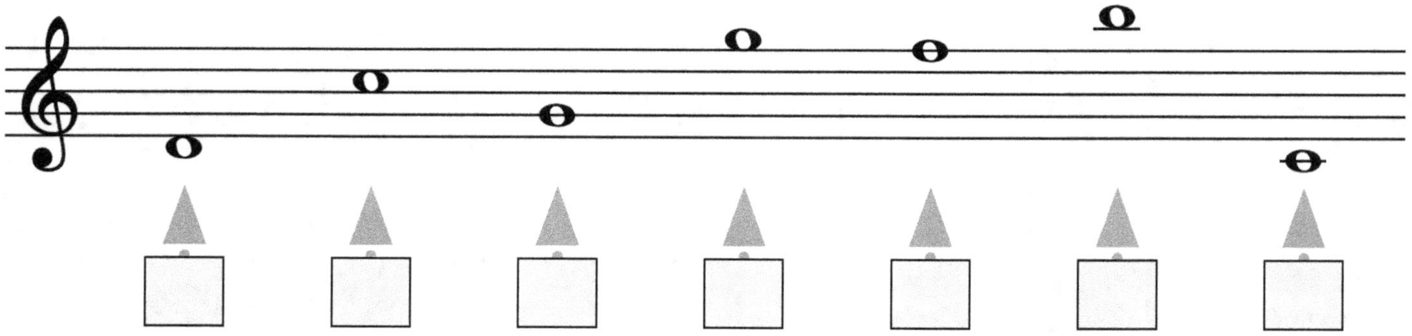

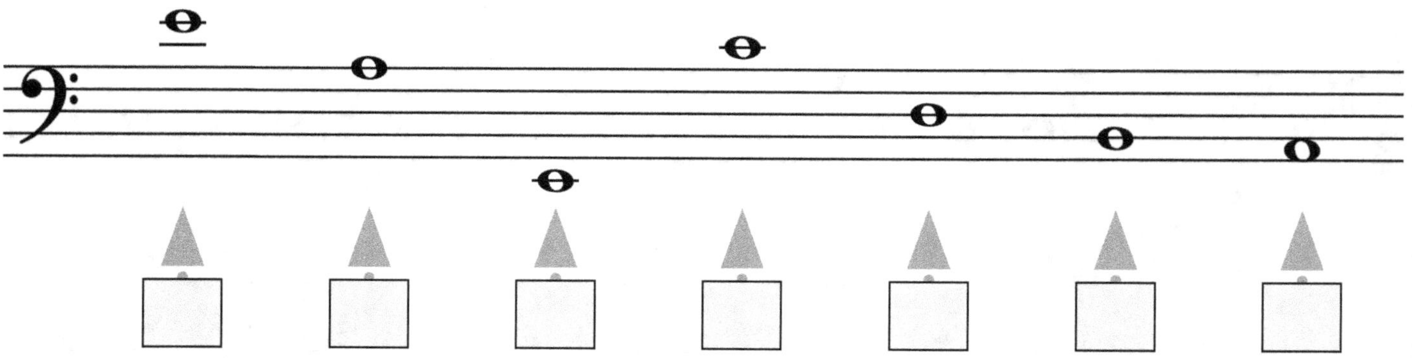

Draw the correct **notes** *(whole notes)* on the staff. Pay **attention** to / **draw** the **clefs**.

  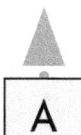    

     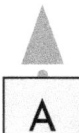  

Draw the correct **notes** *(whole notes)* on the staff. Pay **attention** to / **draw** the **clefs**.

| A | E | C4 | G | F | B | D |

| A | D | B | F | G | E | C3 |

      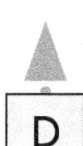

| C6 | E | A | B | G | F | D |

| D | A | C4 | G | A | F | E |

Fill all the **gaps** in the staves / boxes with the correct **notes** and **clefs**.

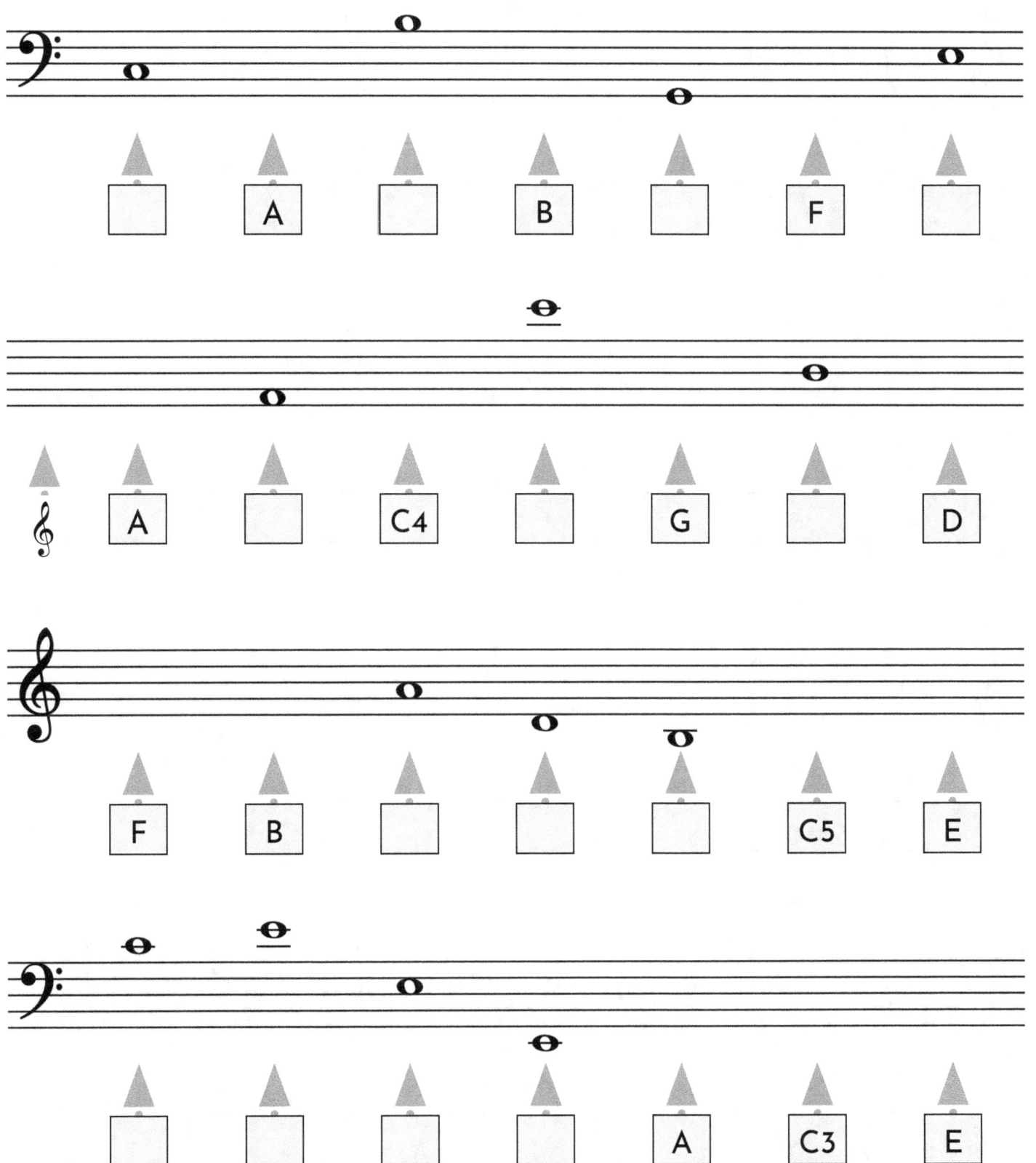

Write the correct note **names** in the boxes. Pay **attention** to and **draw** the **clefs**.

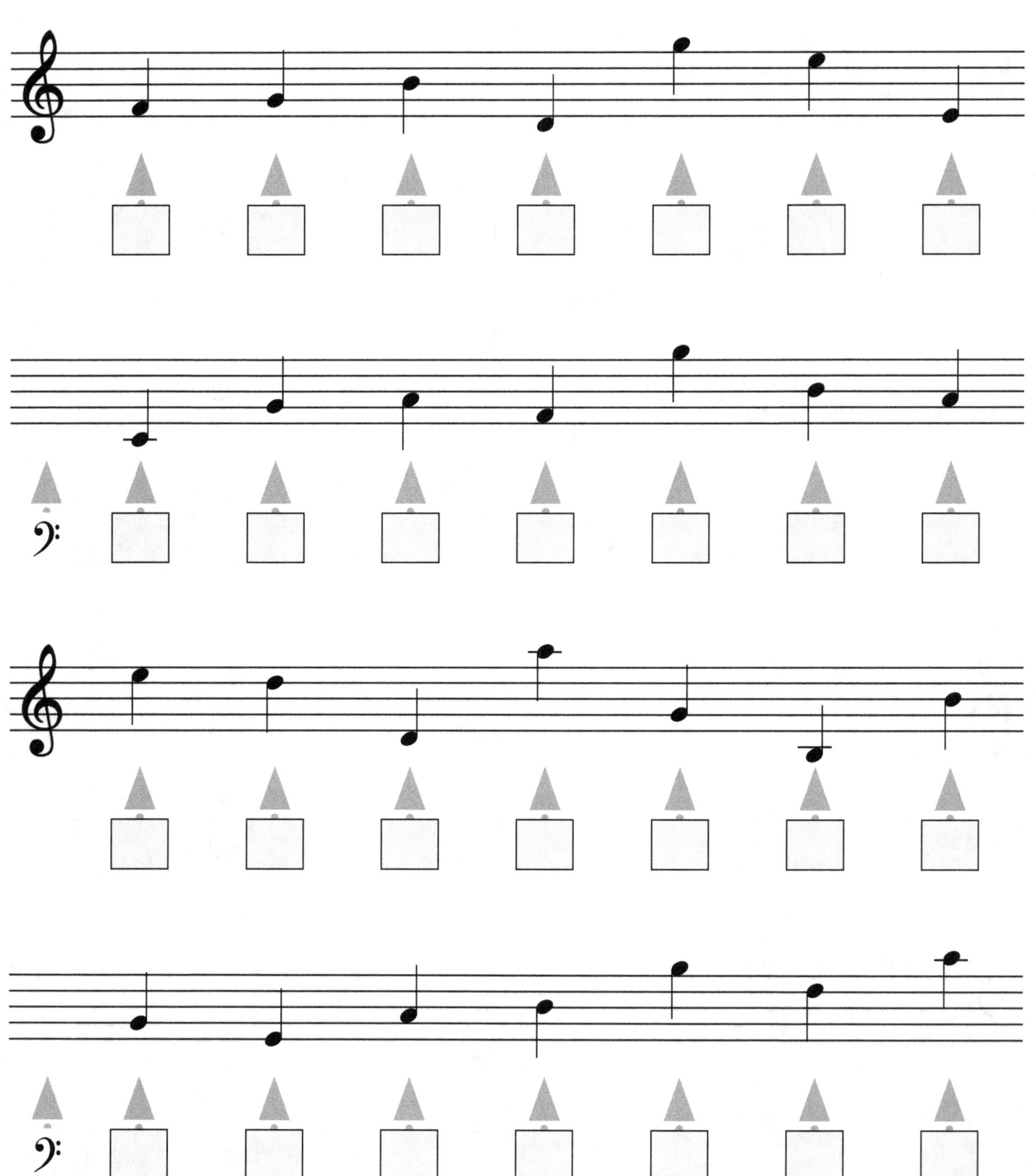

Fill all the **gaps** in the staves / boxes with the correct **notes** and **clefs**.

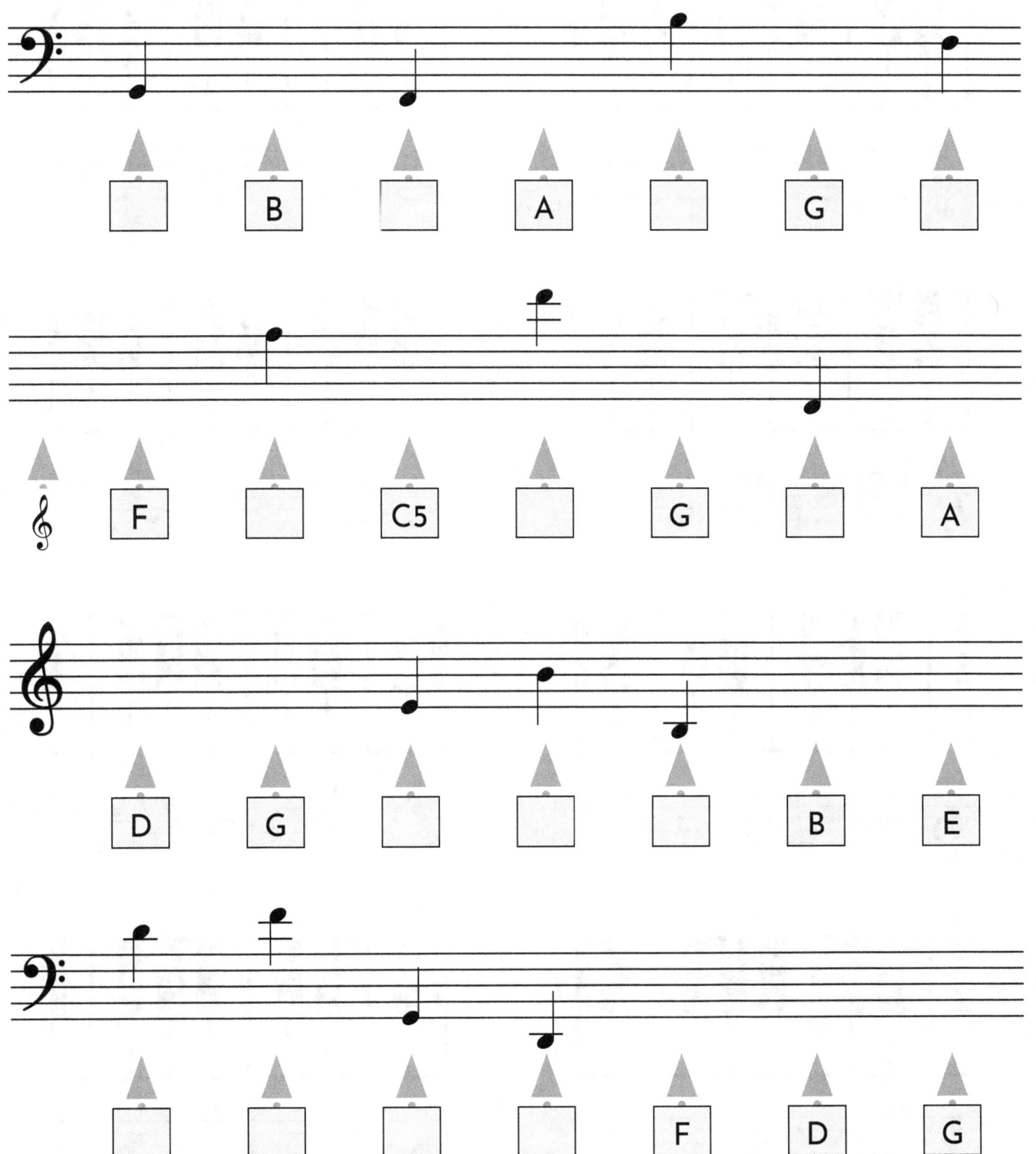

Circle the correct **keys** on the keyboard. Pay **attention** to the keyboard **layout**.

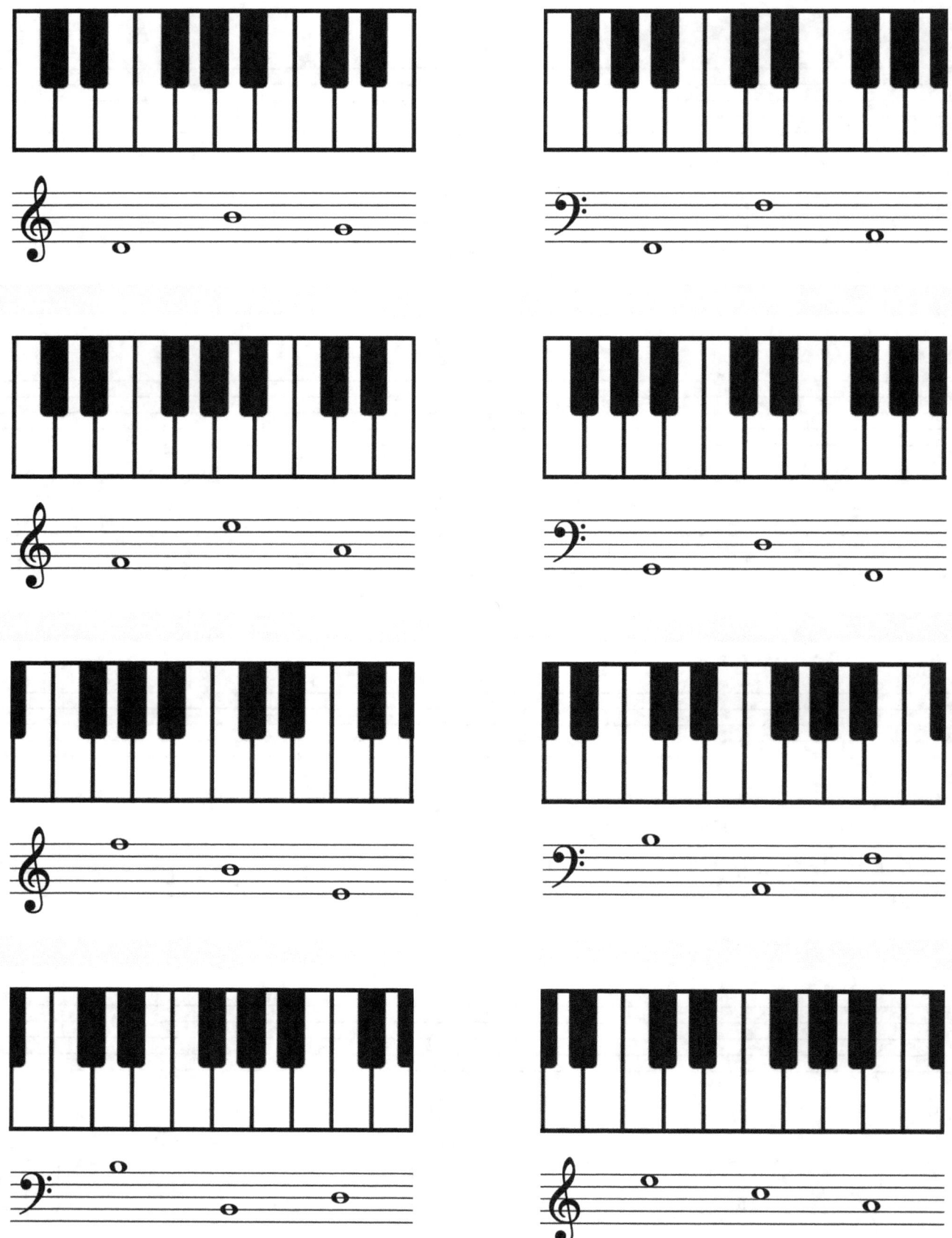

Circle the correct **keys** on the keyboard. Pay **attention** to the keyboard **layout**.

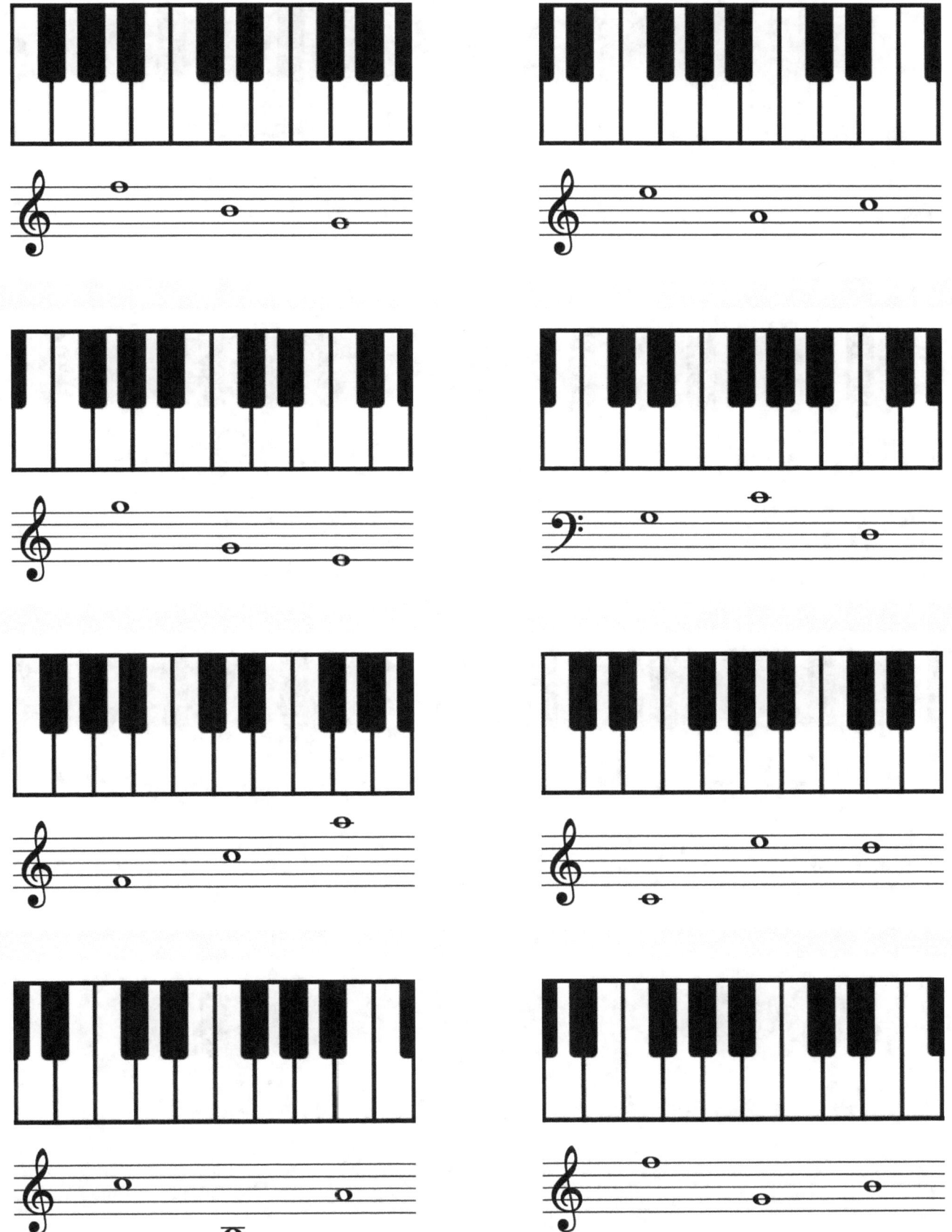

Draw the correct **notes** *(whole notes)* in the staves. Pay **attention** to the **clefs**.

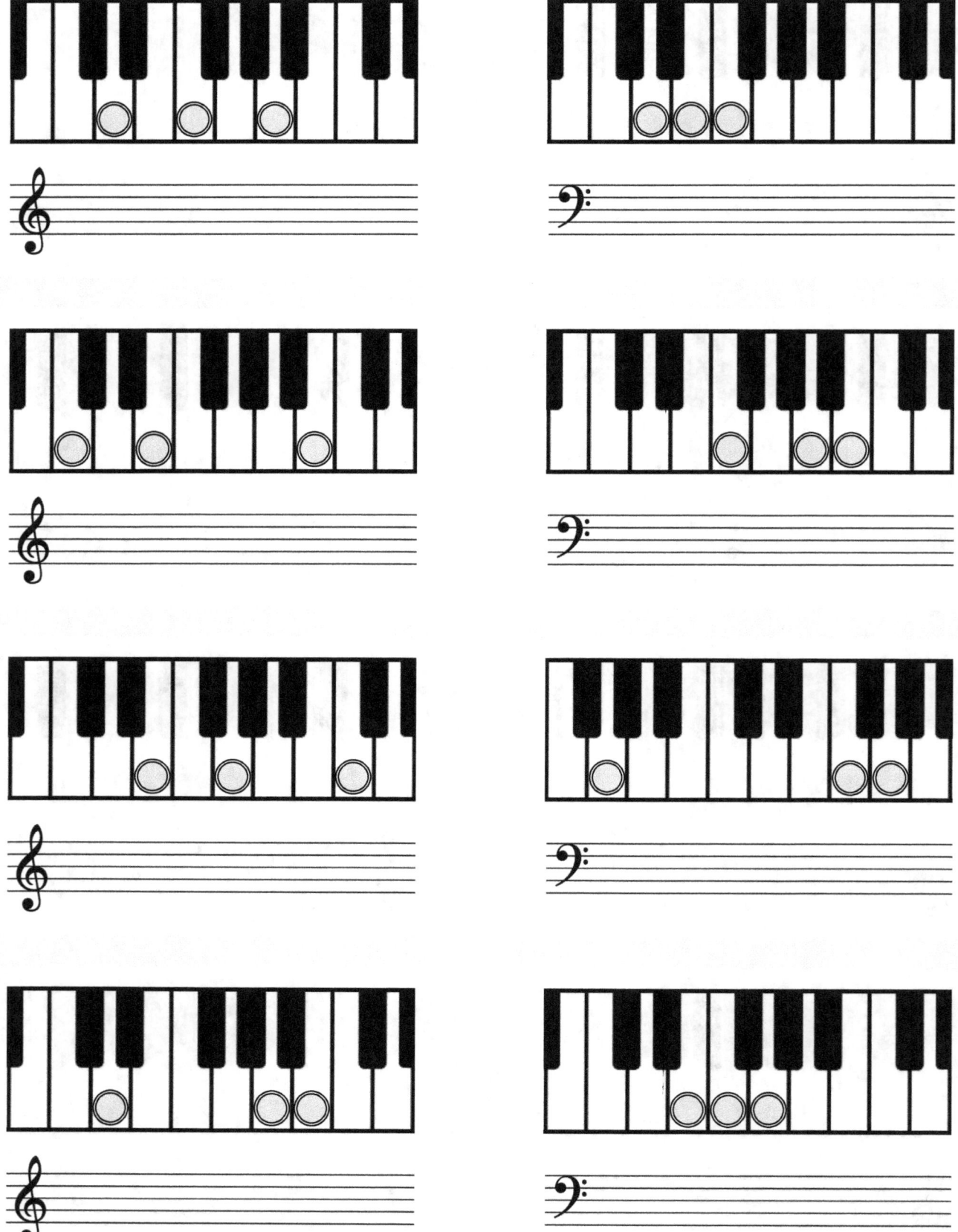

Draw the correct **notes** *(whole notes)* in the staves. Pay **attention** to the **clefs**.

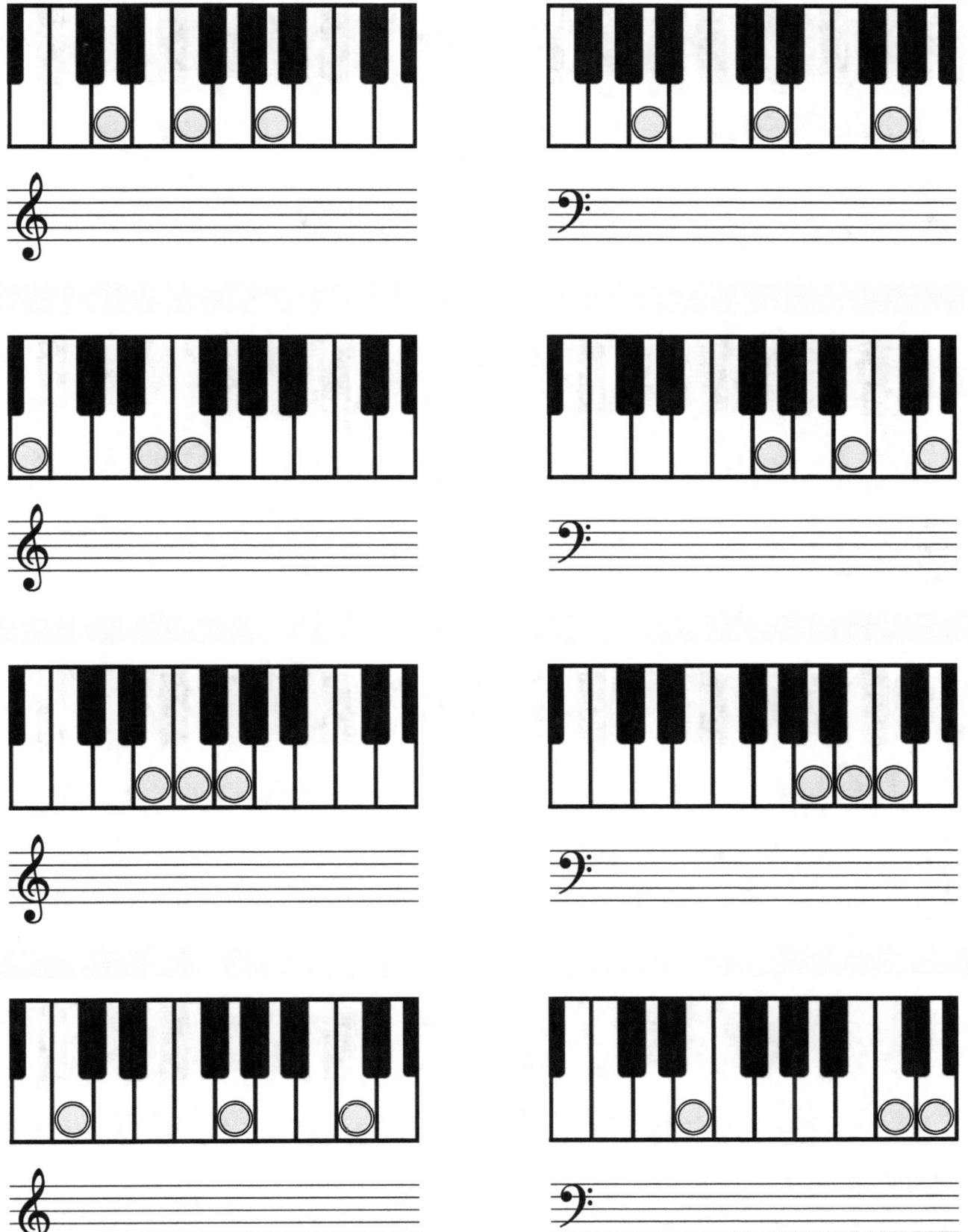

Circle the correct **keys** on the keyboard. Pay **attention** to the keyboard **layout**.

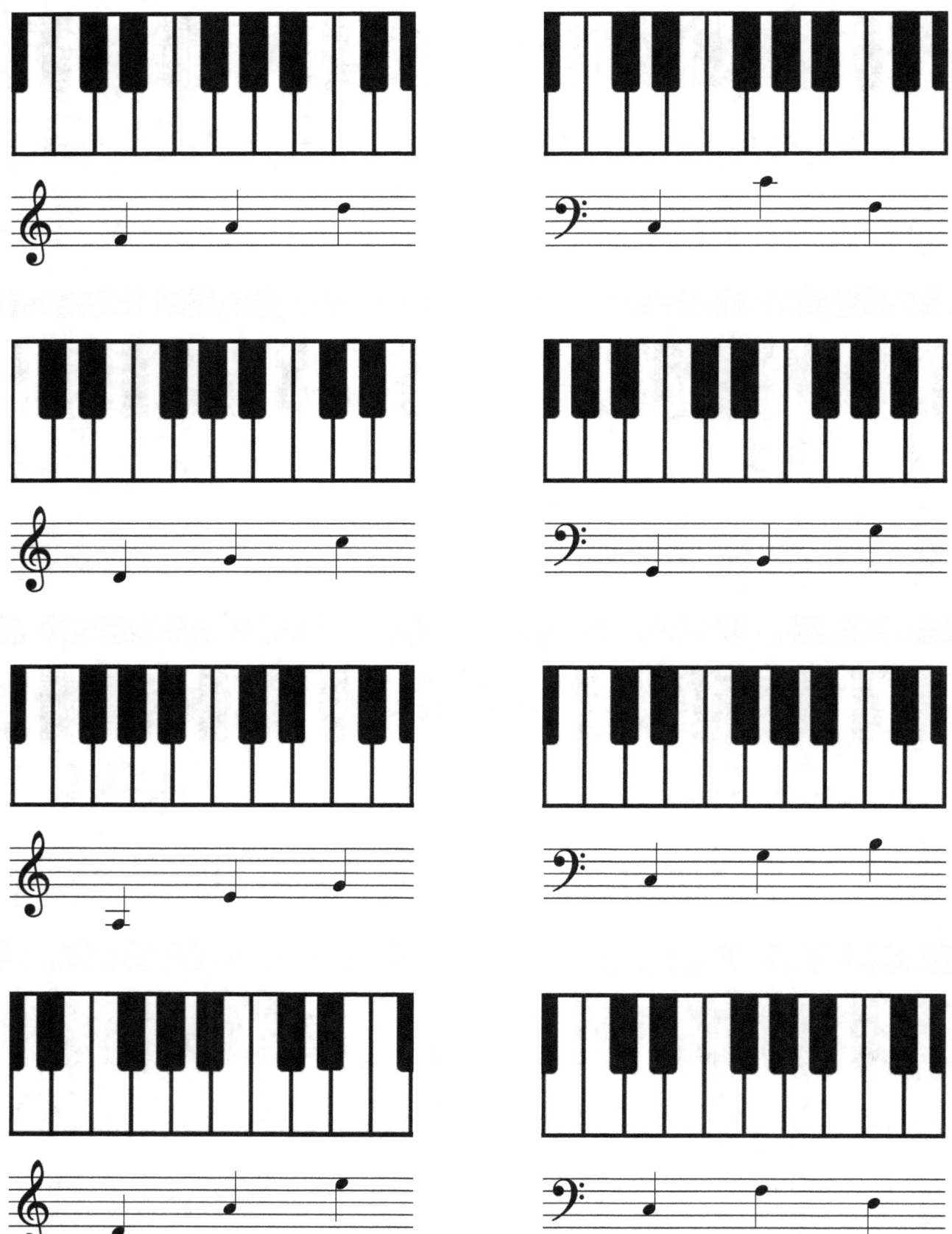

Fill all the **gaps**. **Draw** *(quarter)* **notes** on the staves and **circle** the notes on the **keyboard**.

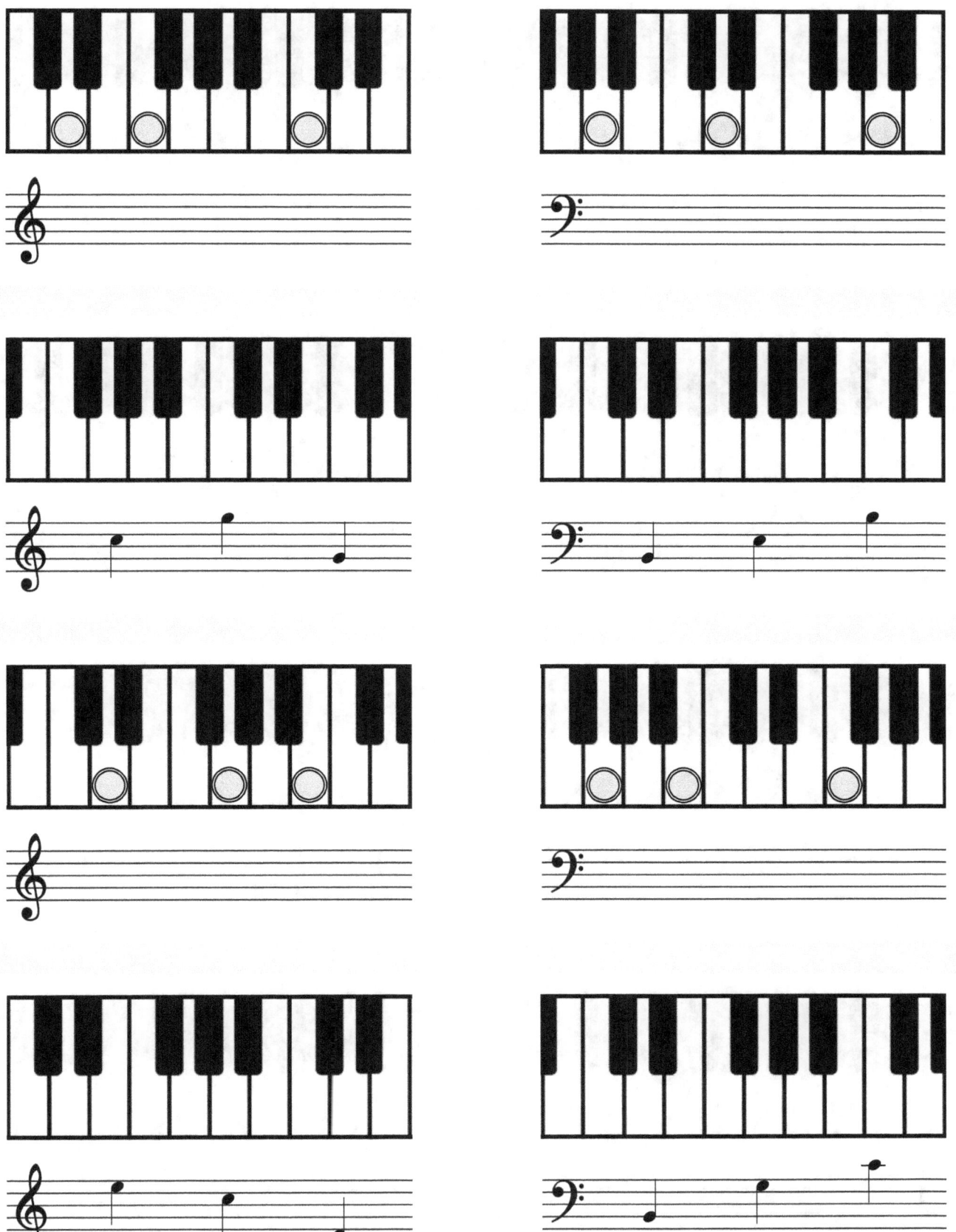

Fill all the **gaps**. Draw *(whole)* **notes** on the staves and **circle** the notes on the **keyboard**.

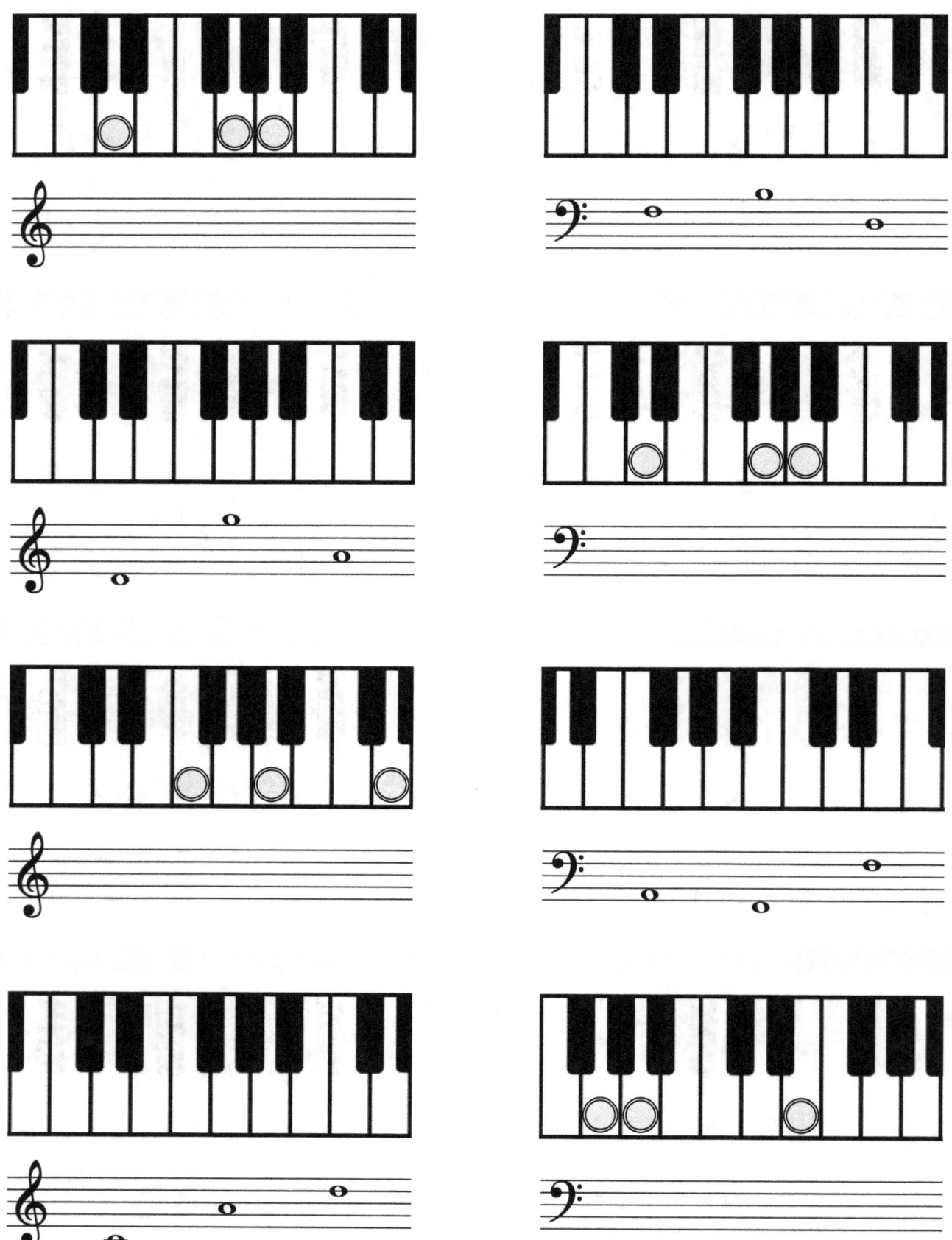

Fill all the **gaps**. **Draw** *(whole)* **notes** on the staves and **circle** the notes on the **keyboard**.

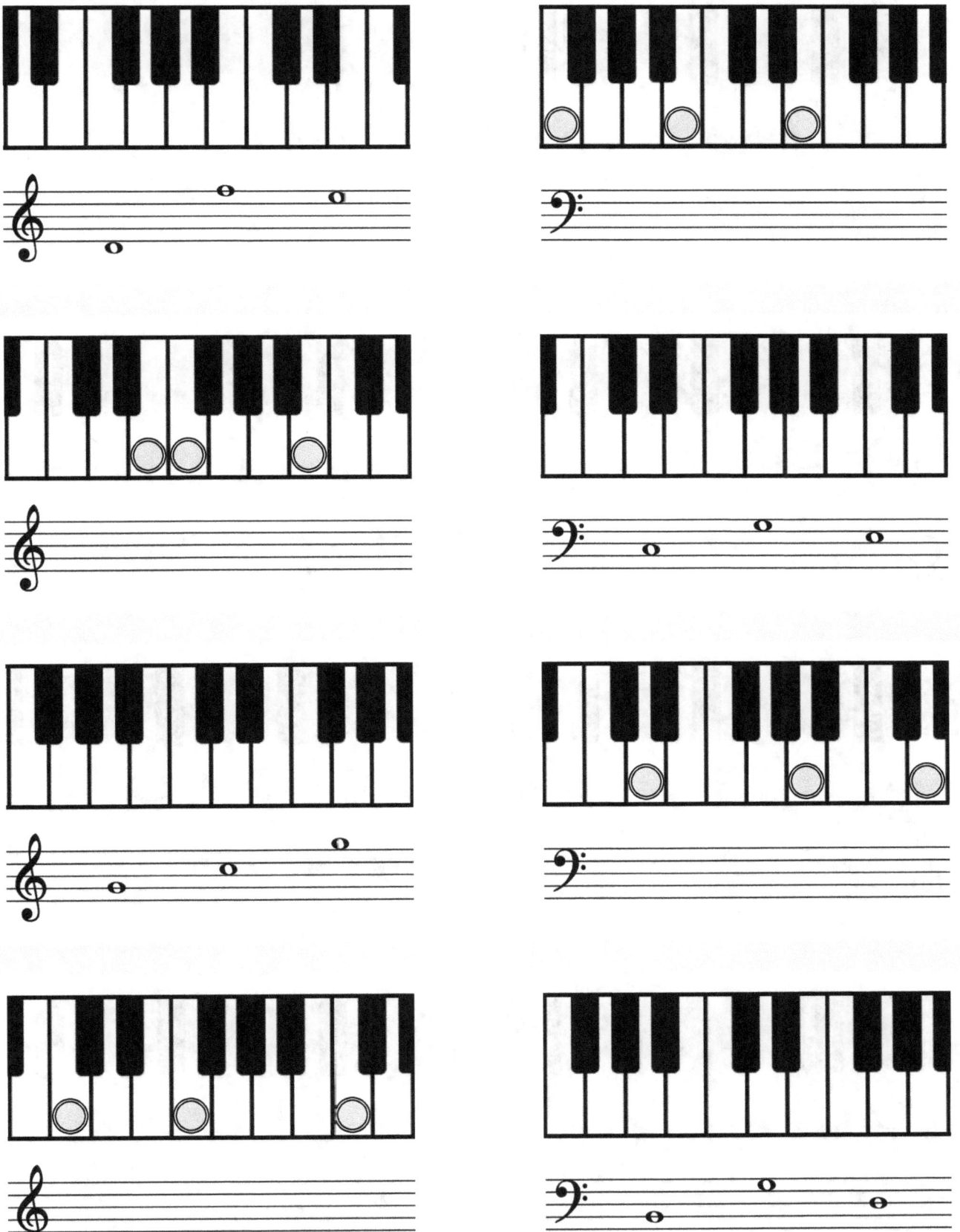

Fill all the **gaps**. **Draw** *(whole)* **notes** on the staves and **circle** the notes on the **keyboard**.

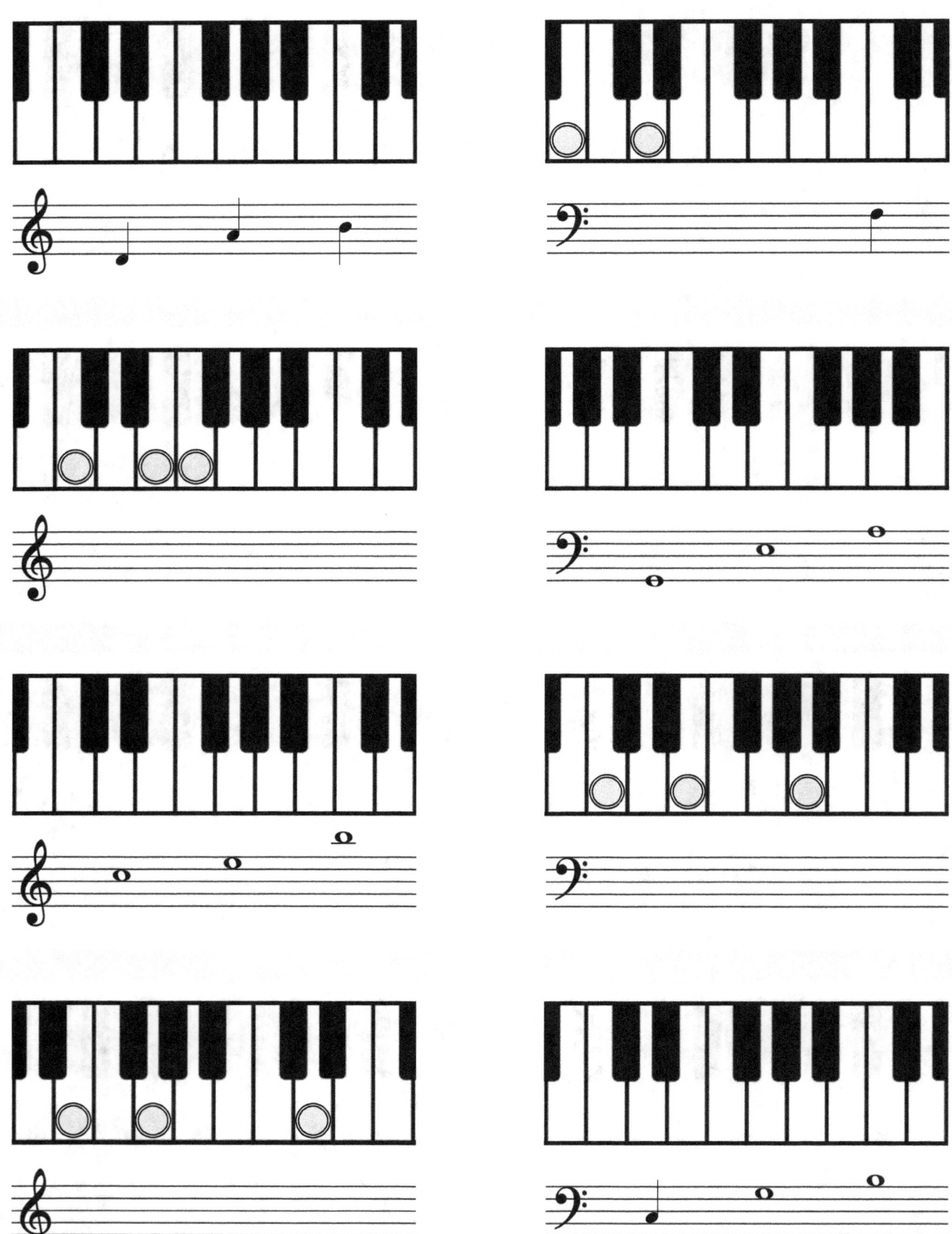

Fill all the **gaps**. **Draw** *(whole)* **notes** on the staves and **circle** the notes on the **keyboard**.

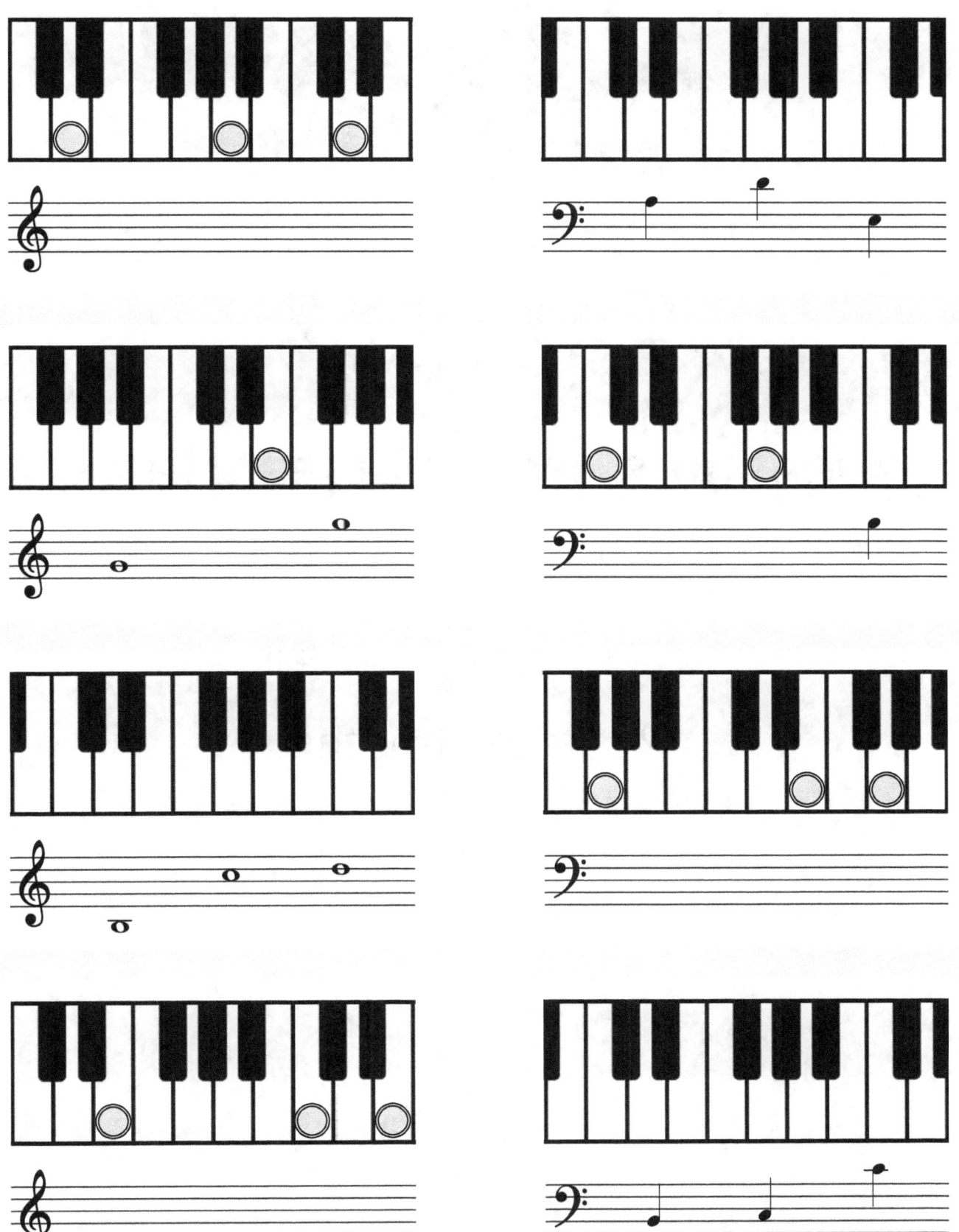

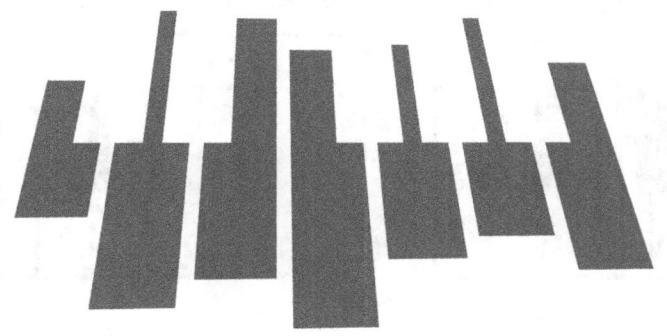

Chapter 2

Measures, Note Values, Rests

---

1. Bars & Bar Lines

2. Note Length

3. Rests

4. Exercises

The Staff: Bar Lines

Vertical lines, called bar lines, separate the staff into smaller parts known as measures or bars. This helps organize the music and makes it easier to read the rhythm. Usually, the key signature and time signature are shown at the beginning of the music, which we will discuss in the next chapters (see p. 66 ff.). Measures help with counting and keeping track of the music, especially in longer or more complex pieces.

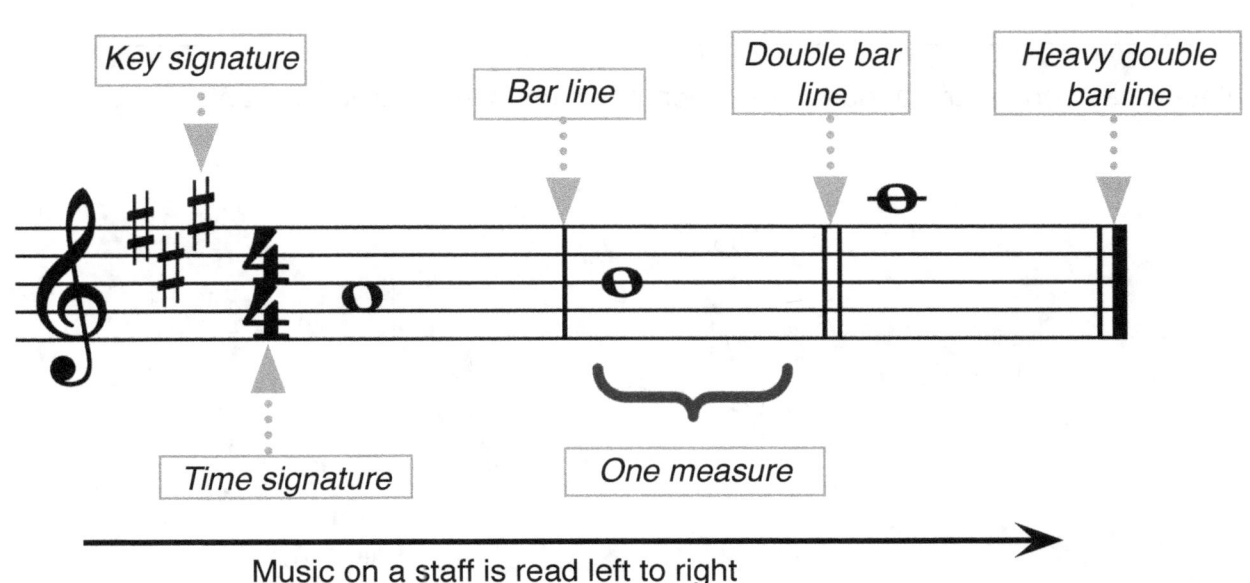

Music on a staff is read left to right

Definitions

Bar line: A vertical line separates one measure from the next in musical notation. This organizes the music and helps musicians to keep track of their position within the piece. These bars are typically numbered for clarity. A common practice is to number every five measures or to place a number at the beginning of each new line. The first bar/measure is labeled as bar 1, the second as bar 2, and so forth.

Double bar line: Two vertical lines signify the end of a piece of music or a section within a piece of music. They can also indicate an important change, such as a key or tempo change.

Heavy bar line: A thicker vertical line often marks the end of a piece or a major section. It can also be used to clearly separate different parts of a piece of music.

Repeat sign: A bar line that is adorned with two dots. It indicates that the section of music should be repeated. There are start and end repeat signs, which mark the beginning and end of the section to be repeated, with the dots placed on the right or left side of the line.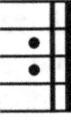

Note Values

In written music, the two most important aspects of reading notes are the pitch of the note (how high or low a note sounds) and its duration (how long the note lasts). Notes can have different values (length of the note). To determine the pitch, we look at the staff and the key signature, and we see on which line or space the note is located. The higher it is placed, the higher it sounds. To determine the length, we first look at the tempo and the time signature, which are defined at the beginning of a piece, and then we see what the note looks like.

Notes may consist of various parts, each of which affect how long it lasts.

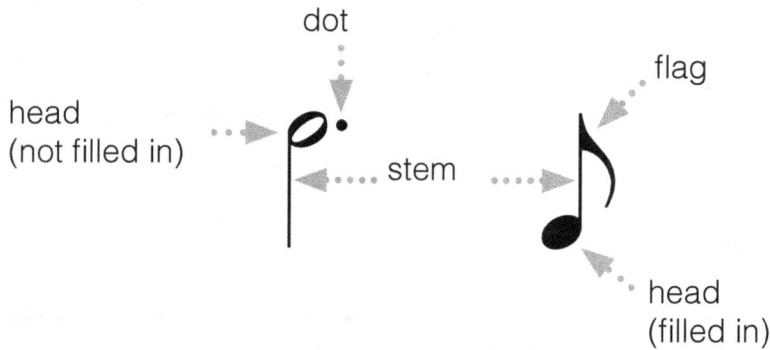

Notes can have multiple flags, be connected by bars, or have several dots.
All these attributes affect the note's duration *(how long it lasts)*.

Duration: Note Lenght

The most common note lenghts:

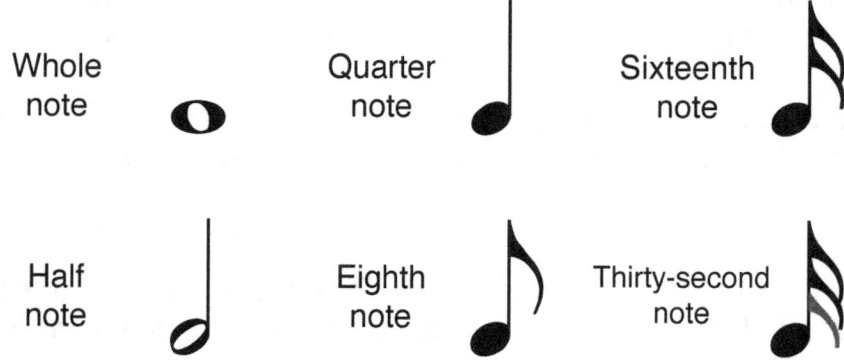

The most basic note, which appears without any stems or flags, is known as a whole note. All other notes are measured in comparison to it. For instance, a half note has a duration that is half of a whole note, whereas a quarter note lasts a quarter of that time. This pattern is consistent for eighth notes, sixteenth notes, thirty-second notes, sixty-fourth notes, and beyond, with each subsequent note type being half the length of the one before it.

More about Note Stems

The note stem has no effect on the note's duration. The basic idea is to write the notes in a way that makes the music as easy as possible to read and understand, and the notes are supposed to be "in the staff" as much as reasonably possible.

1 whole note   = 2 half notes = 4 quarter notes = 8 eighth notes and so on....

You might have also noticed that the note durations sound like fractions in mathematics. Indeed, they function very similarly to fractions: two half notes are equivalent to (last as long as) one whole note; four eighth notes are as long as one half note, and so on.

However, there are no third notes, fifth notes, or tenth notes, etc.

In written music, notes can be subdivided into unusual lengths for more precise timing. Two common ways to do this are by adding dots or ties to the notes.

Dotted Notes

One way to create a different note length is by adding a dot to the note or rest. Dotted notes are one and a half times longer than the equivalent note without a dot. The note retains its original value, while the dot contributes an additional half of that length. With two dots, another half of the previous dot's length is added, and so forth.

Tied Notes

A dotted half note lasts as long as a half note and a quarter note. The same length can also be achieved with a half note tied to a quarter note. Notes of any length can be tied together. The symbol for a tie is a curved line that connects two or more notes of the same pitch. (The notes must be on the same line or space).

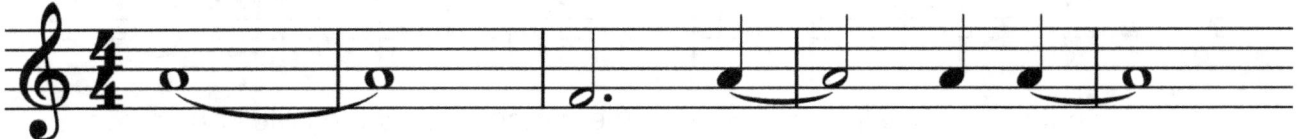

Tied notes are the only way to extend a note across bar lines. The sound produced by tied notes is equivalent to a single note that has the duration of all the tied notes combined. This means that in the diagram above, eight notes are written, but only five notes are played during the performance.

Notes with Beams

You may have noticed that some of the eighth notes in the illustration below do not have flags; instead, they are connected to another eighth note by a beam.

When eighth notes are next to each other, their flags can be replaced by beams that link them into easily readable groups.

These beams can connect notes that fall on the same beat or, in some vocal music pieces, notes sung on the same syllable of text. Each note will have as many beams as it has flags.

Rest Symbols

Each rest symbol in musical notation corresponds to a specific note in terms of duration. However, rests are not merely "silence"; they are active and crucial elements that contribute to shaping the rhythm and dynamics of a piece of music.

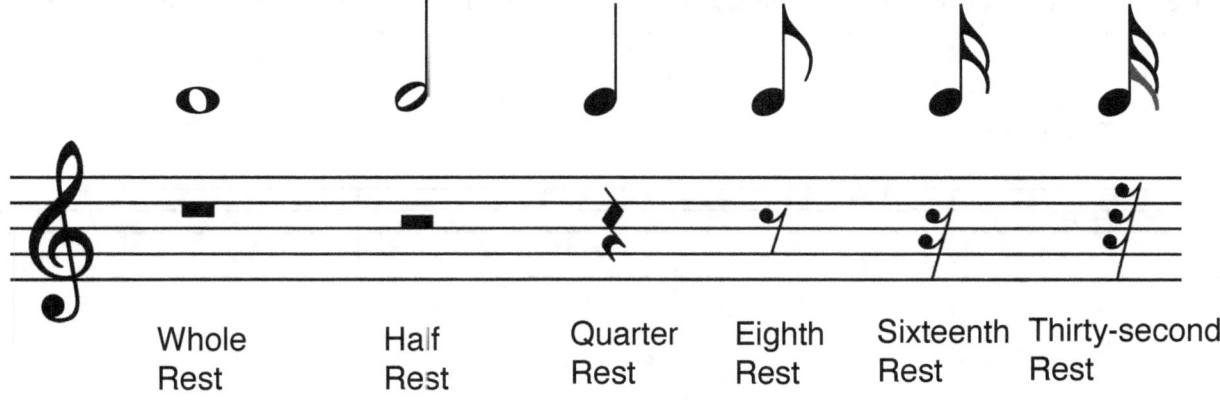

Whole Rest | Half Rest | Quarter Rest | Eighth Rest | Sixteenth Rest | Thirty-second Rest

Rests do not always stand for silence; they act as placeholders in polyrhythmic contexts, even when one musician plays both parts, adding complexity and texture to the music.

Basic rules for the direction of note stems:

Notes below the middle line should have upward stems to avoid cluttering the staff. Notes on or above the middle line should have downward stems, ensuring a balanced visual layout in the score

In chords, the orientation of the note stem is typically dictated by the note furthest from the staff's middle line.

Here, too, the direction of the note stems usually depends on the note that is furthest from the center of the staff to keep the beam close to the staff.

In instances of varying rhythms, the note stems can be written in opposite directions to make the music easy and clear to read.

Single Notes

Chords

Notes with Beams

Rhythms

Complete the musical staff:

Numbering for all measures / **Double bar line** after measure 4 / **Whole rest** in each measure

Example

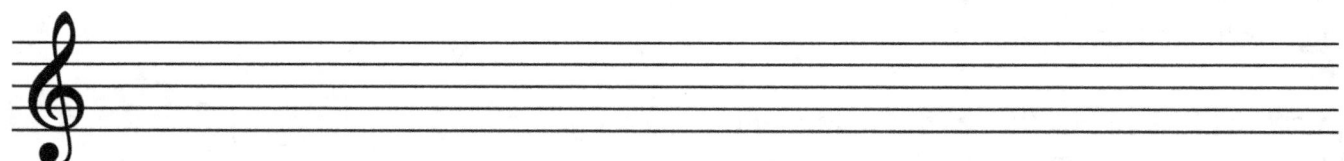

Bar __1__   Bar ____   Bar ____

Bar ____   Bar ____   Bar ____

Draw on the musical staff:

Eight measures / **Heavy bar line** in measure 8 / **Repeat sign** in measure 4 *(repeat first 4 measures)*

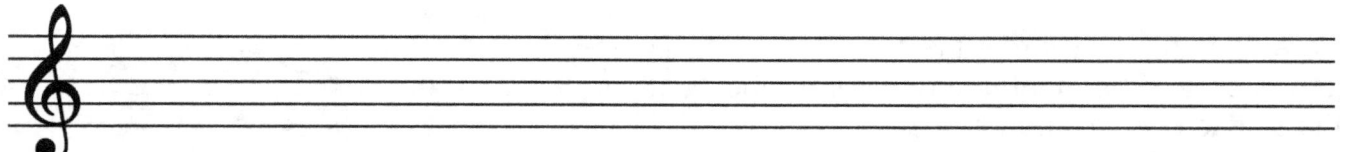

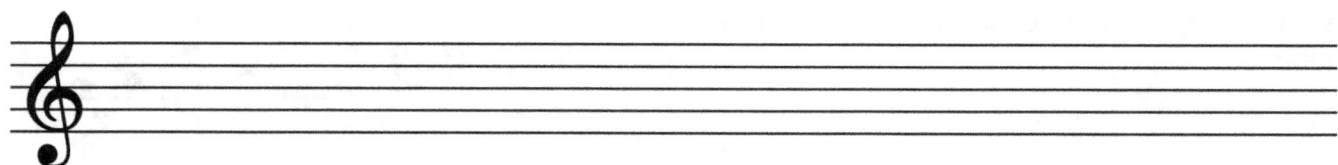

Complete the musical staff:

Draw the specified **symbols** into the measures.

Example

Whole Rest　　　　　　　Half Rest　　　　　　　Quarter Rest

2 Eighth Rests　　　Start (Bar5)　　　End (Bar6)
　　　　　　　　　Repeat Sign　　　Repeat Sign

Draw on the musical staff:

Six bars / A **heavy double bar** in measure 6 / A **whole rest** in Bar 2,4,5

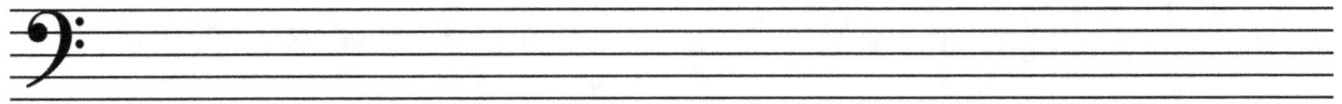

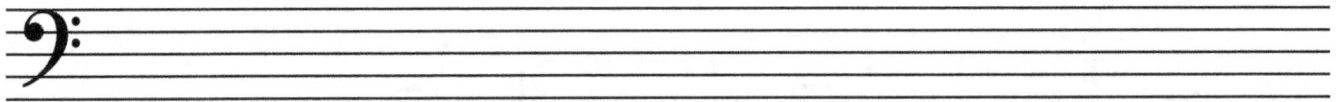

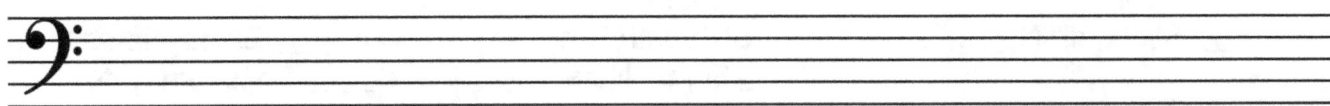

Complete the diagrams:

Draw the notes in the boxes and **add the note value** underneath in numbers

𝅝 = [ ]

1 Whole Note
= ____ Quarter

𝅗𝅥 = [ ]

1 Half Note
= ____ Quarter

𝅝 + 𝅗𝅥 = [ ]

1 Whole + 1 Half
= ____ Half + ____ Eighth

𝅝 = [ ]

1 Whole Note
= ____ Eighths

𝅗𝅥 = [ ]

1 Half
= 1 Quarter + ___ Eighth

𝅗𝅥 𝅗𝅥 = [ ]

2 Half
= 1 dotted Half + ____ Quarter

Complete the diagrams:

Convert notes with beams into individual, **standalone notes**

♫ = [ ]

Beam
= ____ Eighth Notes

𝅘𝅥𝅯𝅘𝅥𝅯 = [ ]

Beam
= ____ Sixteenth Notes

♫♫ = [ ]

Beam
= ____ Eighth Notes

𝅘𝅥𝅯𝅘𝅥𝅯𝅘𝅥𝅯𝅘𝅥𝅯 = [ ]

Beam
= ____ Sixteenth Notes

𝅘𝅥𝅯𝅘𝅥𝅯♪ = [ ]

Beam
= ____ Sixteenth Notes +
____ Eighth Note

♪𝅘𝅥𝅯𝅘𝅥𝅯 = [ ]

Beam
= ____ Eighth Notes
+ ____ Sixteenth Notes

Complete the diagrams:

Draw the notes in the boxes and **add the note value** underneath in numbers

♩ = [ ]

1 Quarter Note
= _____ Eighths

♩. = [ ]

1 dotted Half
= _____ Quarter

𝗈. = [ ]

1 dotted Whole
= _____ Halfs

𝗈•• = [ ]

1 Whole with 2 dotts
= _____ Halfs + _____ Quarter

♩•• = [ ]

1 Quarter with 2 dotts
= _____ Eights +
_____ Sixteenth

♩ + ♩ = [ ]

1 Half + 1 Quarter
= _____ Eights

Complete the diagrams:

Connect the standalone notes into **beamed notes**

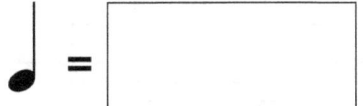 = [ ]

3 Eights
= _____ Beamed eight

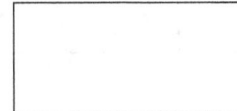 = [ ]

Sixteenth + Eighth
= _____ & _____ beams

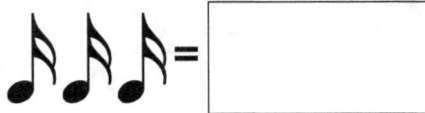 = [ ]

3 Sixteenth
= _____ beams

 = [ ]

2 Eights + 1 Sixteenth
= ___ & ___ beams

 = [ ]

4 Thrity-second
= ___ beams

 = [ ]

2 Sixteenth + 1 Eighth
= ___ & ___ & ___ beams

Complete the scores:

For each note, **draw** a **rest of the same length**. The first measure is done for you.

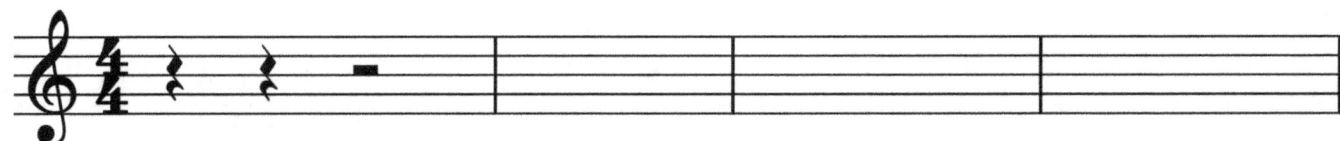

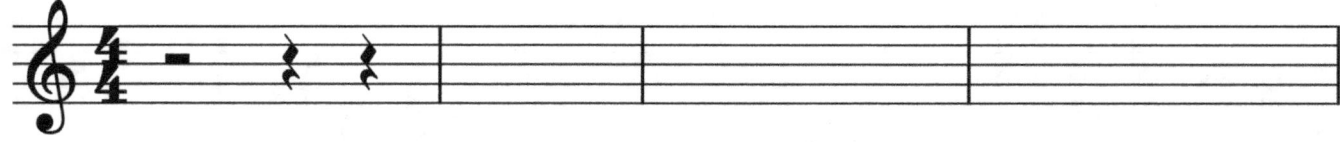

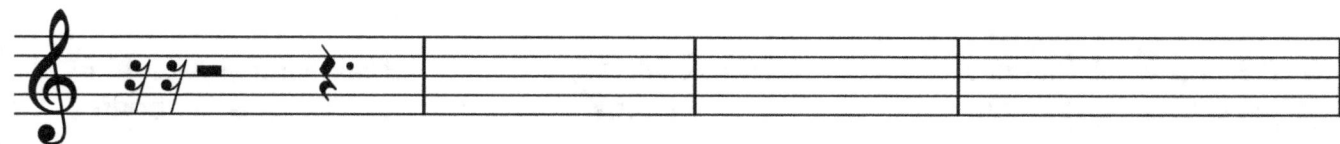

Complete the scores:

For each note, **draw** a **rest of the same length**. The first score is done for you.

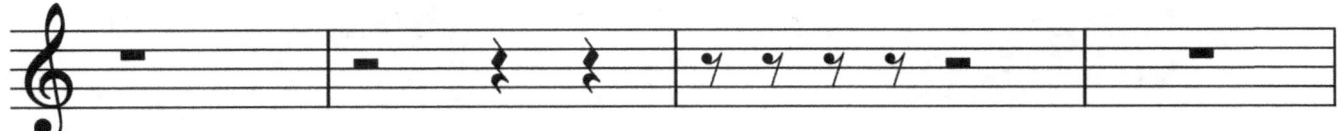

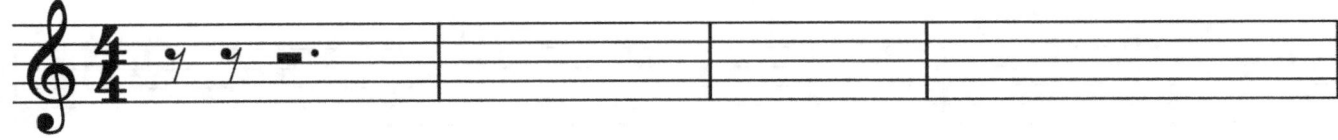

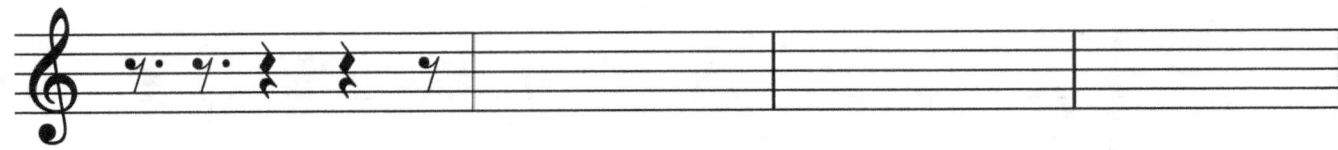

Complete the musical staffs:

For each box, **draw** the number of **notes / rests** into the measures above.

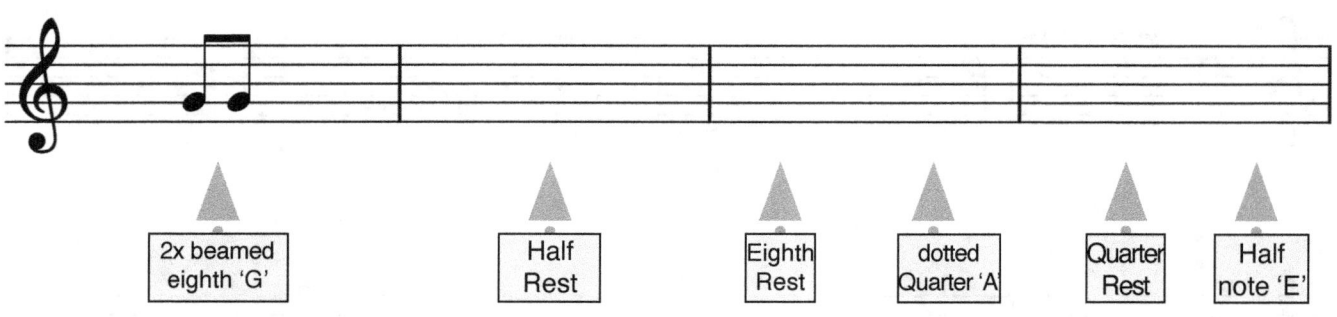

| 2x beamed eighth 'G' | Half Rest | Eighth Rest | dotted Quarter 'A' | Quarter Rest | Half note 'E' |

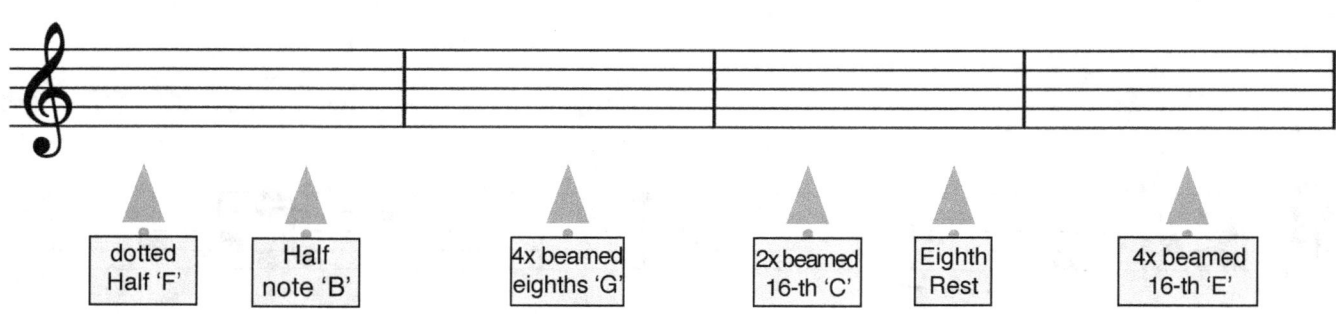

| dotted Half 'F' | Half note 'B' | 4x beamed eighths 'G' | 2x beamed 16-th 'C' | Eighth Rest | 4x beamed 16-th 'E' |

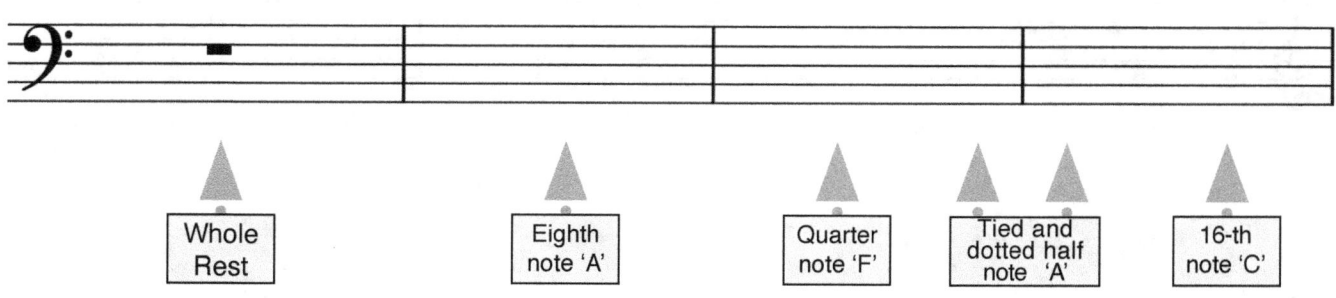

| Whole Rest | Eighth note 'A' | Quarter note 'F' | Tied and dotted half note 'A' | 16-th note 'C' |

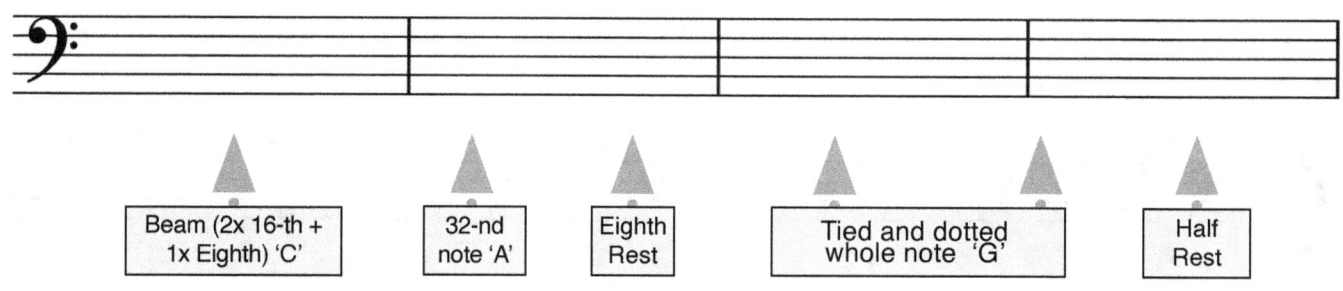

| Beam (2x 16-th + 1x Eighth) 'C' | 32-nd note 'A' | Eighth Rest | Tied and dotted whole note 'G' | Half Rest |

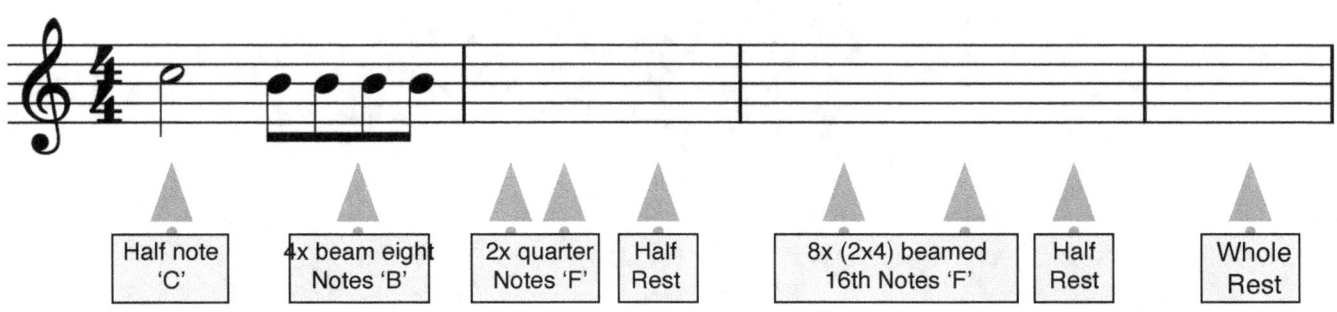

Complete the musical staffs:

For each box, **draw** the number of **notes / rests** into the measures above.

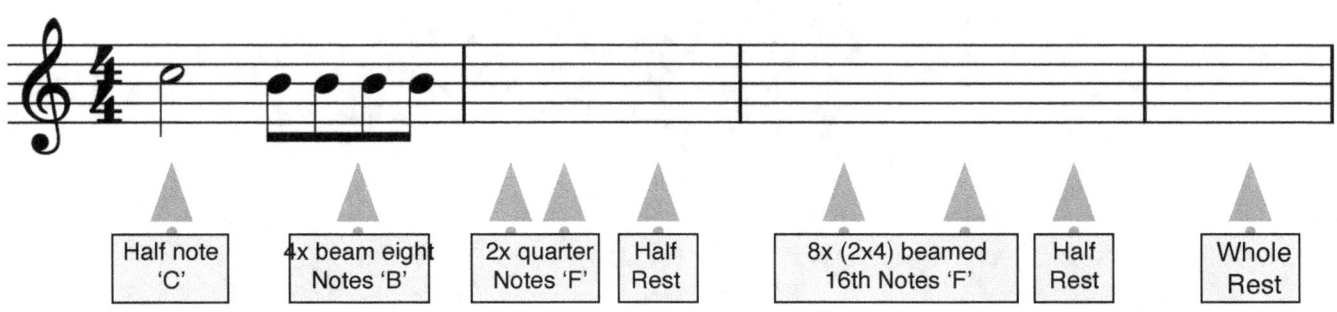

| Half note 'C' | 4x beam eight Notes 'B' | 2x quarter Notes 'F' | Half Rest | 8x (2x4) beamed 16th Notes 'F' | Half Rest | Whole Rest |

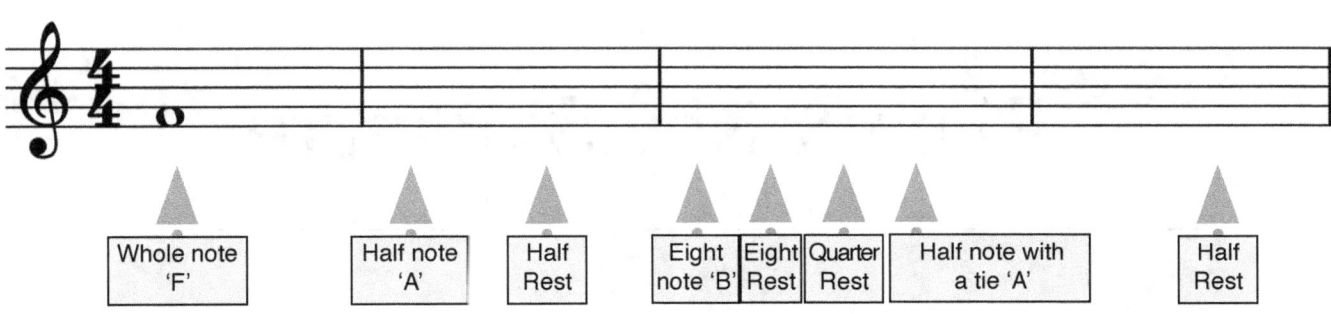

| Whole note 'F' | Half note 'A' | Half Rest | Eight note 'B' | Eight Rest | Quarter Rest | Half note with a tie 'A' | Half Rest |

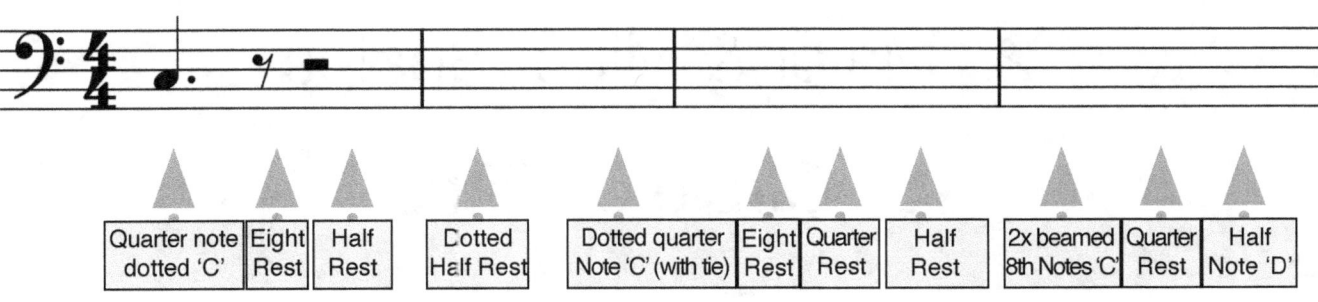

| Quarter note dotted 'C' | Eight Rest | Half Rest | Dotted Half Rest | Dotted quarter Note 'C' (with tie) | Eight Rest | Quarter Rest | Half Rest | 2x beamed 8th Notes 'C' | Quarter Rest | Half Note 'D' |

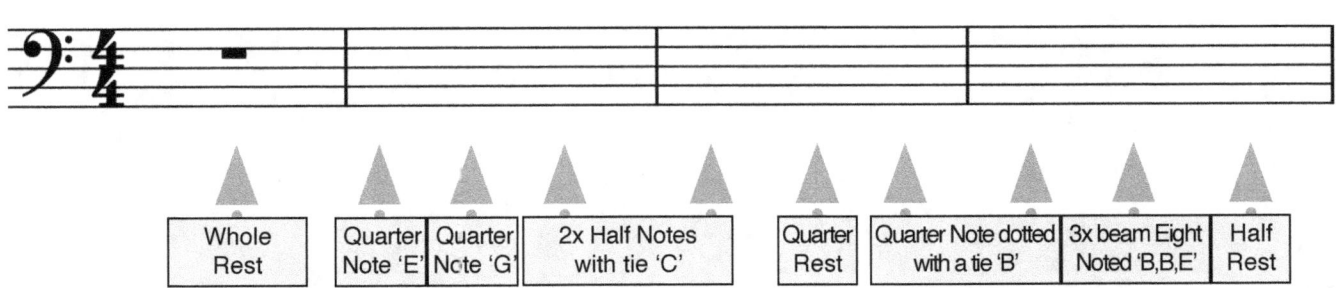

| Whole Rest | Quarter Note 'E' | Quarter Note 'G' | 2x Half Notes with tie 'C' | Quarter Rest | Quarter Note dotted with a tie 'B' | 3x beam Eight Noted 'B,B,E' | Half Rest |

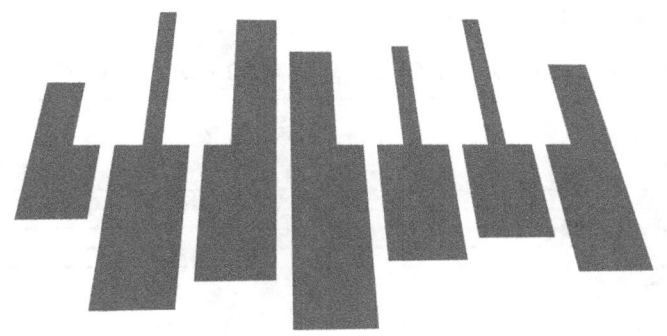

Chapter 3

Pitch & Key Signature

1. Accidentals & Pitch

2. Major & Minor Scales

3. Circle of Fifths

4. Exercises

Pitch

The pitch of a note describes how high or low it sounds. Musicians assign different letter names to the various pitches: A, B, C, D, E, F, and G.

These seven letters name all the natural tones (on a keyboard, these are all the white keys) within an octave.

An octave is the interval between two notes of the same name. When you reach the eighth natural tone, you begin the next octave with another A.

These seven letters represent the natural notes (all the white keys) within an octave. The next 'C' (note 8) marks the beginning of the next octave *(from the Latin "octo," meaning eight)*.

In Western music, each octave consists of twelve standard notes. What are the names of the five additional notes found on a keyboard, specifically the black keys?

In music notation, there are three important symbols: the "flat" symbol (♭), the "sharp" symbol (#), and the "natural" symbol (♮). These symbols modify the pitch of a note and are essential for describing the black keys on a piano keyboard.

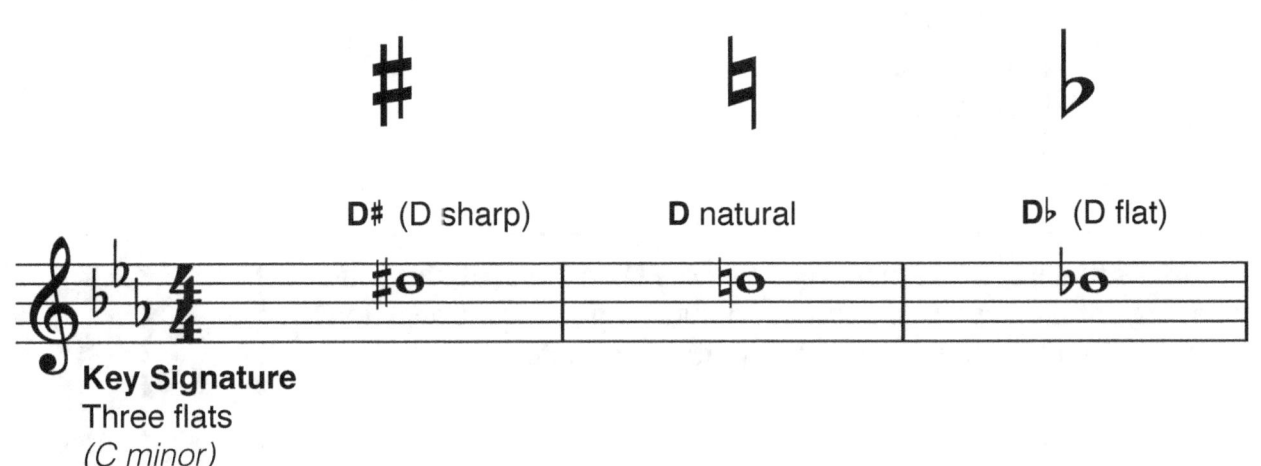

Sharps, flats, and naturals can be written either in the key signature or directly before the notes they modify.

An octave consists of seven white keys and five black keys. The seven white keys are named A, B, C, D, E, F, and G, while the five black keys are named C#, D#, F#, G#, and A# when raised, or D♭, E♭, G♭, A♭, and B♭ when lowered, depending on the musical context. For example, from C to C is an octave, from F to F, or from G to G, and so on.

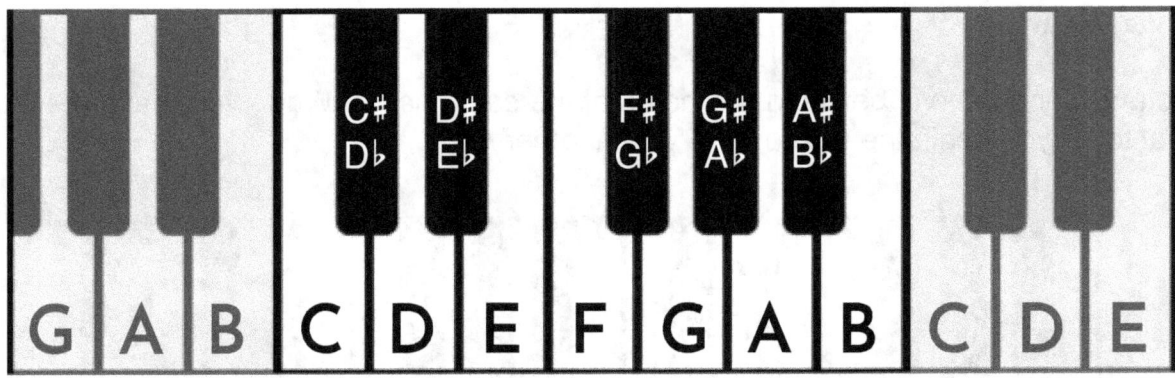

Sharp Sign	The sharp symbol increases a note by a half step (semitone). A note altered by a sharp is thus played a half tone higher.

For example:
F becomes F#
C becomes C#

Natural Sign

The natural sign cancels any previous alteration made by a sharp or flat, returning the note to its natural pitch.

For example:
F#(F sharp) is returned to F by the natural sign.
C#(C sharp) is returned to C by the natural sign.

Flat Sign

The flat symbol lowers a note by a half step. Therefore, a note altered by a flat is played a half tone lower.

For example:
D becomes D♭
B becomes B♭

This means that in our example with the note D on the staff, the sharp raises it by a half step to D#, and the natural sign brings it back to D natural. The flat lowers it by a half step, turning D into D♭.

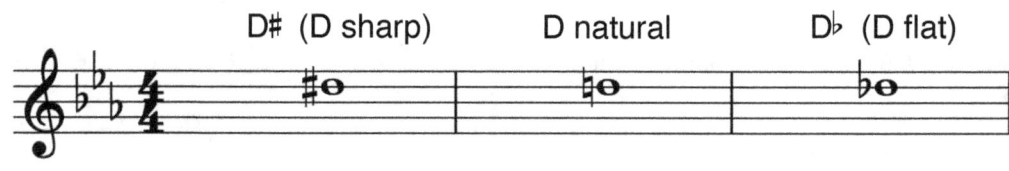

D# (D sharp)   D natural   D♭ (D flat)

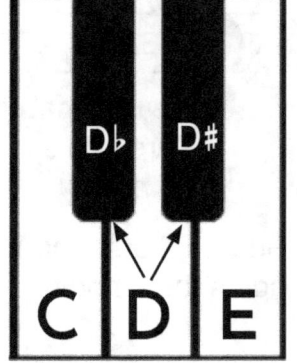

A semitone, or half step, on the piano is the smallest distance between two adjacent keys (for example, from a white key to the next black key). A whole tone step consists of two semitone steps (for example, from a white key to the second next white key). When two white keys have no black key between them, this represents a semitone step from white to white (such as B to C and E to F).

C# and D♭ sound identical because the same key is played, but they are notated differently depending on whether a sharp or a flat is used.

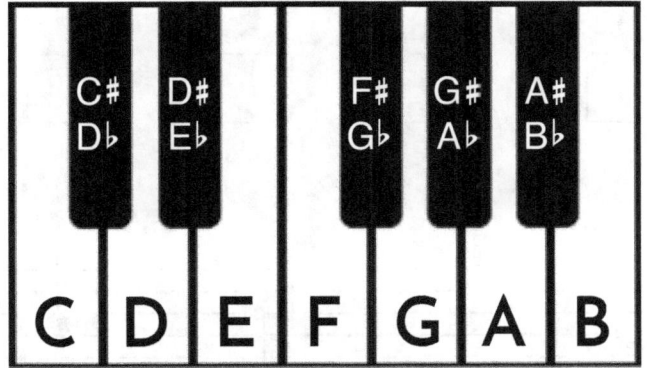

Natural Notes	Sharp-Notes #	Flat-Noten ♭
C	C#	C♭
D	D#	D♭
E	E#	E♭
F	F#	F♭
G	G#	G♭
A	A#	A♭
B	B#	B♭

The table above shows the relationship between sharp notes, flat notes, and natural notes, and serves as a learning aid.

Examples

Flat sign

♭

Notes with flats do not always fall on a black key.

F → F♭ (This is a white key, natural E)

G → G sharp

B → B flat

F → F flat

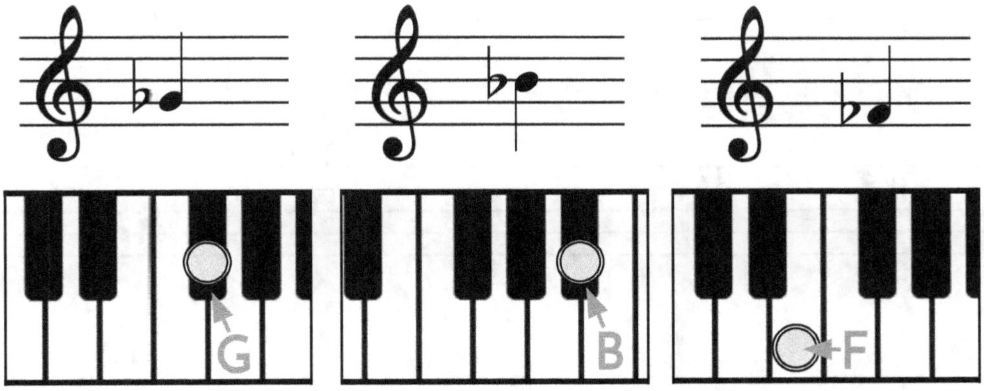

Sharp sign

#

Notes raised by a sharp can also be on a white key.

E → E# (This is a white key, natural F)

G → G sharp

F → F sharp

E → E sharp

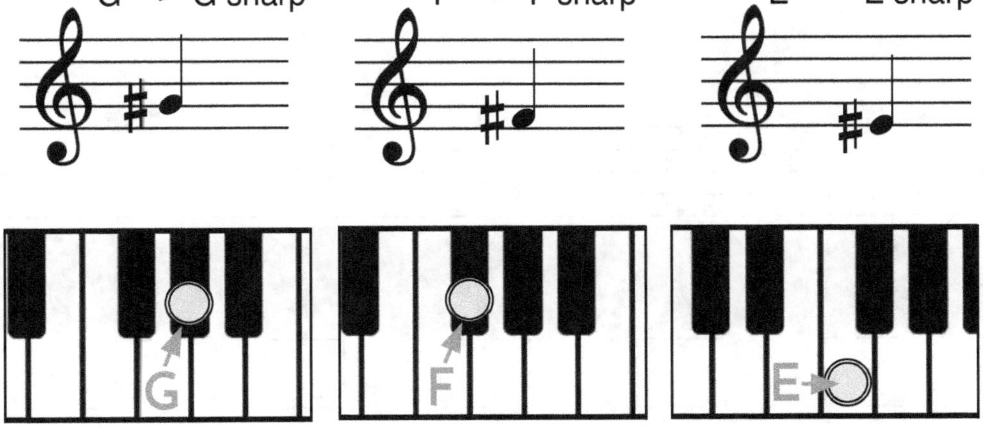

Write the correct note **names** in the boxes. Pay **attention** to and **draw** the **clefs**.

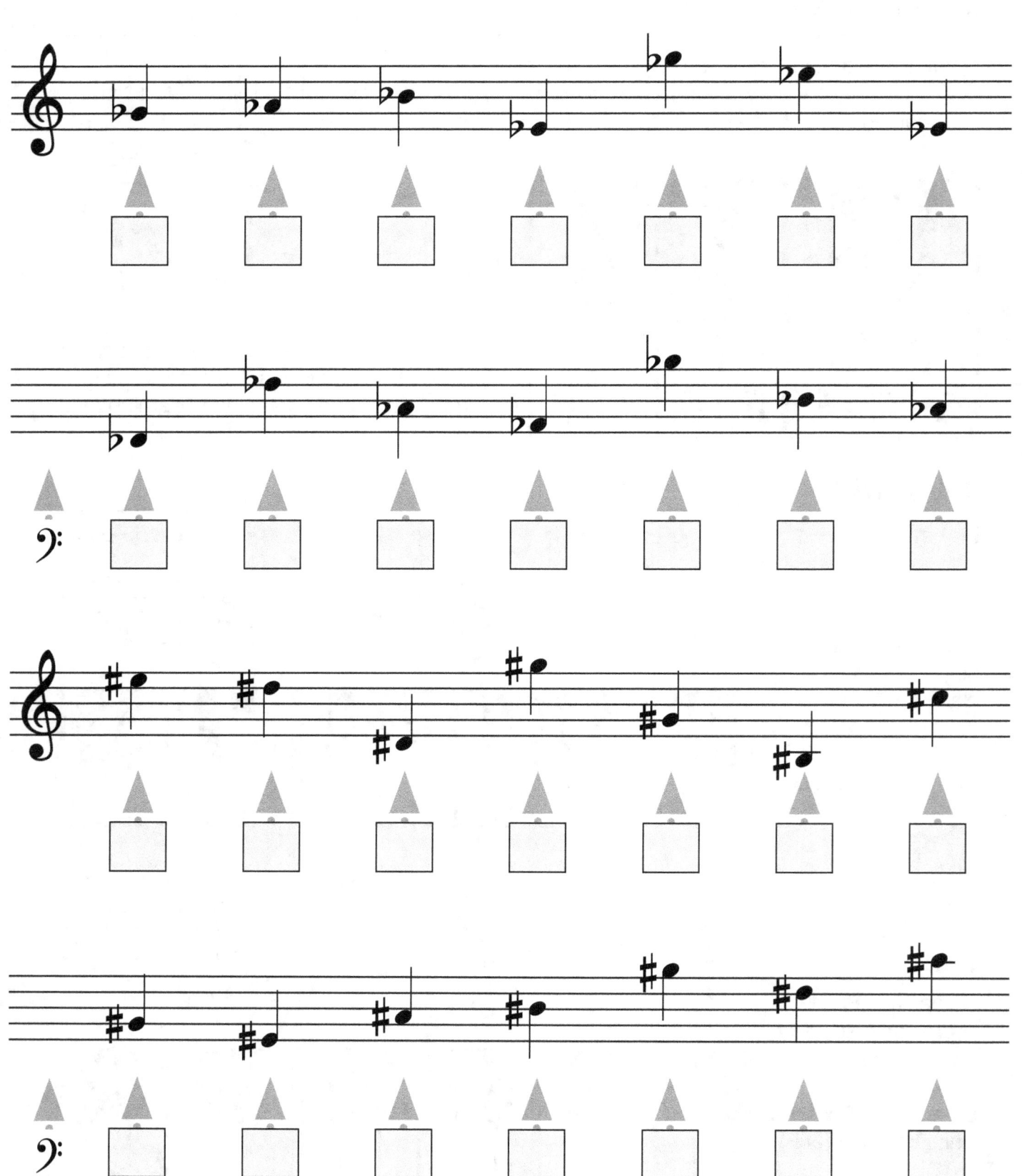

Write / Draw the correct note **names** in the boxes. Pay **attention** to and **draw** the **clefs**.

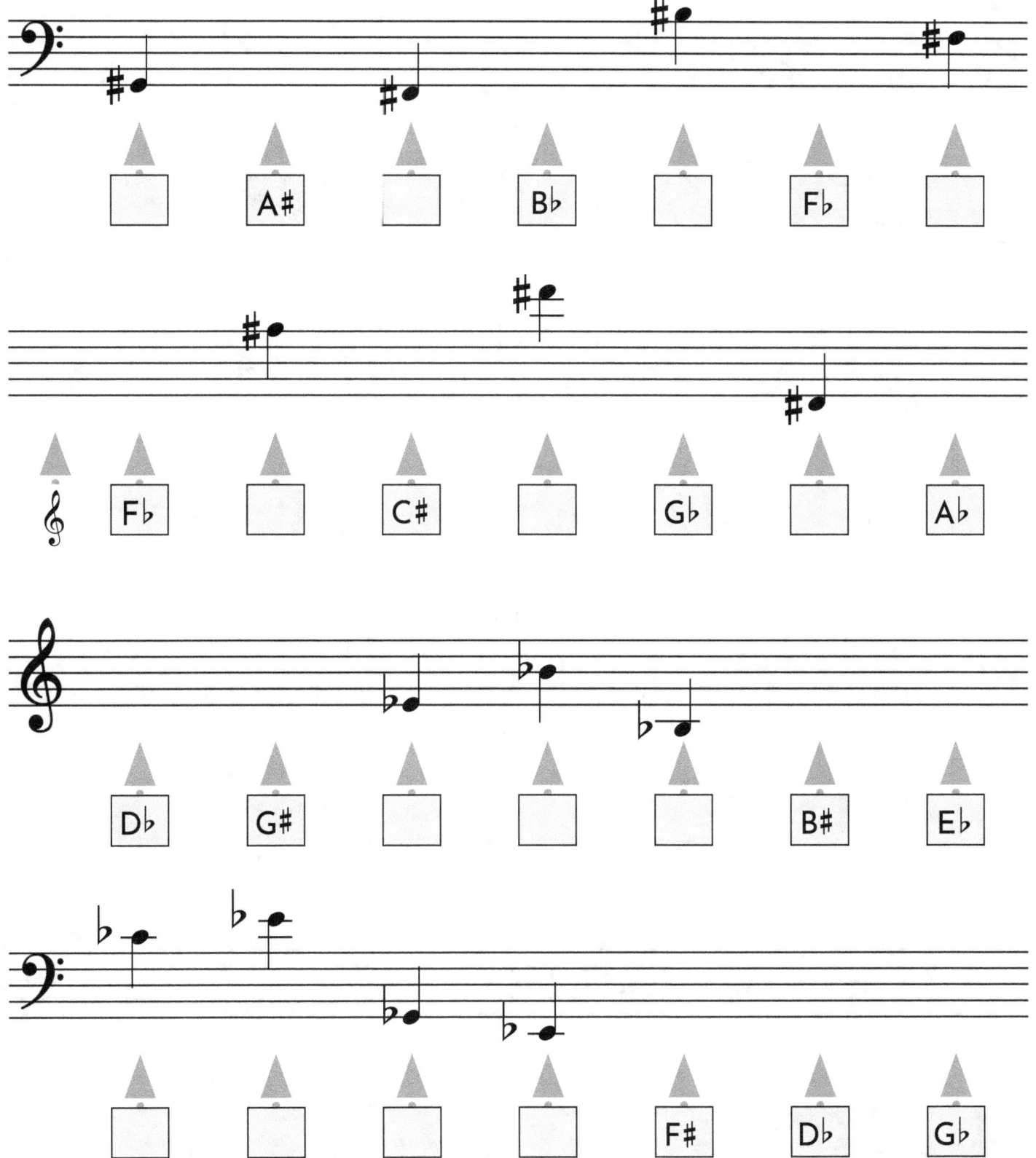

Write the correct note **names** in the boxes. Pay **attention** to and **draw** the **clefs**.

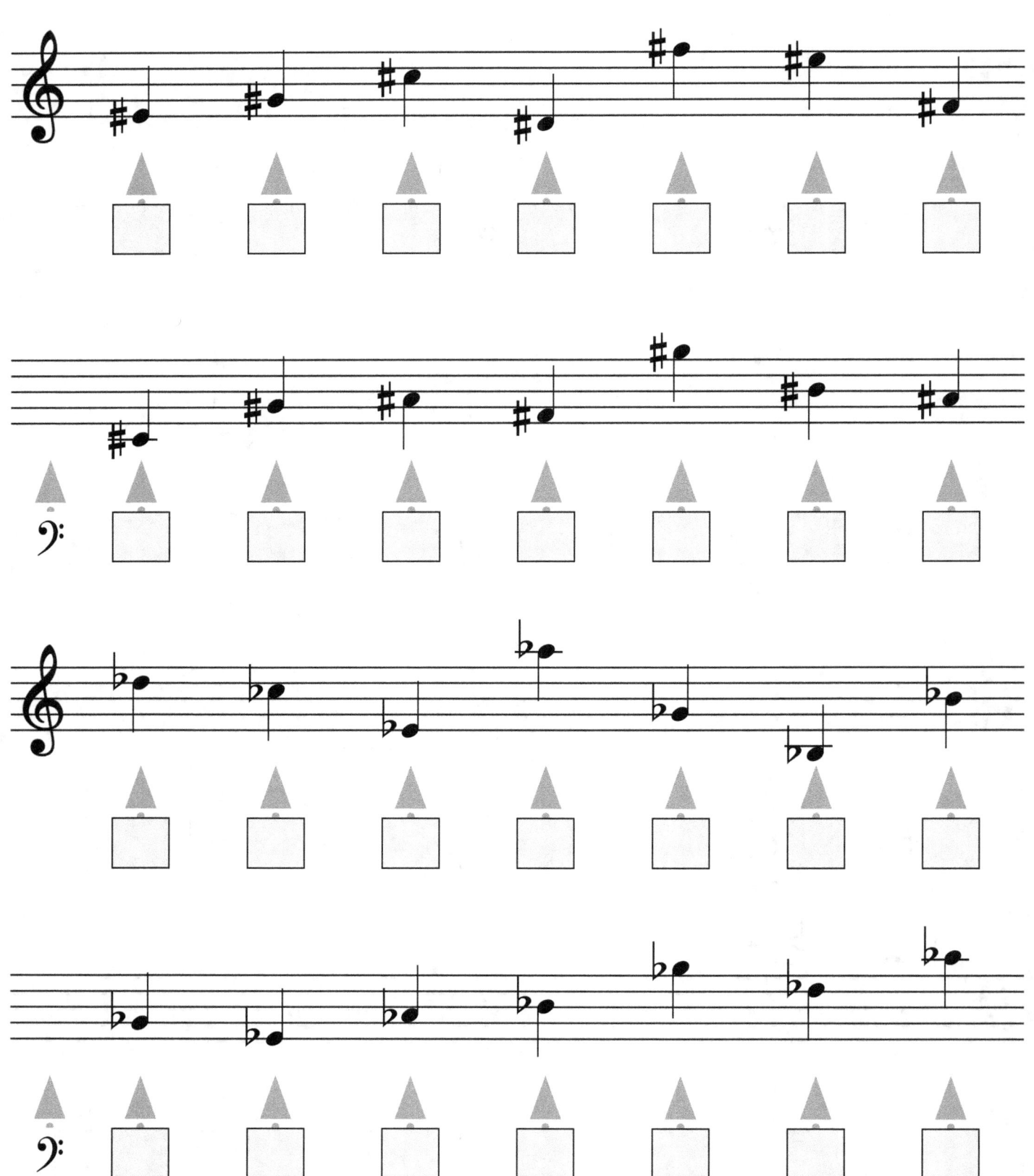

Write / Draw the correct note **names** in the boxes. Pay **attention** to and **draw** the **clefs**.

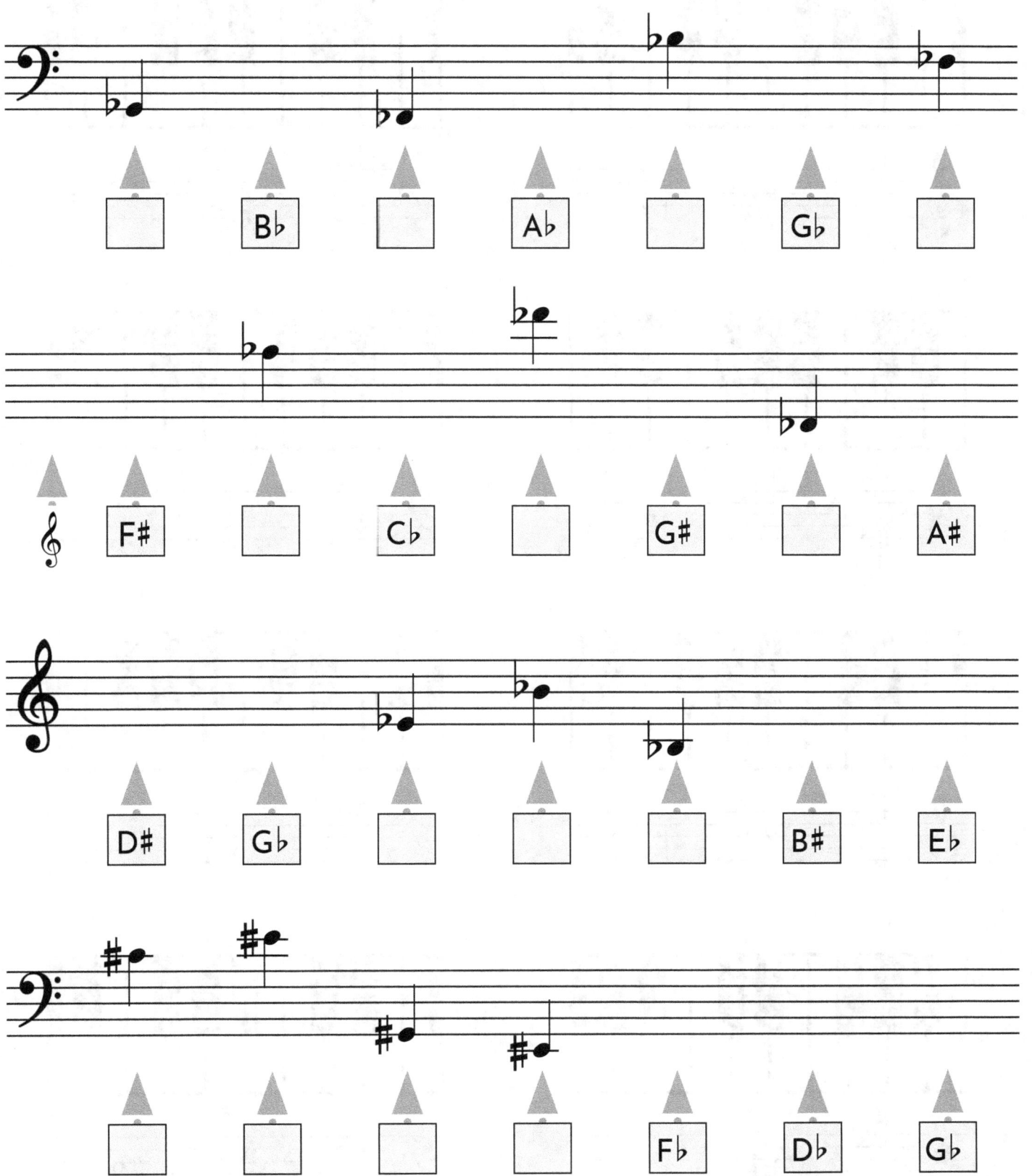

Circle the correct **keys** on the keyboard. Pay **attention** to the keyboard **layout**.

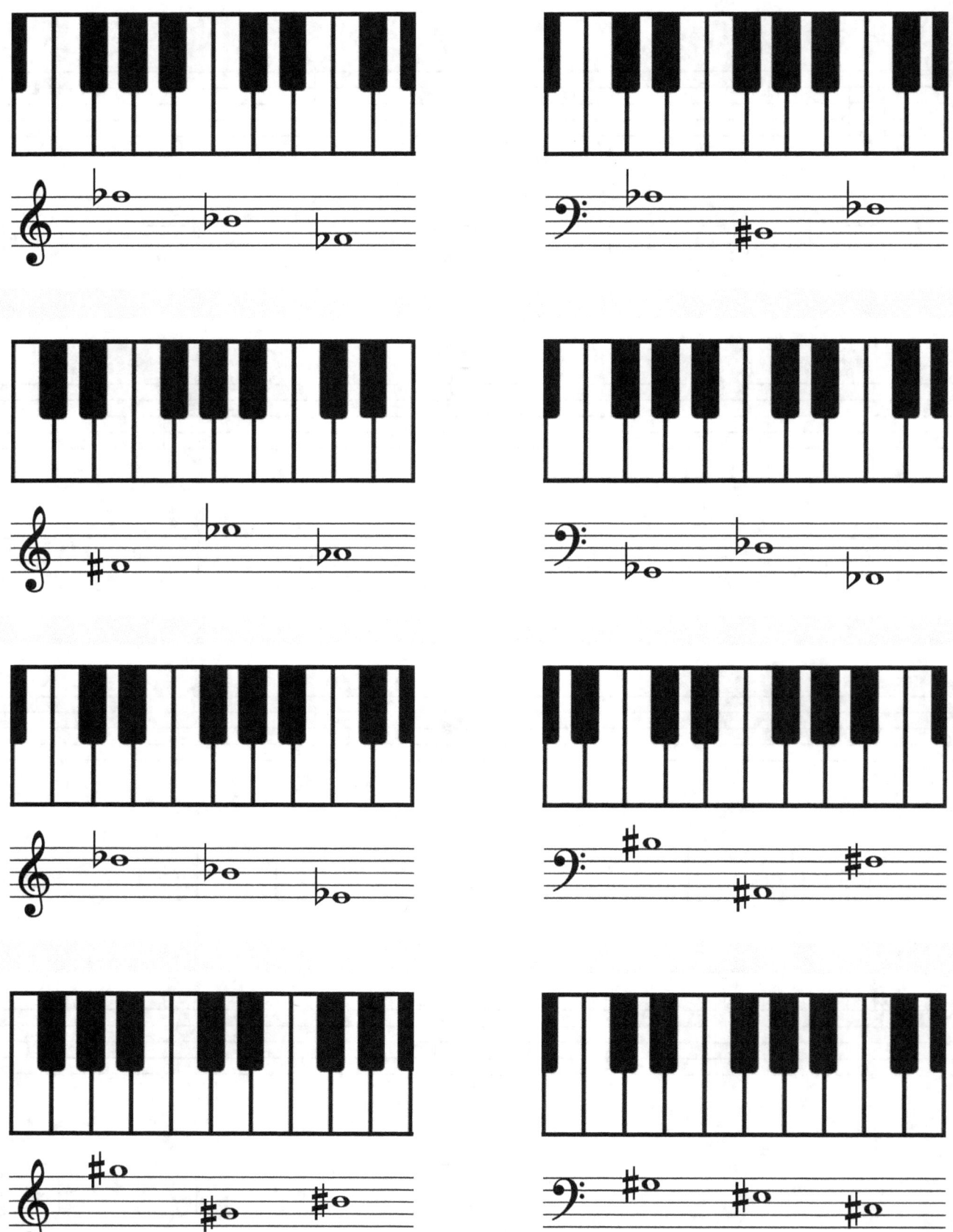

Circle the correct **keys** on the keyboard. Pay **attention** to the keyboard **layout**.

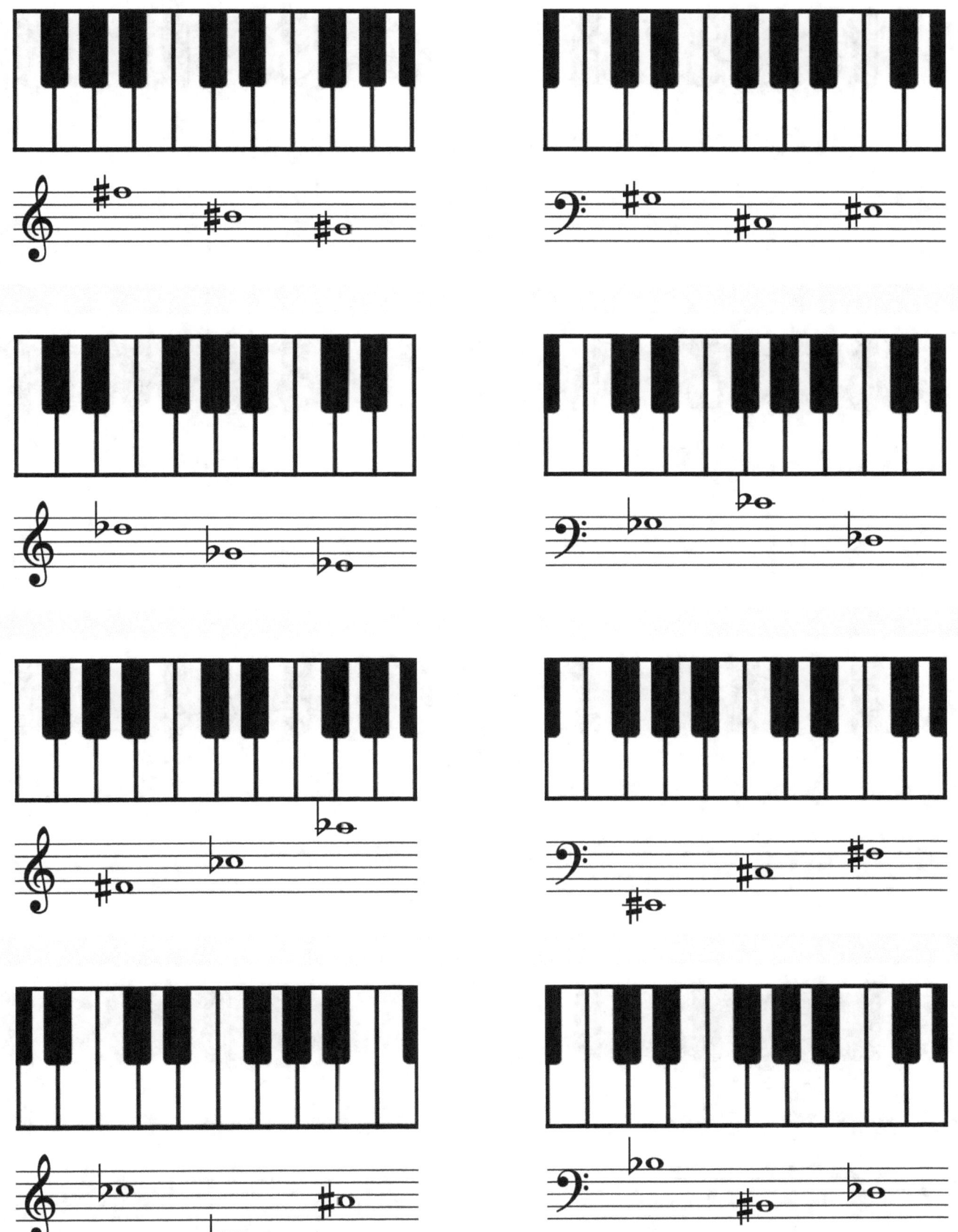

Draw the correct **notes** *(quarter notes)* in the staves. Use **only flats** & pay **attention** to the **keyboard**.

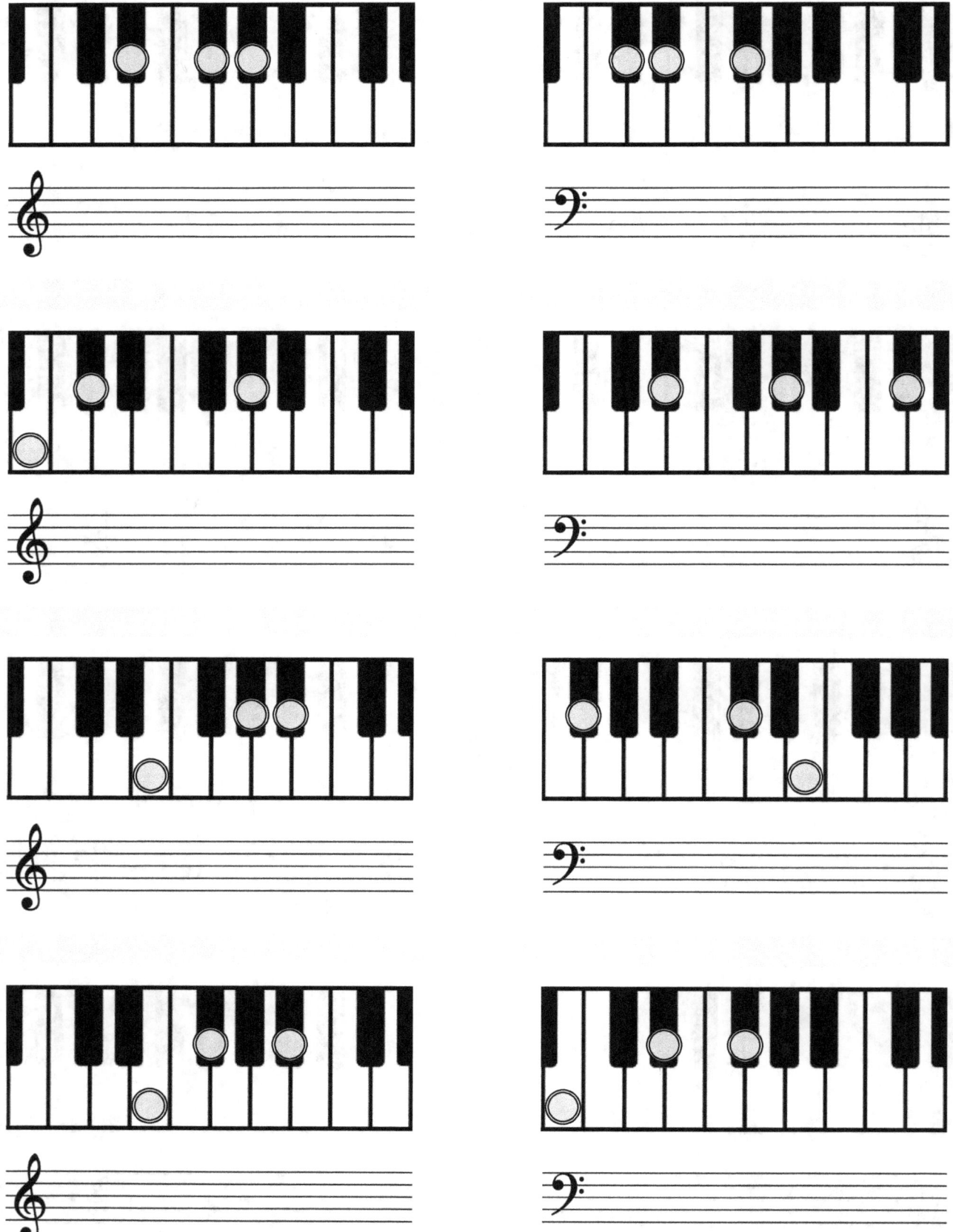

Draw the correct **notes** (quarter notes) in the staves. Use **only sharps** & pay **attention** to the **keyboard**.

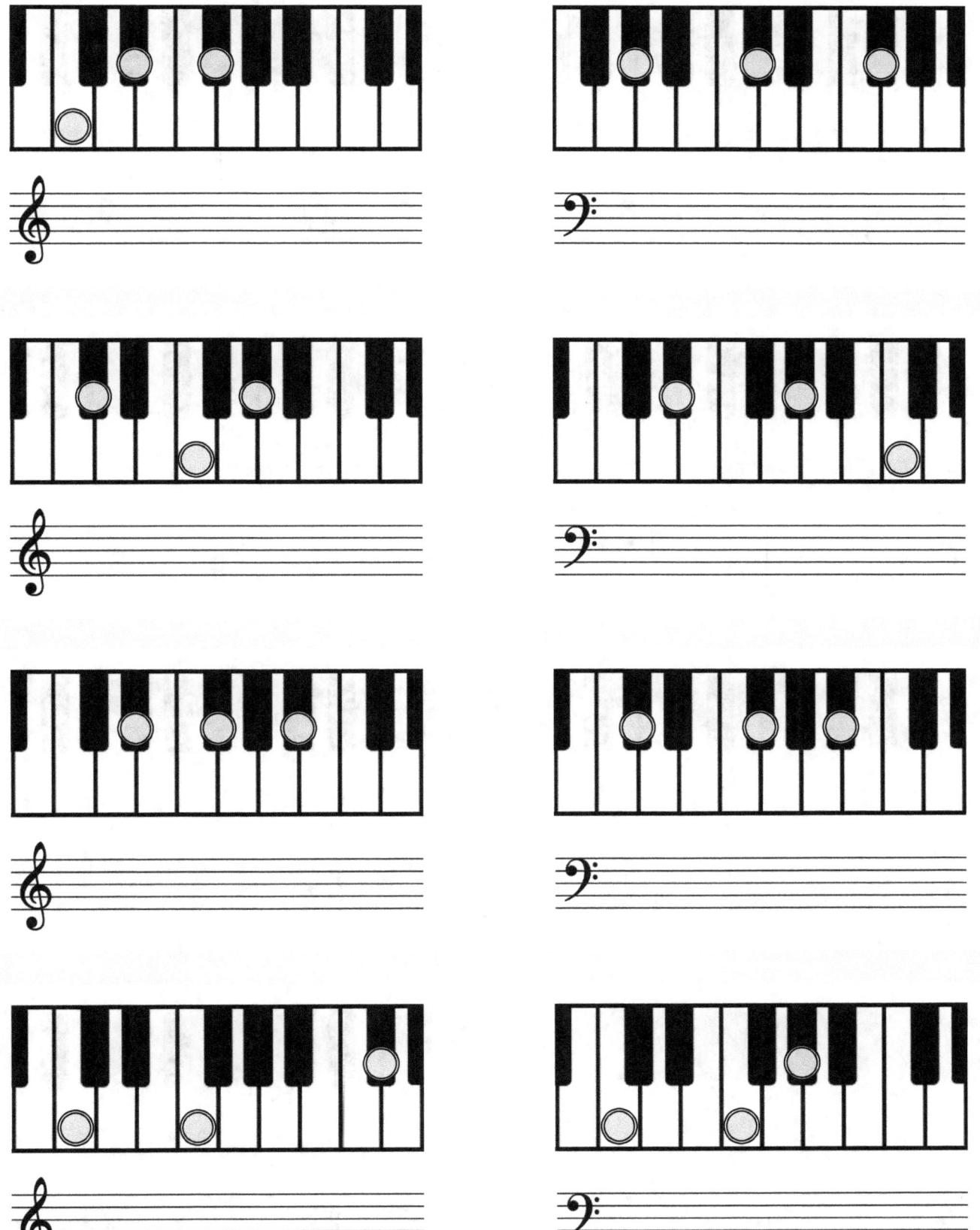

Circle the correct **keys** on the keyboard. Pay **attention** to the keyboard **layout**.

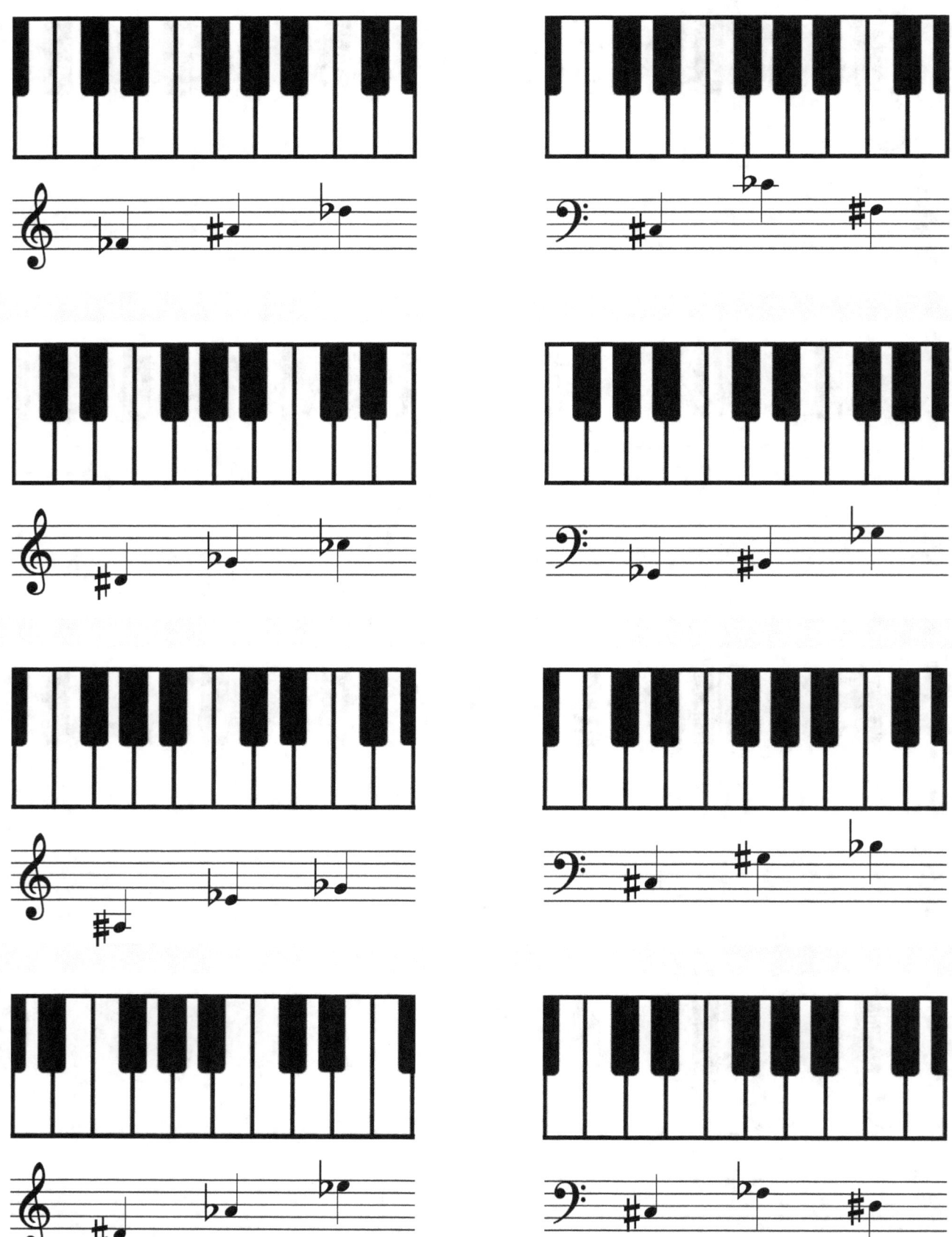

Fill all the **gaps**. **Draw** *(quarter)* **notes** (♯) on the staves and **circle** the notes on the **keyboard**.

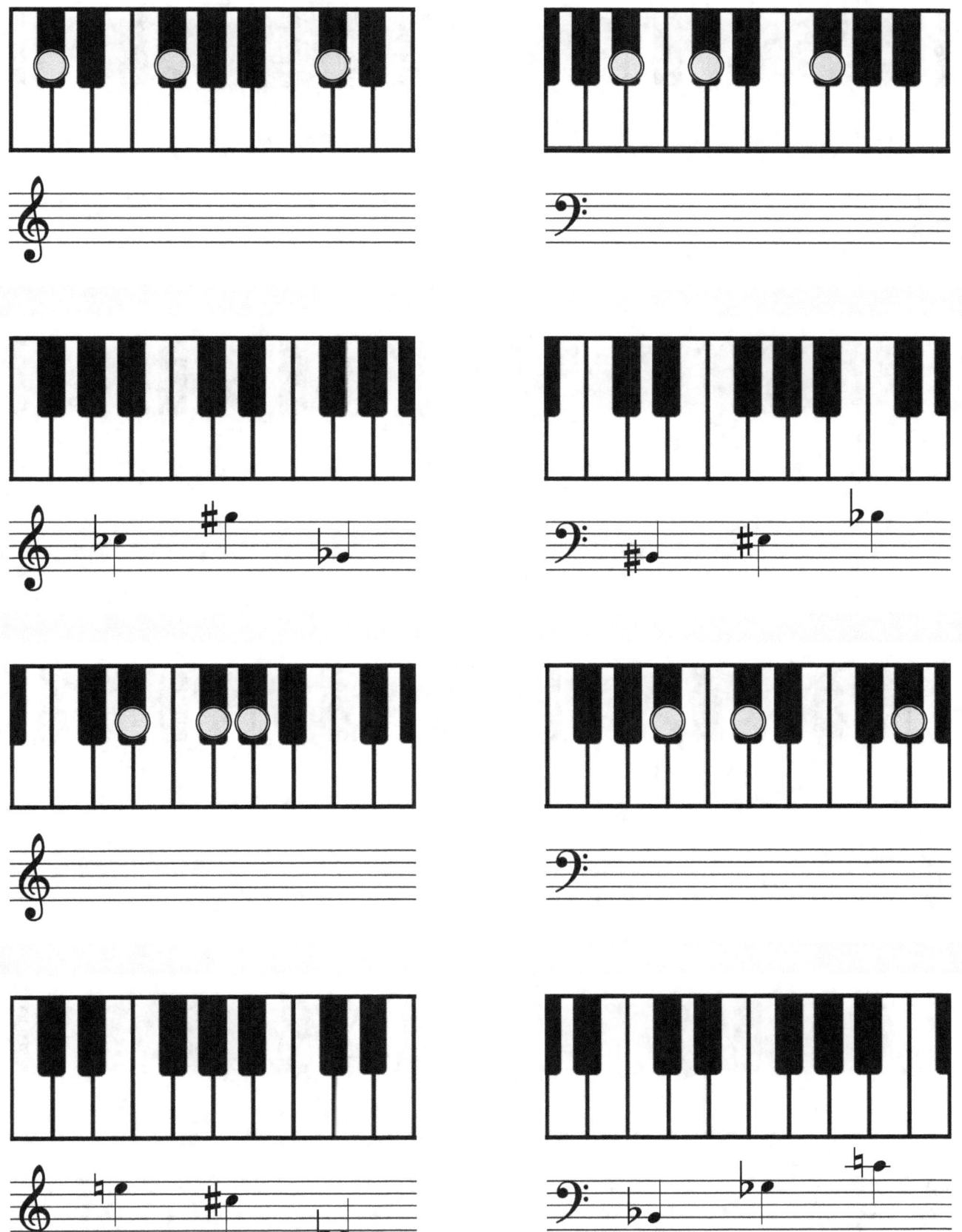

Fill all the **gaps**. **Draw** *(whole)* **notes** (♭) on the staves and **circle** the notes on the **keyboard**.

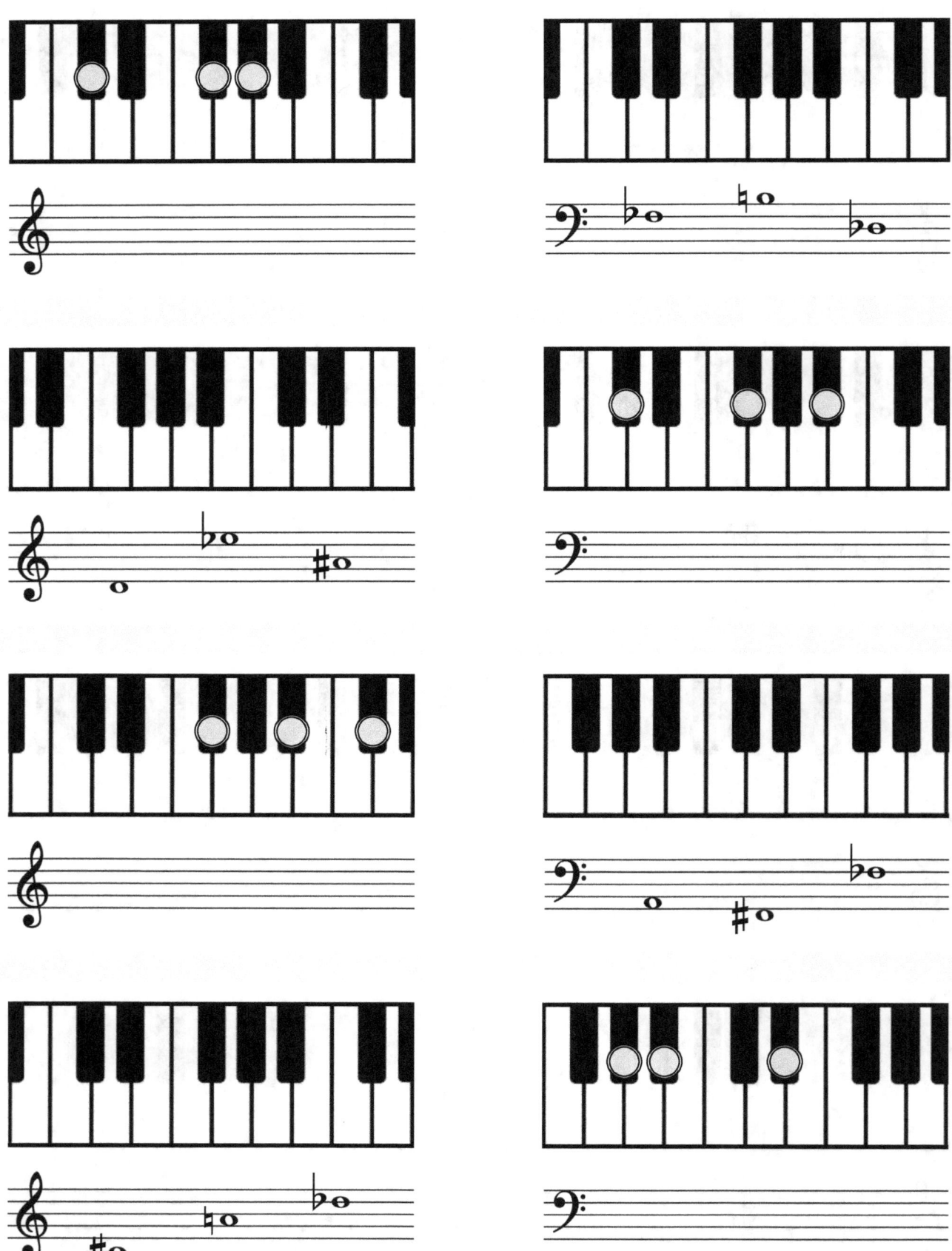

Fill all the **gaps**. **Draw** *(whole)* **notes (♯)** on the staves and **circle** the notes on the **keyboard**.

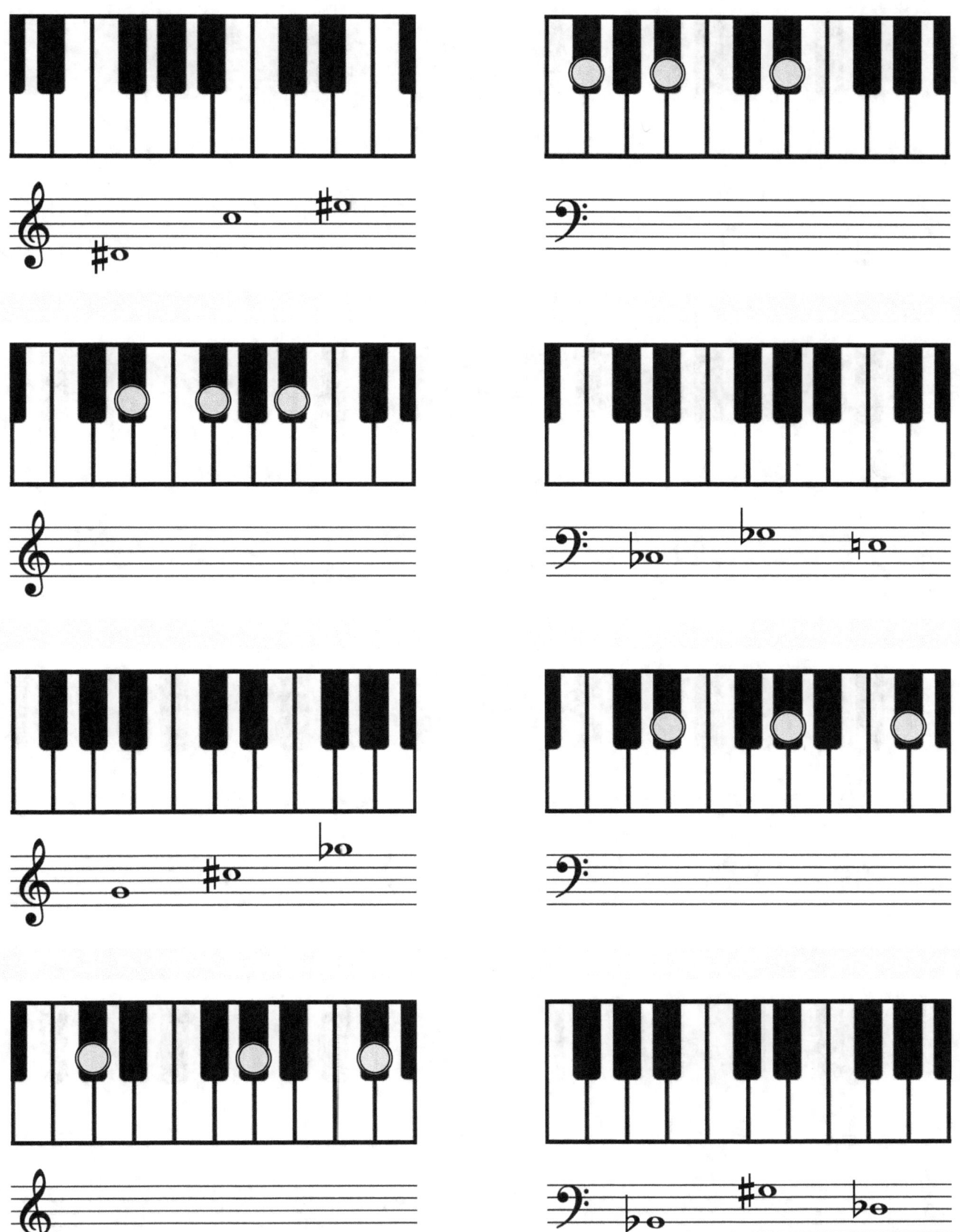

Fill all the **gaps**. **Draw** (quarter) **notes** (♯) on the staves and **circle** the notes on the **keyboard**.

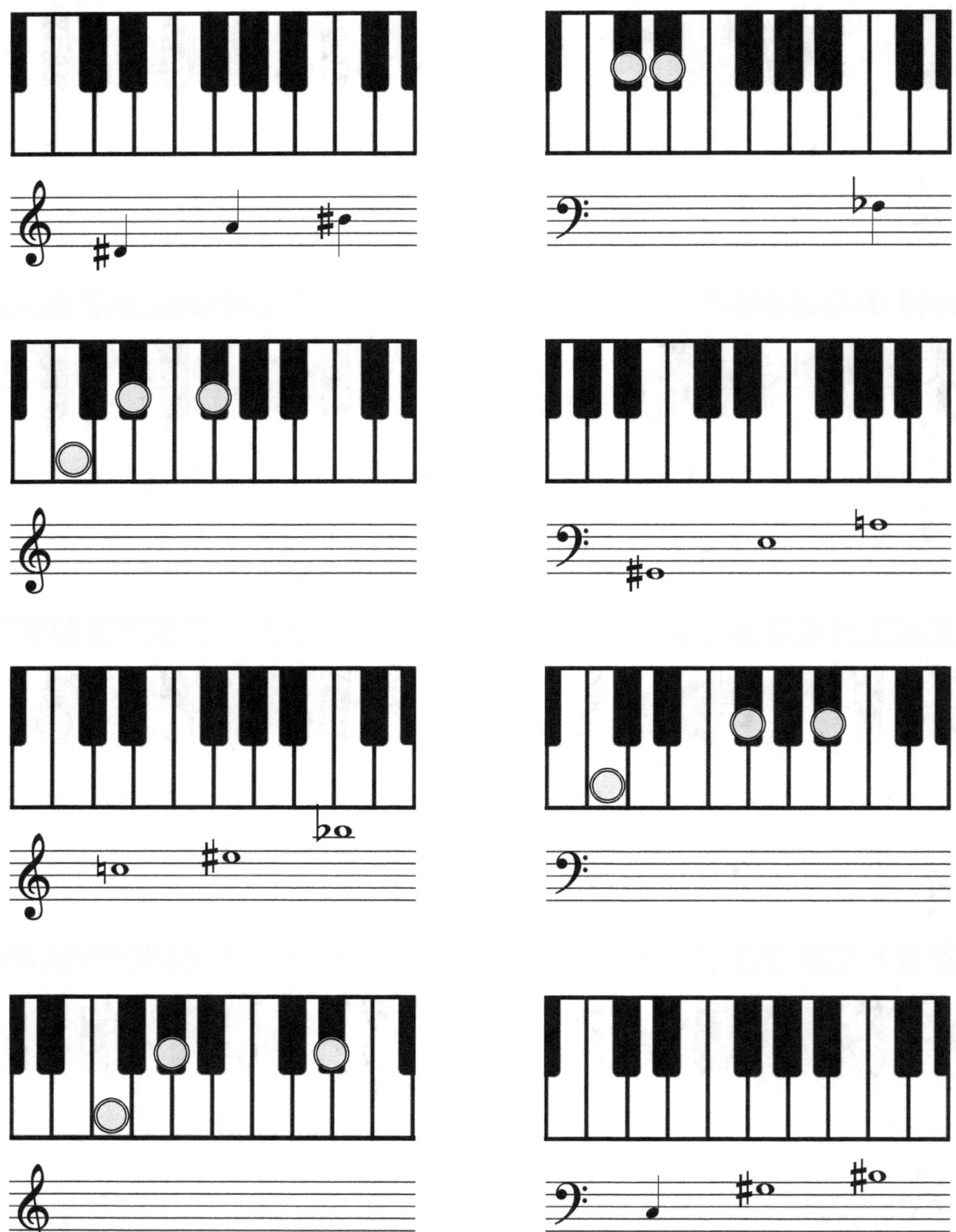

Fill all the **gaps**. **Draw** *(whole)* **notes (♯)** on the staves and **circle** the notes on the **keyboard**.

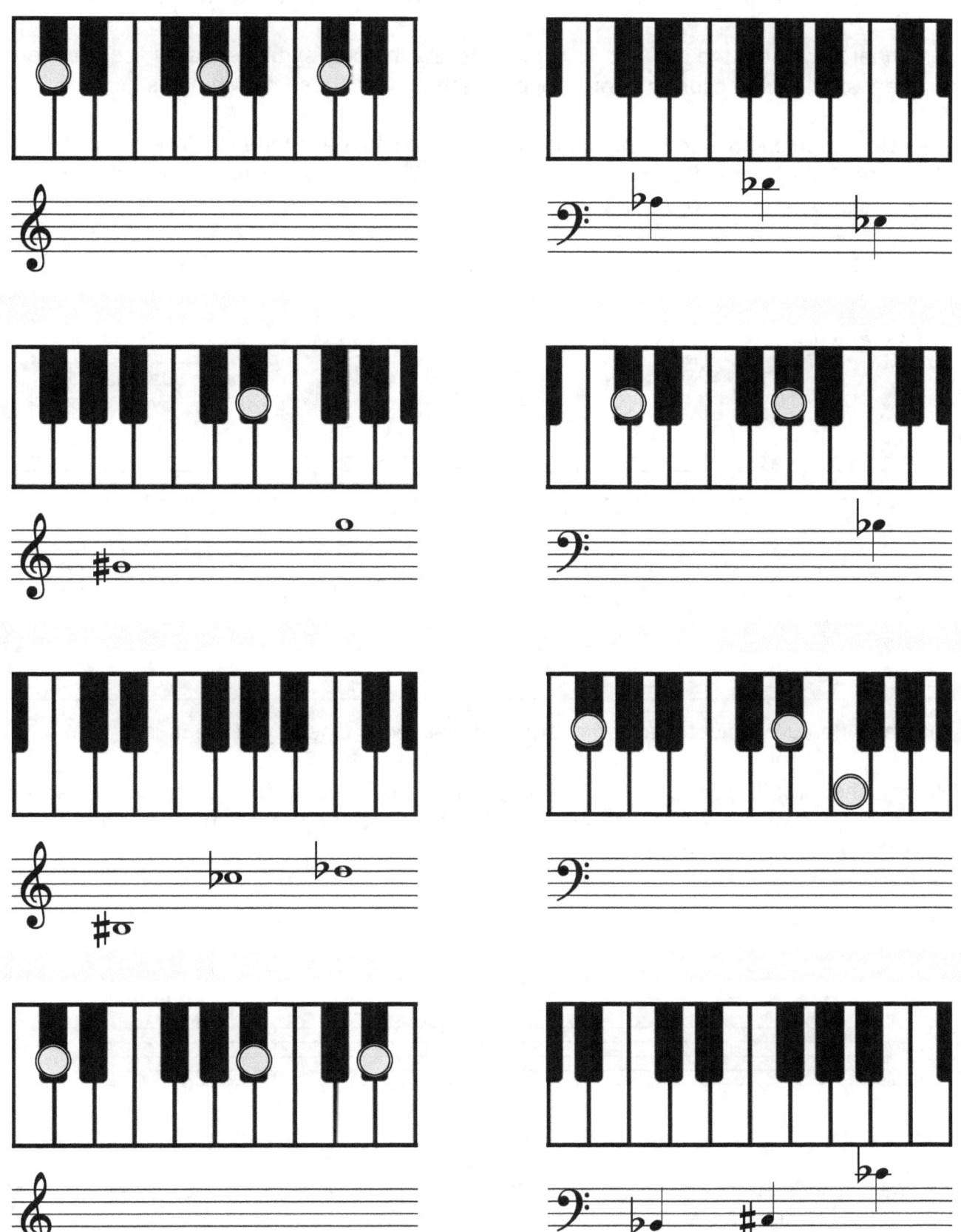

Key Signature

The key signature is placed right after the clef on the staff. It may contain either sharps on certain lines or spaces or some flats also on specific lines or spaces. If no flats or sharps are listed after the clef symbol, then the key signature means that "all notes are natural."

In standard notation, the clef and key signature are the only symbols that typically appear on every staff. They occur so frequently because they are essential symbols.

They signify which note corresponds to each line and space of the staff. The clef indicates which note letters are in the spaces or on the lines (C, D, E, etc.), while the key determines if the note is sharp, flat, or natural.

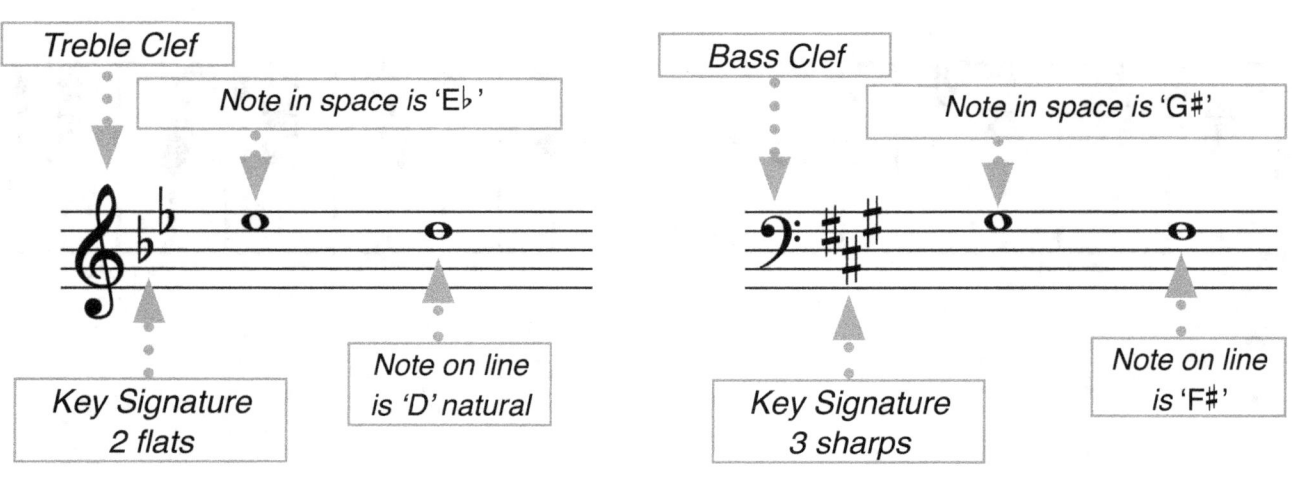

The key signature indicates all the sharps and flats within the key of the music.

When a sharp (or flat) appears on a line or space in the key signature, all notes on that line or space are raised (or lowered), and all other notes sharing the same letter in different octaves are also raised (or lowered).

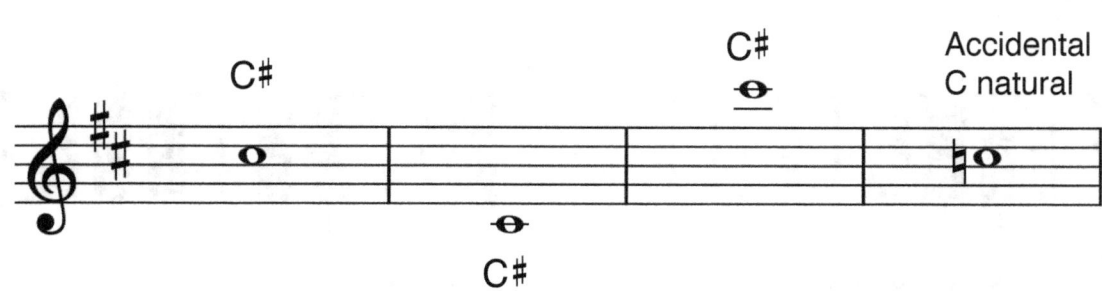

If a sharp is indicated in the C space on the staff, then all Cs are C-sharp unless a natural or another accidental alters this.

Sharps and flats always appear in the same order across all key signatures (up to 7 sharps or flats, but never both). For instance, if a key (G major or E minor) has only one sharp, it will be F-sharp; therefore, F-sharp is always the first sharp listed in a sharp key signature. The keys with two sharps (D major and B minor) have F-sharp and C-sharp; thus, C-sharp is always the second sharp in a key signature, and so on.

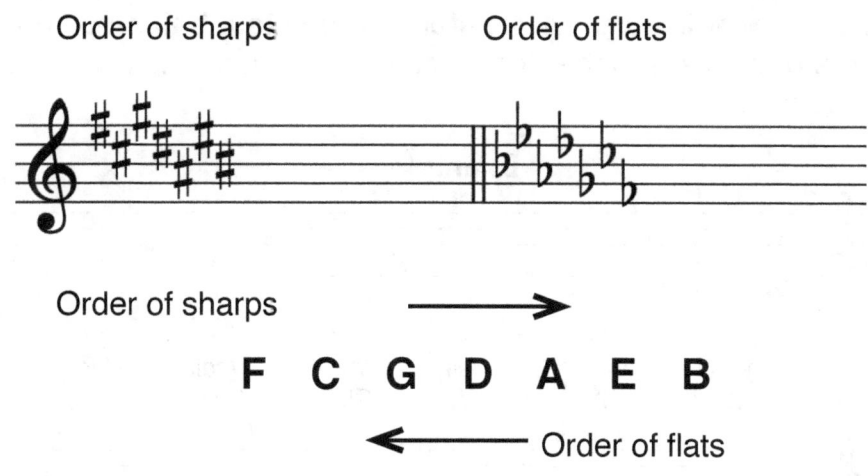

Order of sharps   Order of flats

Order of sharps   ⟶

F C G D A E B

⟵   Order of flats

The order of sharps is: F-sharp, C-sharp, G-sharp, D-sharp, A-sharp, E-sharp, B-sharp. The order of flats is the reverse of the order of sharps: B-flat, E-flat, A-flat, D-flat, G-flat, C-flat, F-flat.

Thus, the keys with only one flat (F major and D minor) have a B-flat; the keys with two flats (B-flat major and G minor) have B-flat and E-flat; and so on.

The sequence of flats and sharps, like the order of the keys themselves, follows the circle of fifths *(see next page)*.

Example

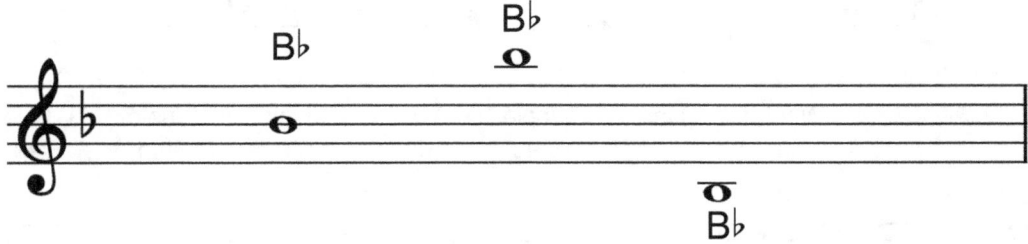

If the key signature has a B-flat on the B line, then all B notes on the staff are marked with a flat. This is indicated once at the beginning and applies to all subsequent notes on this line and across all octaves.

This is logical when most notes in the piece of music feature this B-flat, which is then added to the key signature. If it only occurs occasionally, individual notes are marked with accidentals as needed.

Major and minor keys

The arrangement of sharps (♯) and flats (♭) in music helps us recognize different types of scales, known as major and minor. Each scale begins with a specific note, which also names the scale. For example, a C major scale starts with the note C. These scales, called diatonic scales, follow a pattern of seven notes that are spaced in a sequence of whole steps (like walking up two stairs at a time) and half steps (like walking up one stair at a time).

Major scale

To find the notes in a major key, start on the root note and follow this pattern: **whole step, whole step, half step, whole step, whole step, whole step, half step**. This pattern leads you to the root note one octave higher than where you began, and it includes all the notes of the key in that octave.

Example

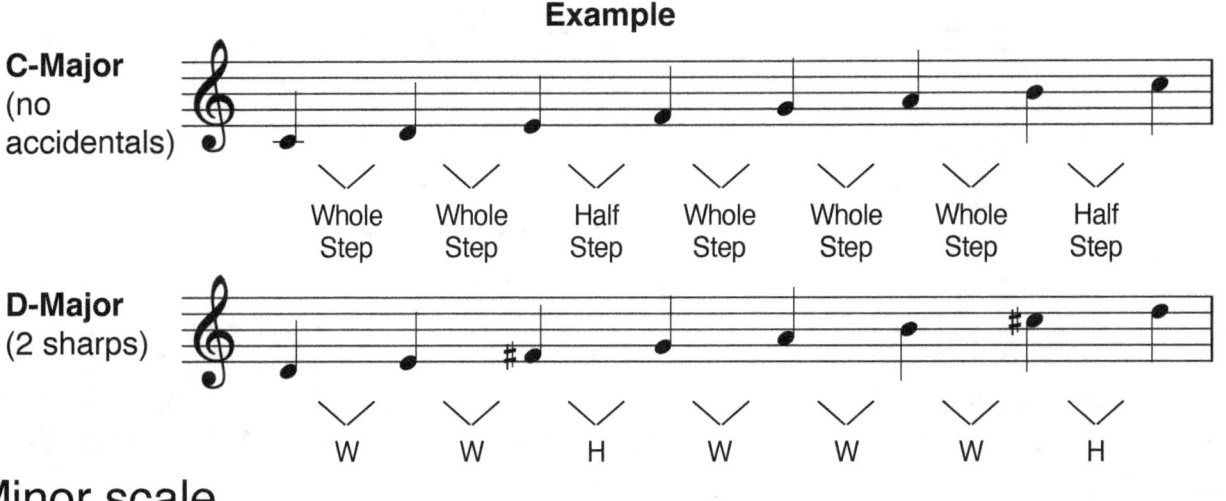

Minor scale

To find the notes in a minor key, begin on the root note and follow this pattern: **whole step, half step, whole step, whole step, half step, whole step, whole step**. This sequence will lead you to the root note one octave higher than where you started, covering all the notes of the key within that octave.1

Example

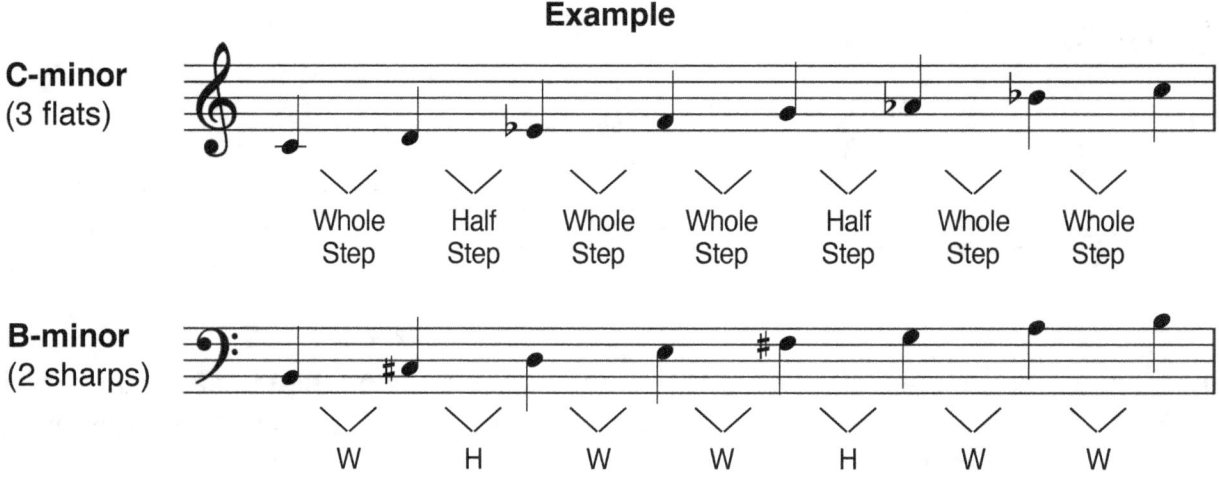

In both examples, the accidentals are placed directly in front of the notes. In the key signature, these are written on the respective lines (or spaces), thus eliminating the need to repeatedly mark the accidentals throughout the piece.

Circle of Fifths

The circle of fifths visually illustrates the relationships among the 12 major and minor keys. Each major key has a corresponding related minor key. Moving clockwise, each step adds a sharp, while moving counterclockwise, each step adds a flat.

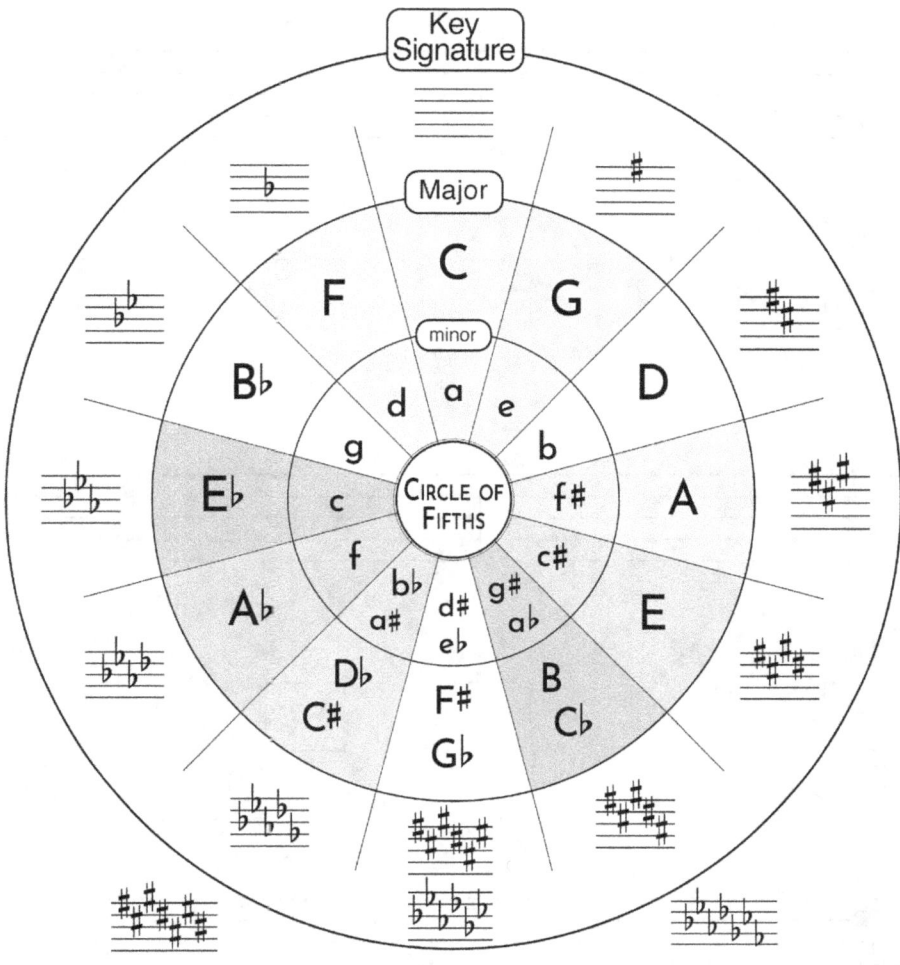

The keys in the same "slice" contain the same set of notes, just in a different order. For example, C minor is the relative minor of E-flat major.

Example

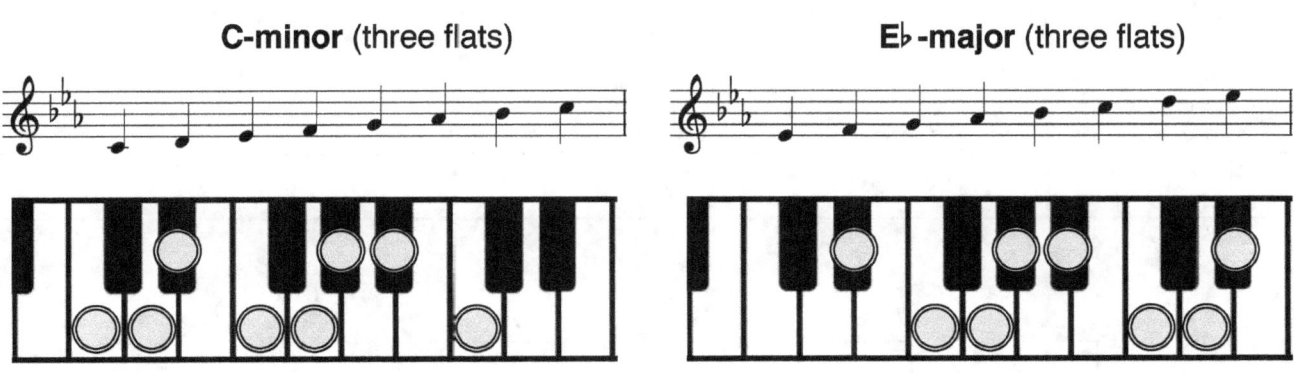

C-minor (three flats)   **E♭-major** (three flats)

C minor and E-flat major start on different notes but have the same key signature.

Write the correct note **names** in the boxes. Pay **attention** to the **key signature** and **accidentals**.

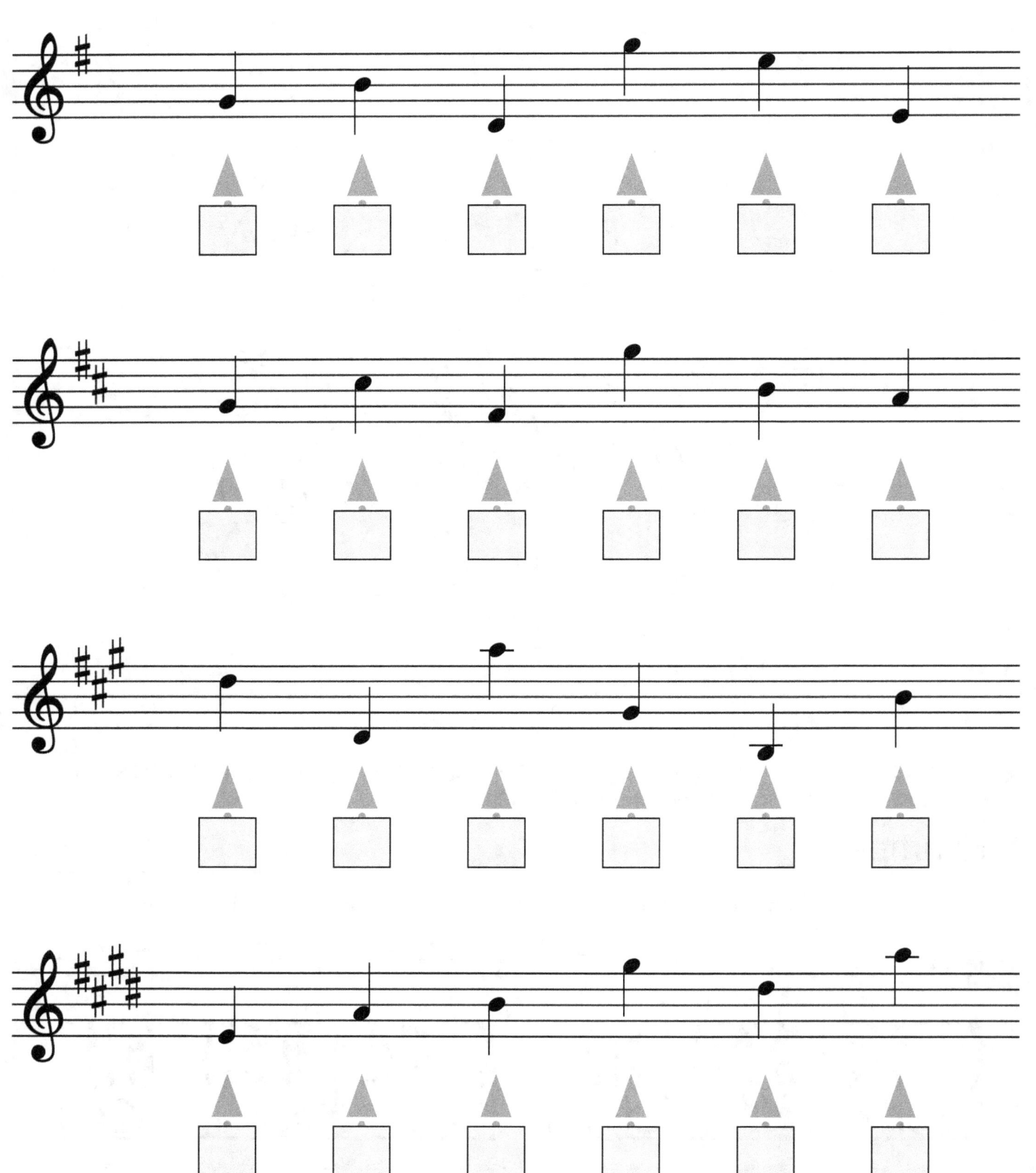

Write the correct note **names** in the boxes. Pay **attention** to the **key signature** and **accidentals**.

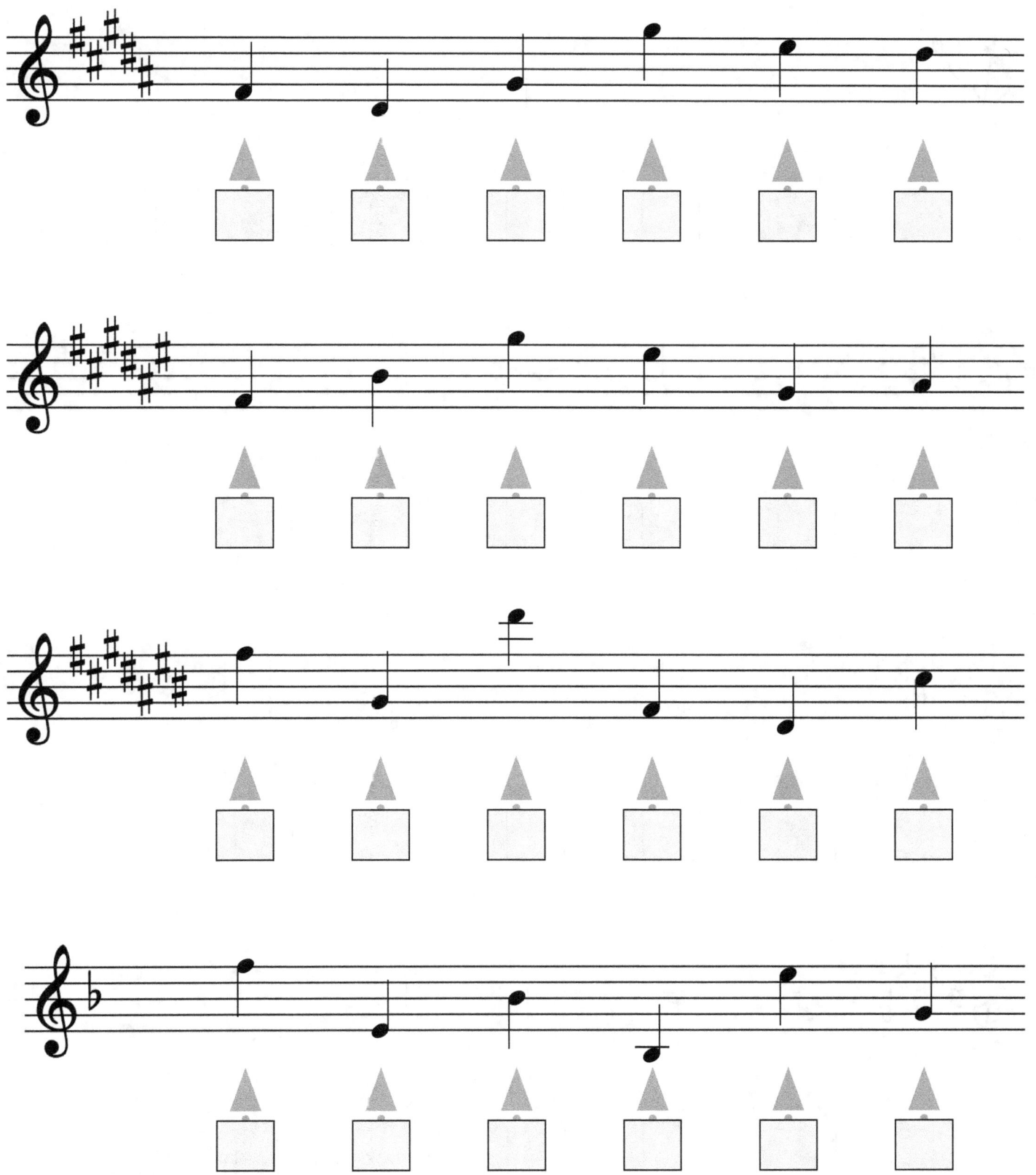

Write the correct note **names** in the boxes. Pay **attention** to the **key signature** and **accidentals**.

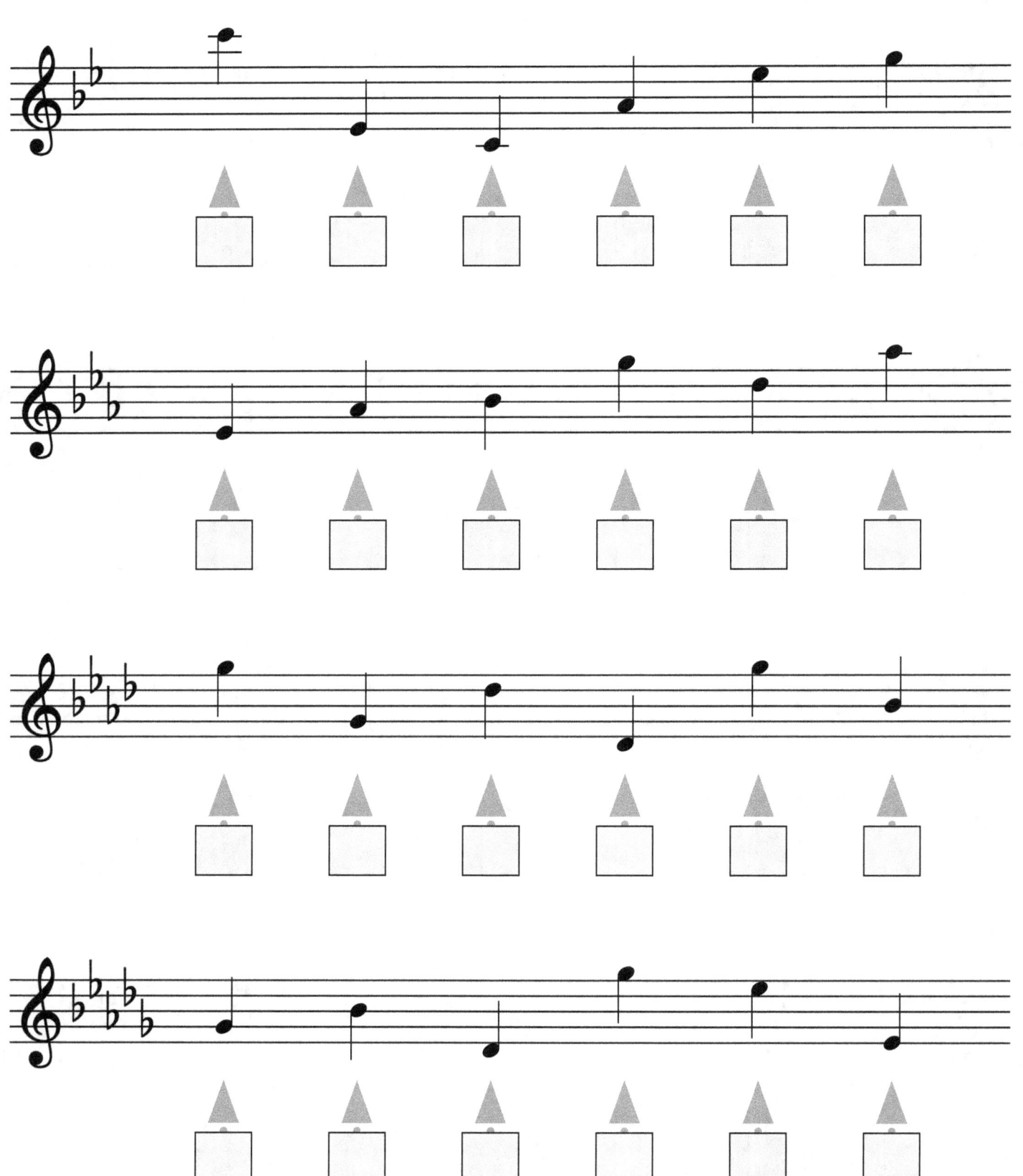

Write the correct note **names** in the boxes. Pay **attention** to the **key signature** and **accidentals**.

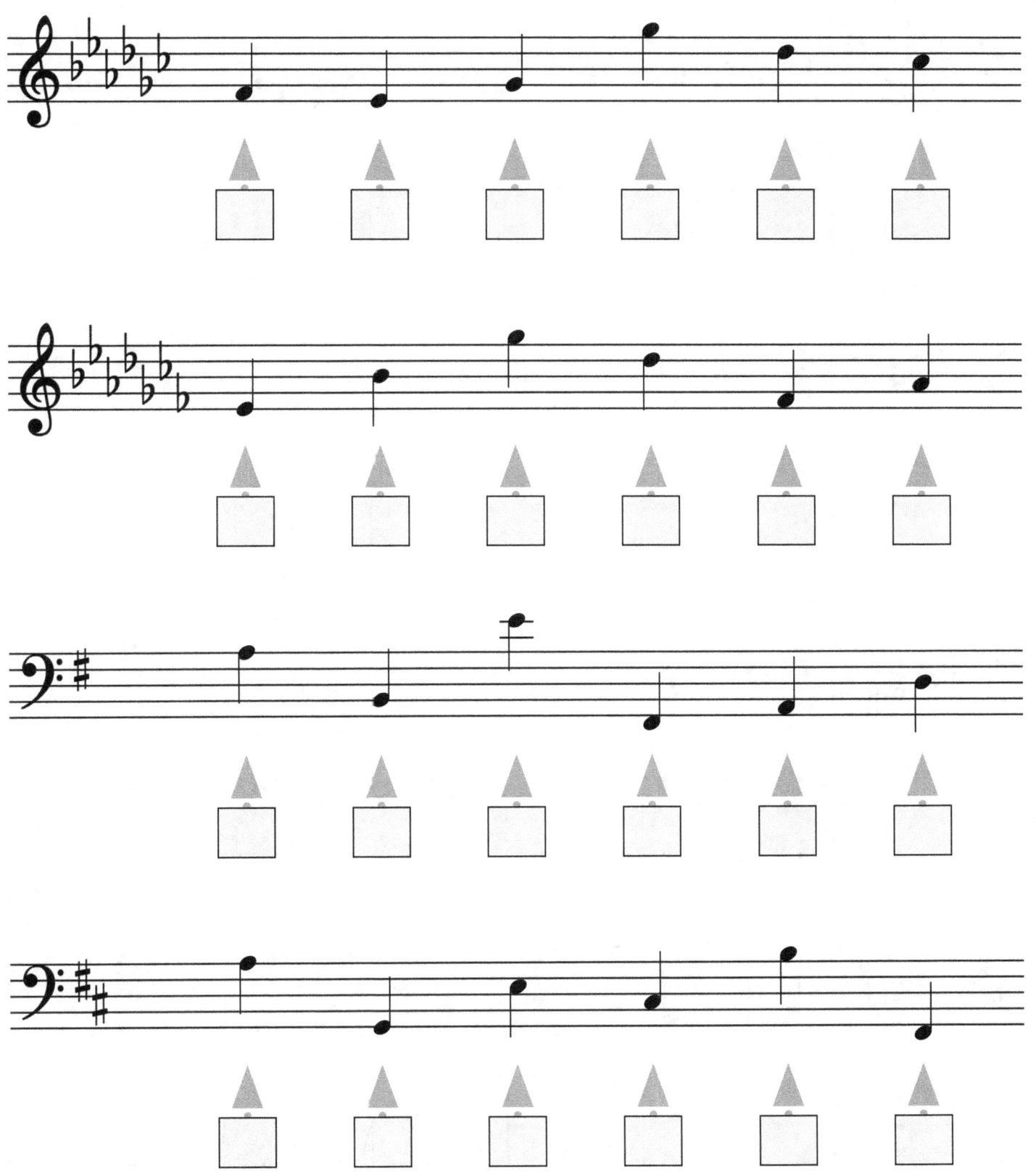

Write the correct note **names** in the boxes. Pay **attention** to the **key signature** and **accidentals**.

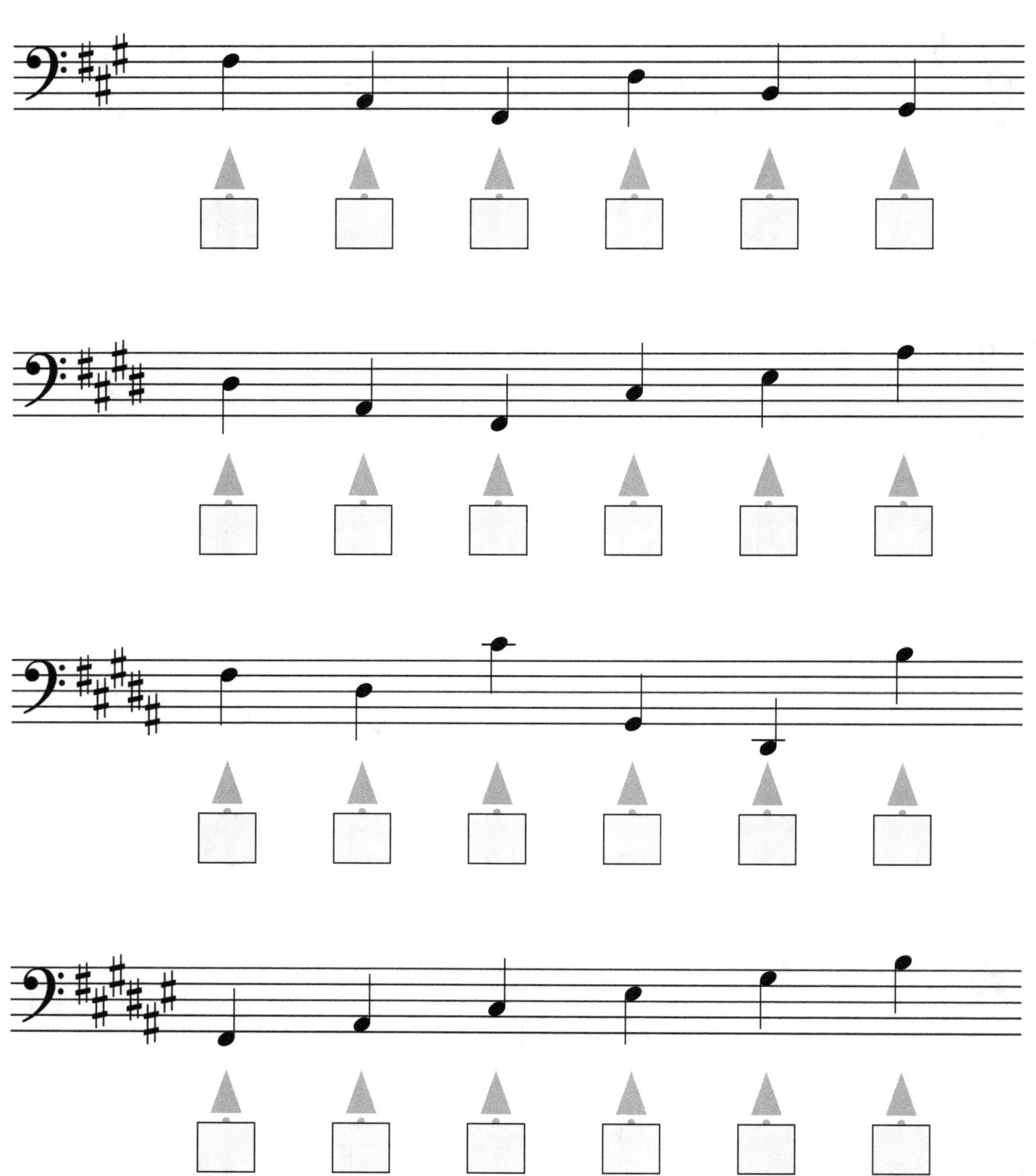

Write the correct note **names** in the boxes. Pay **attention** to the **key signature** and **accidentals**.

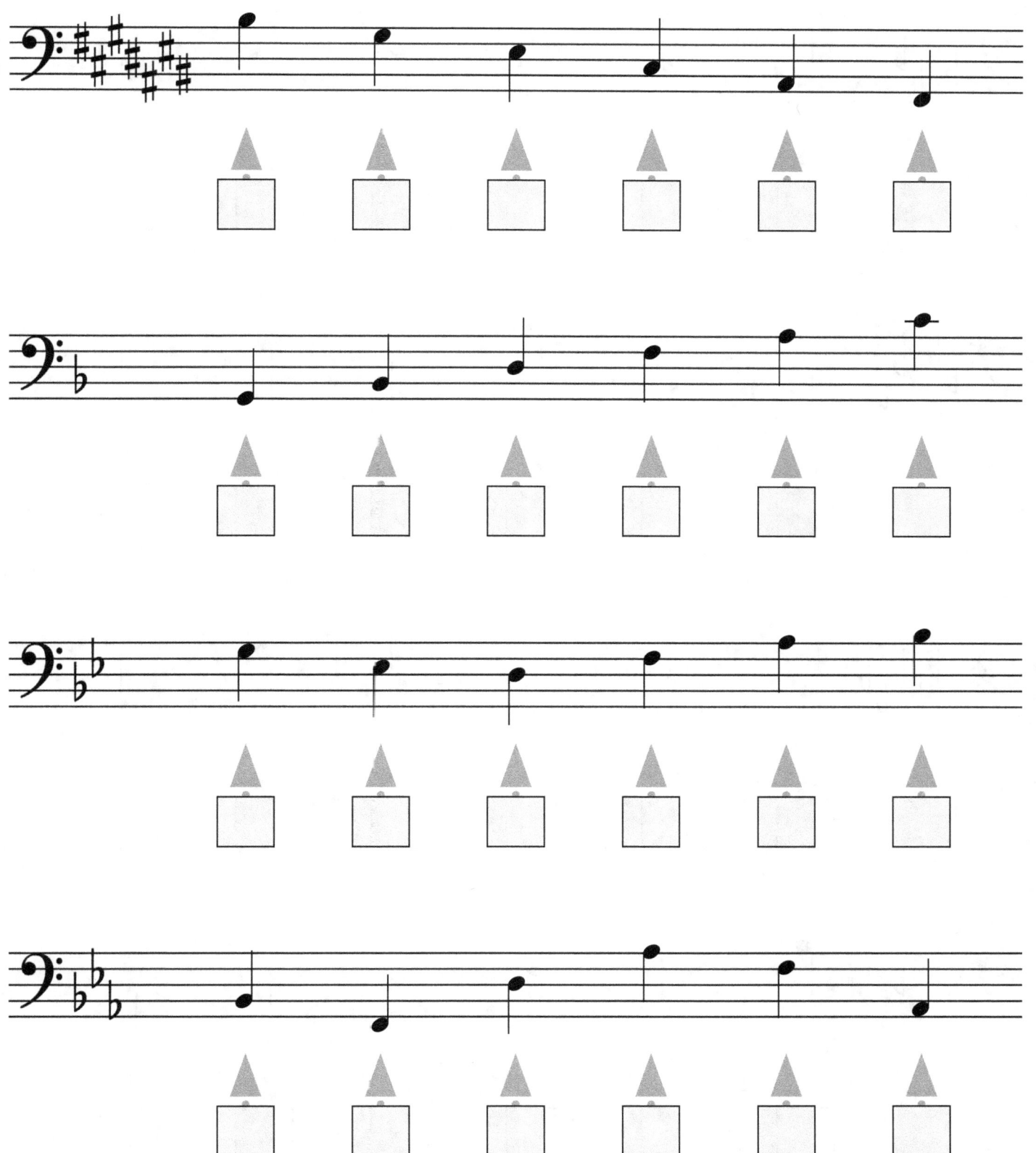

Write the correct note **names** in the boxes. Pay **attention** to the **key signature** and **accidentals**.

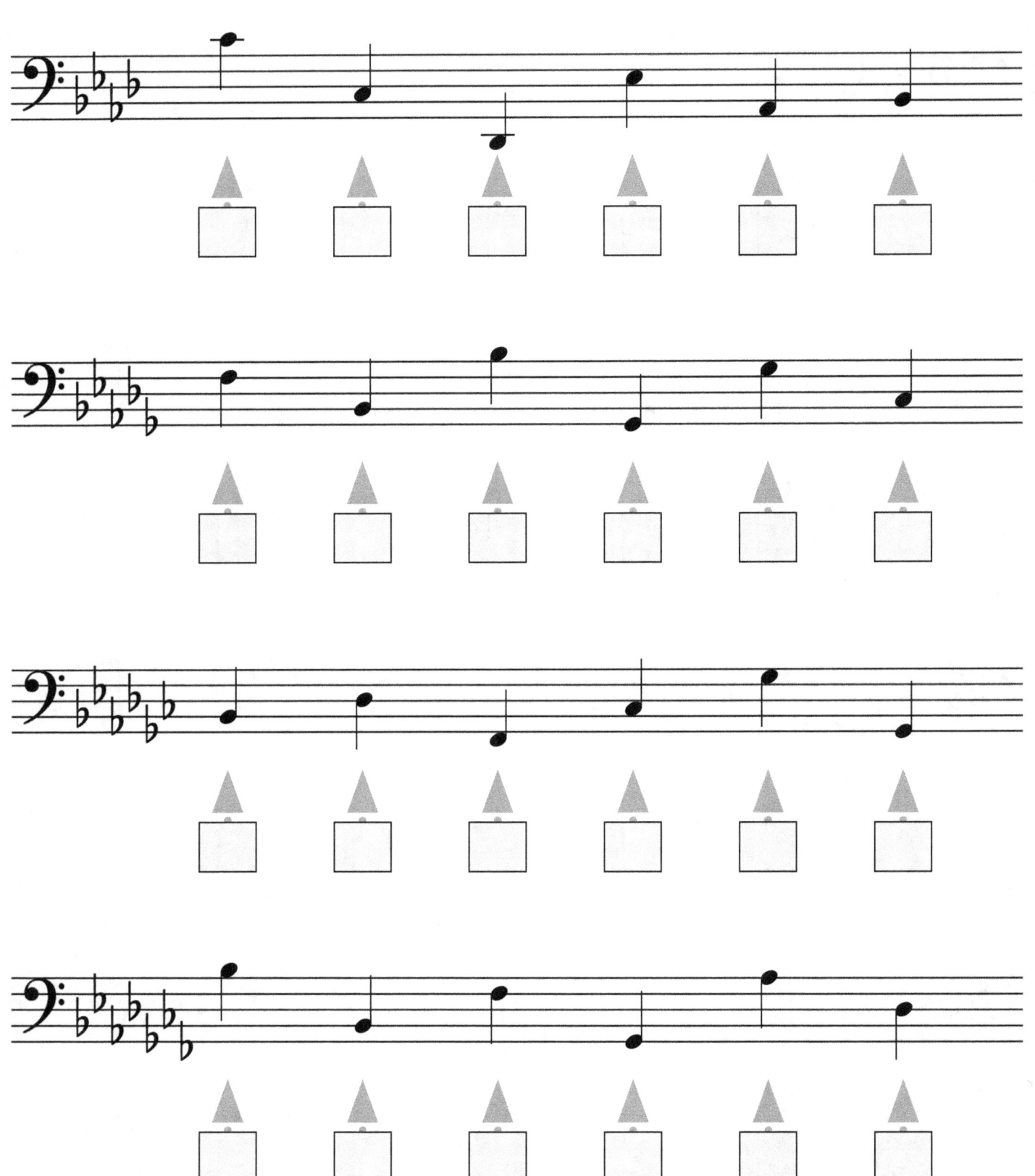

Write the correct note **names** in the boxes. Pay **attention** to the **key signature** and **accidentals**.

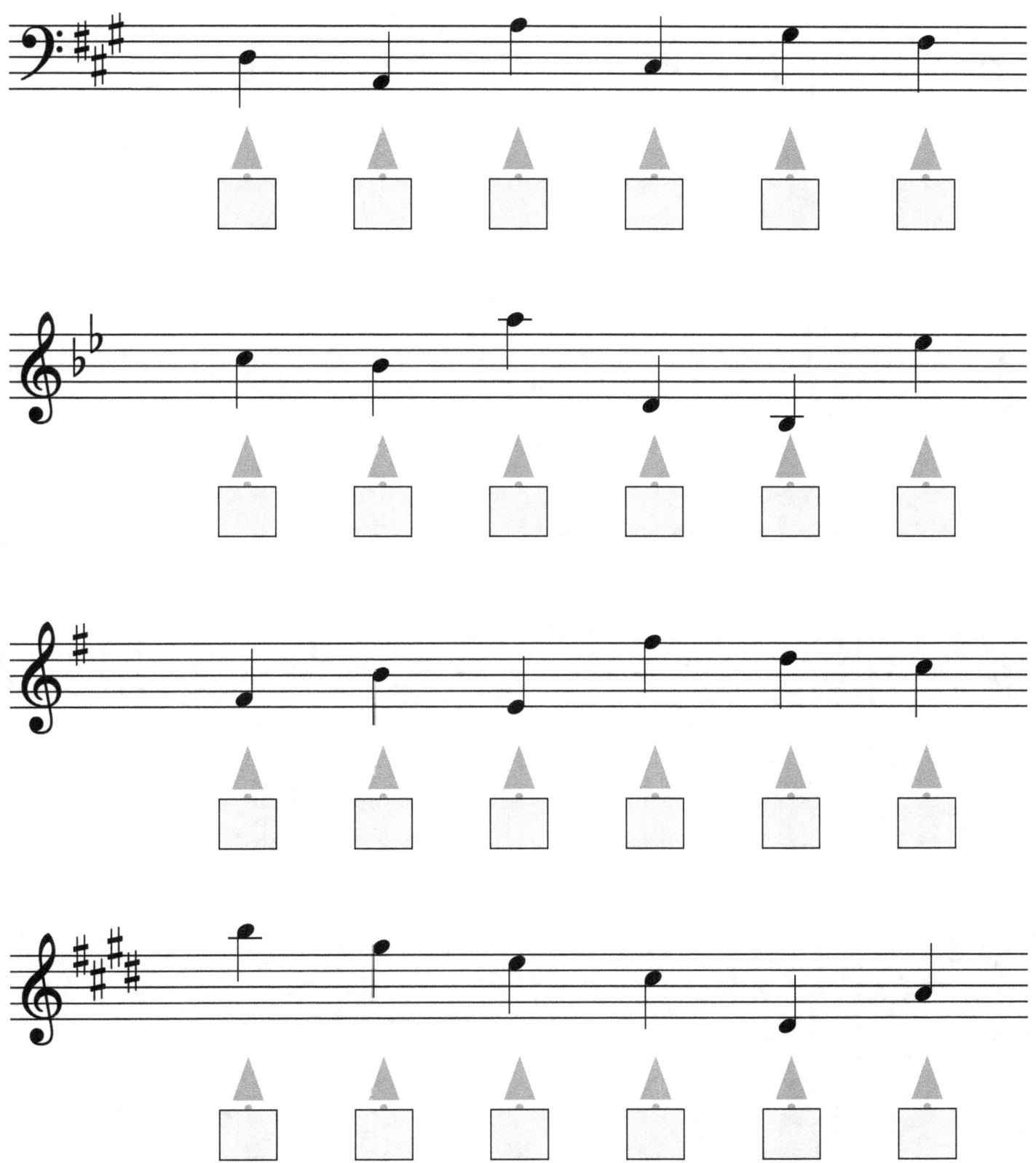

Write the correct note **names** in the boxes. Pay **attention** to the **key signature** and **accidentals**.

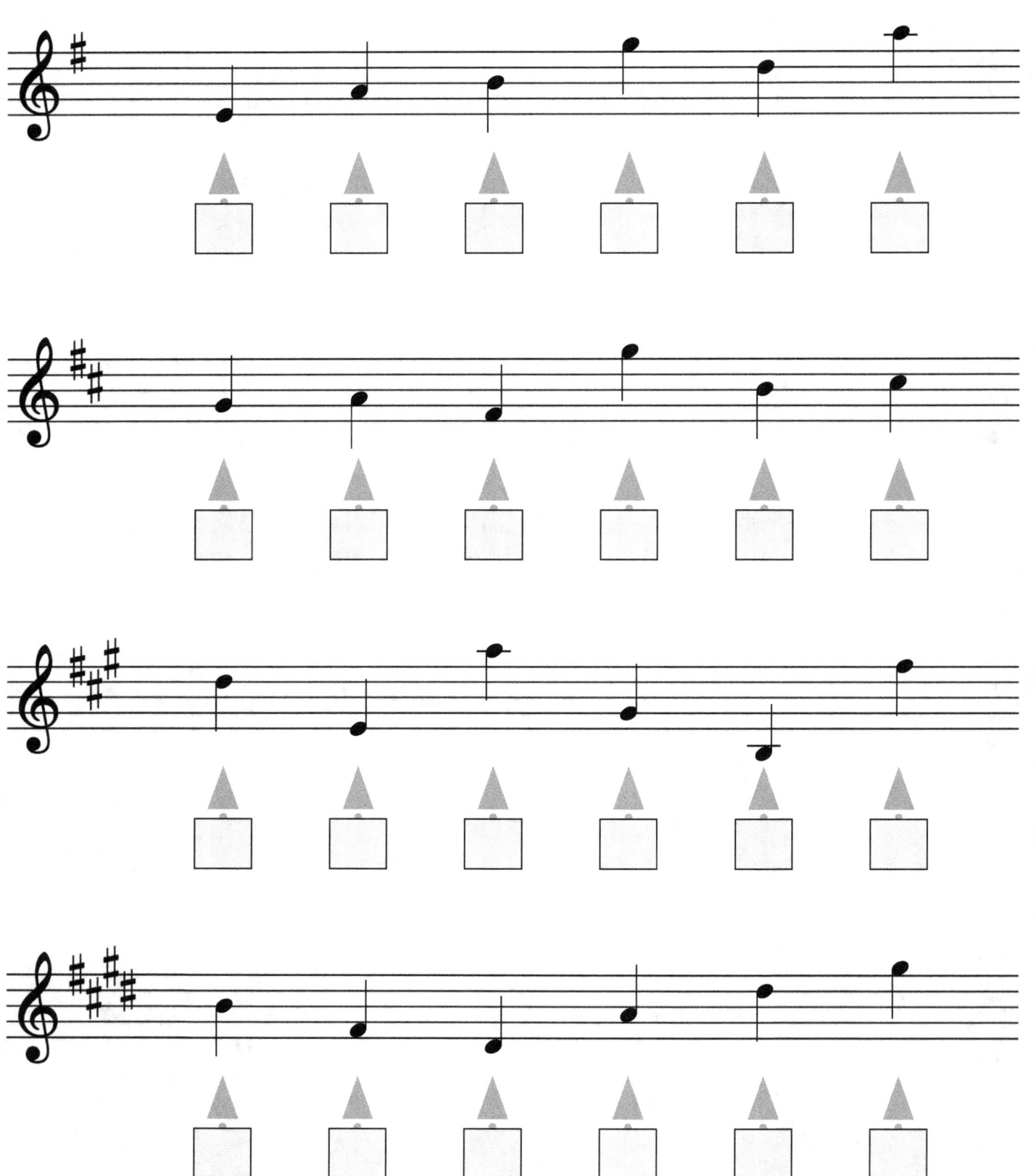

Write the correct note **names** in the boxes. Pay **attention** to the **key signature** and **accidentals**.

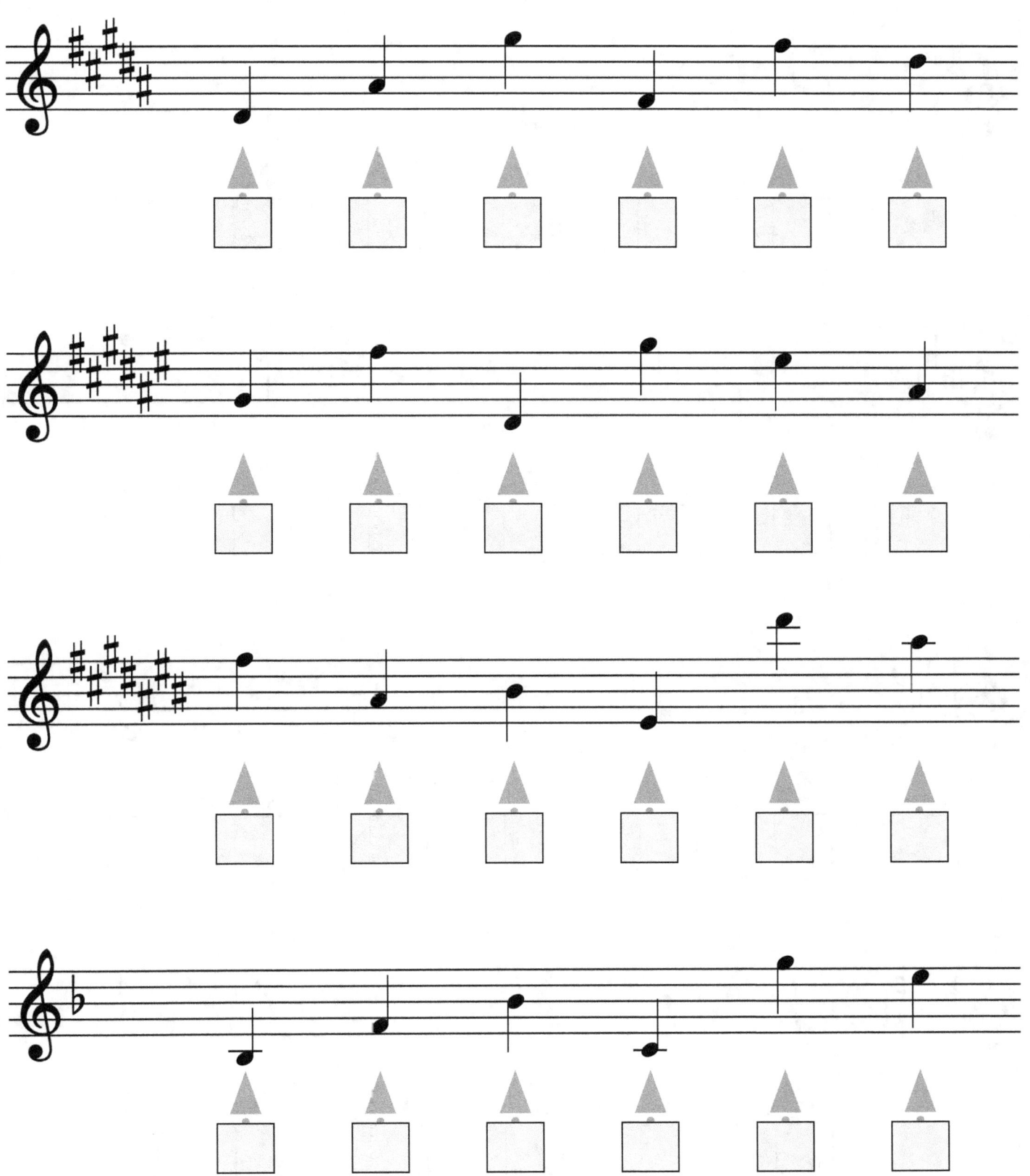

Write the correct note **names** in the boxes. Pay **attention** to the **key signature** and **accidentals**.

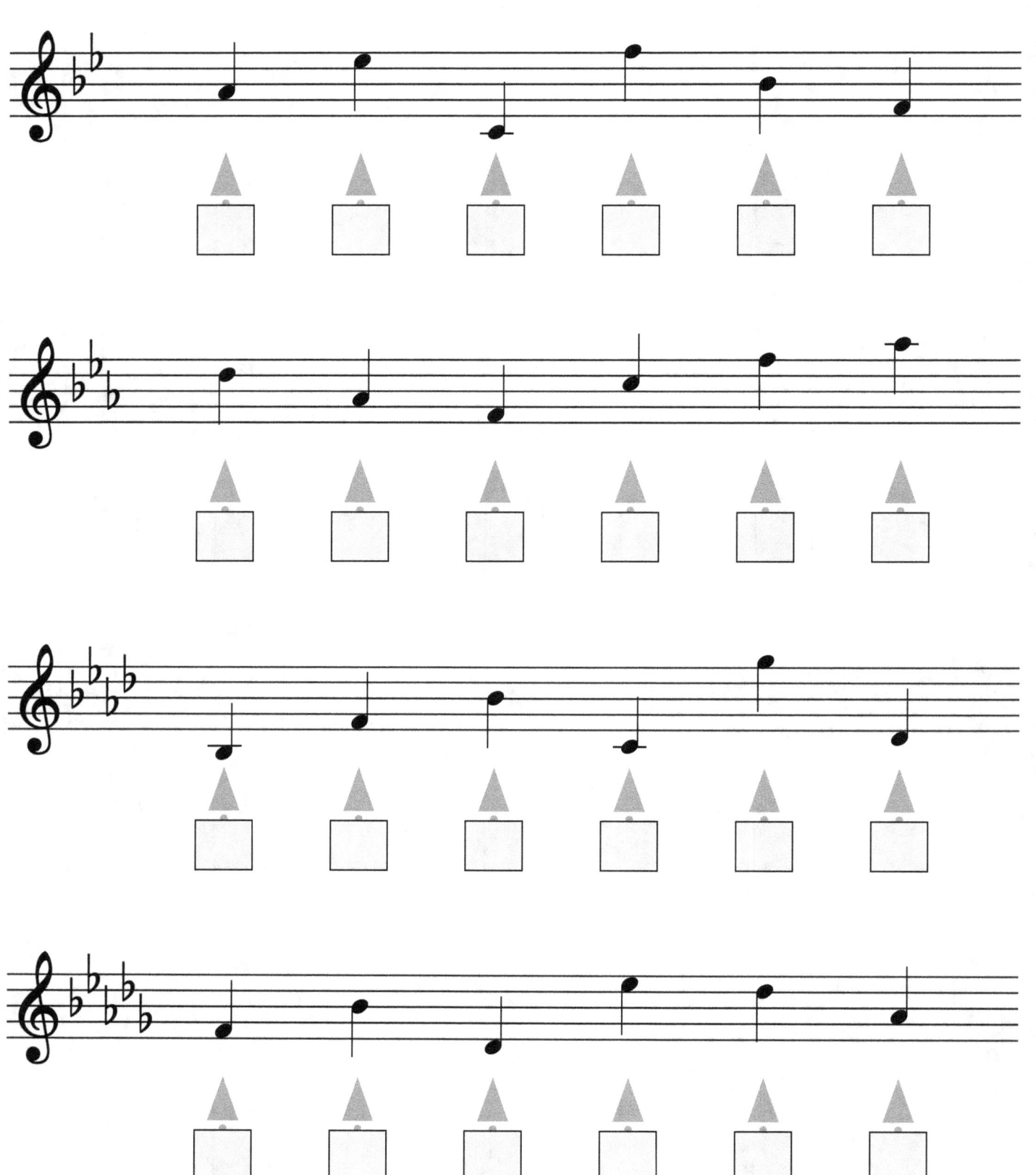

Write the correct note **names** in the boxes. Pay **attention** to the **key signature** and **accidentals**.

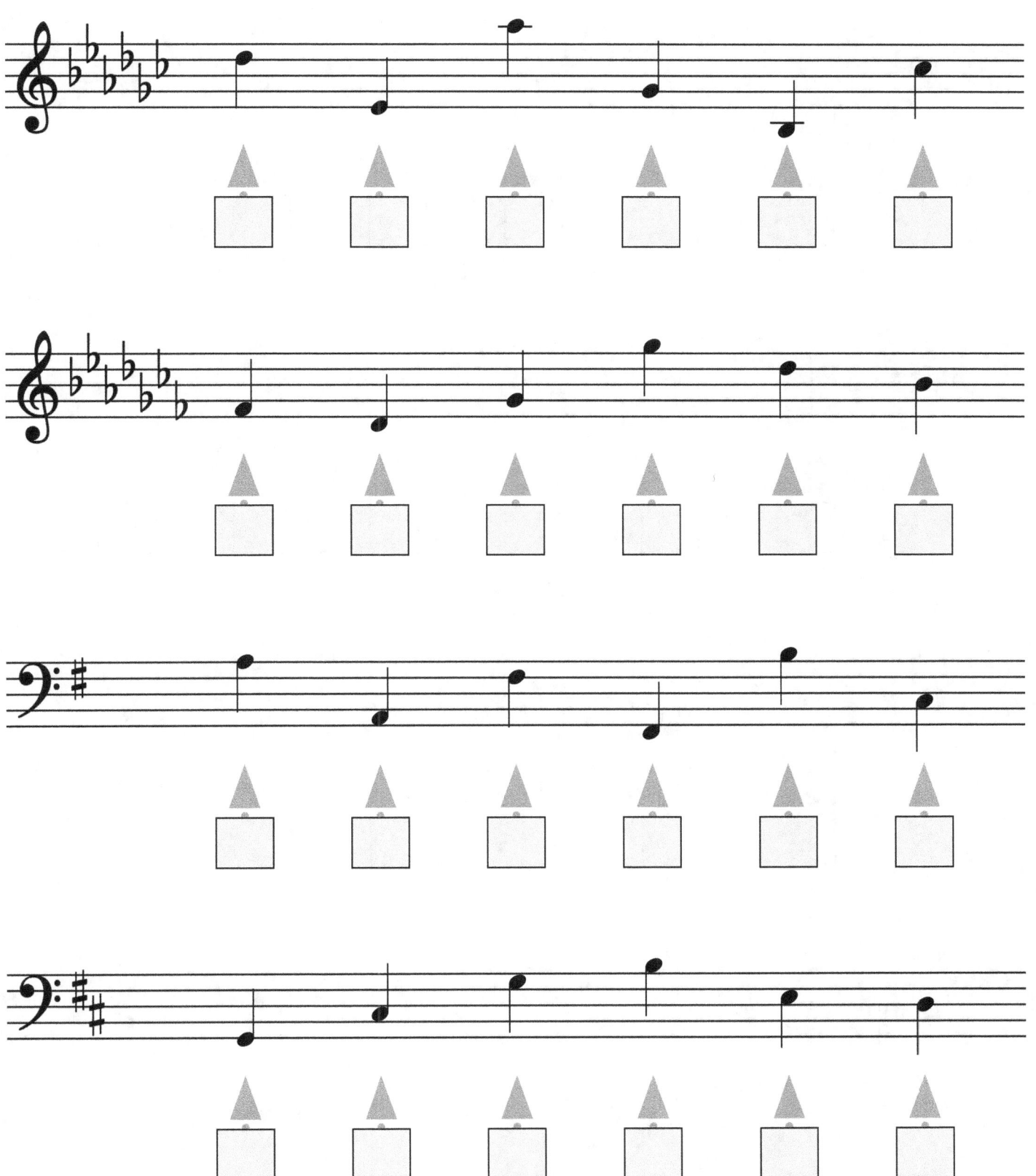

Write the correct note **names** in the boxes. Pay **attention** to the **key signature** and **accidentals**.

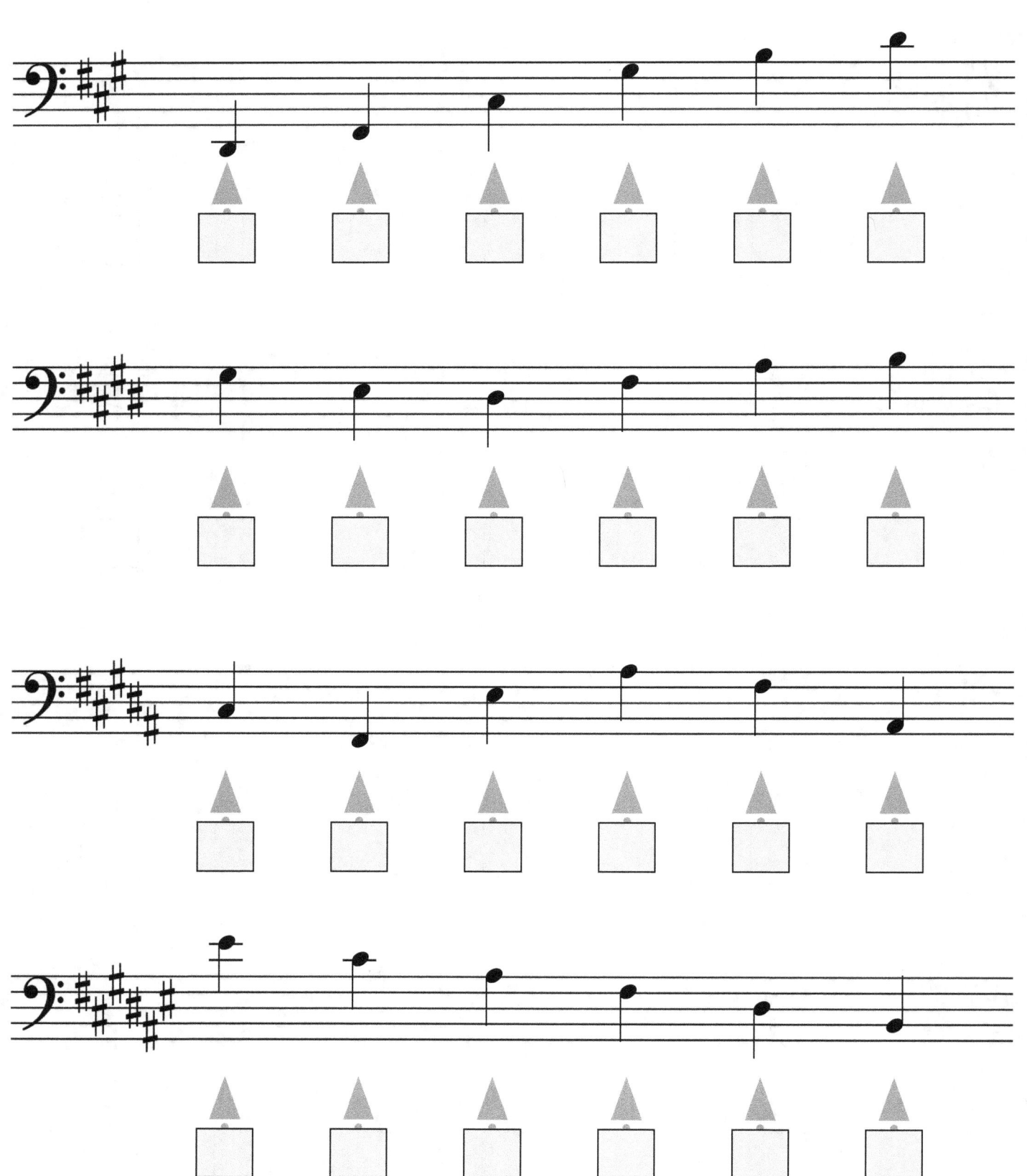

Write the correct note **names** in the boxes. Pay **attention** to the **key signature** and **accidentals**.

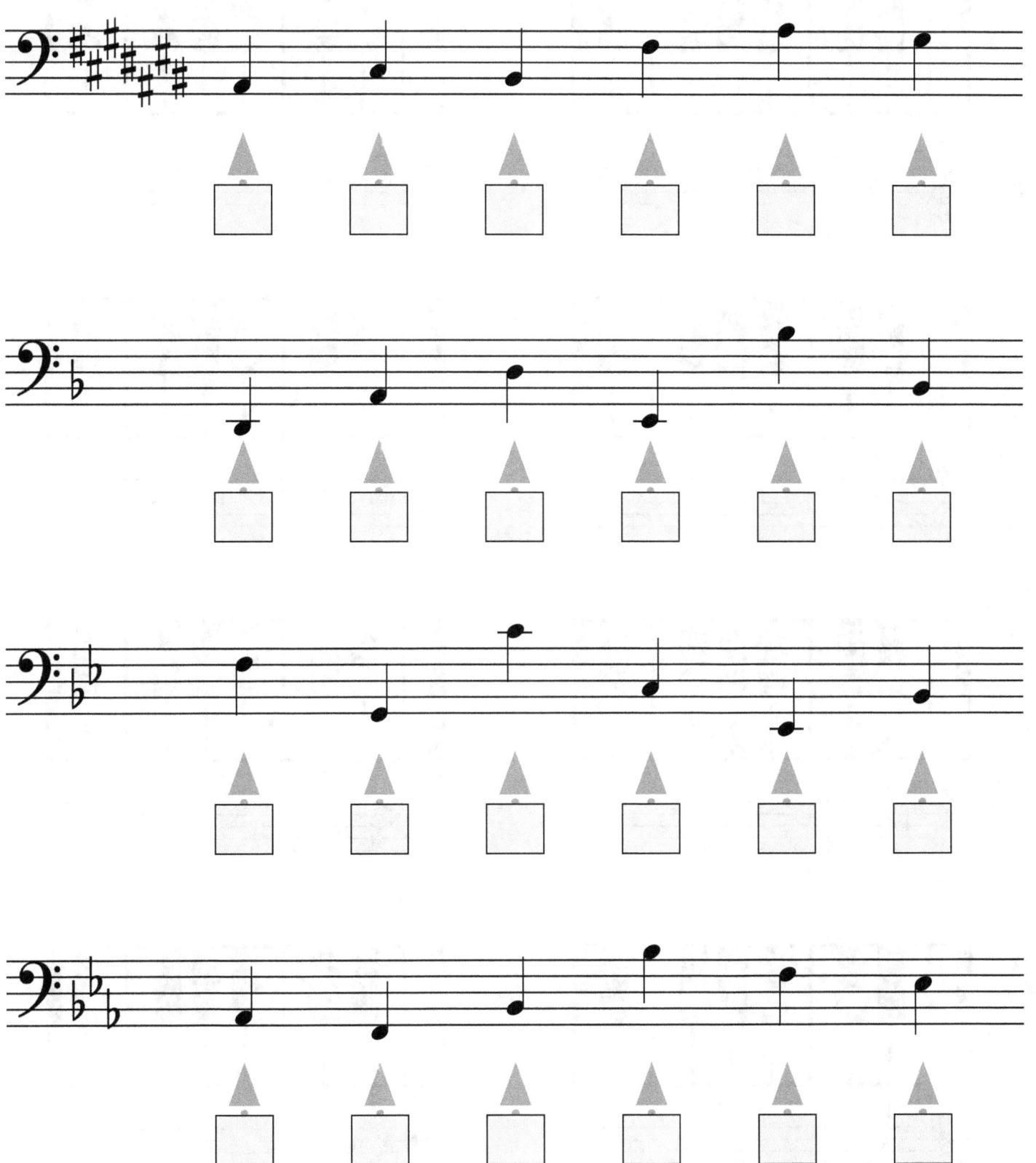

Draw the correct **notes** *(whole notes)* in the staves. Pay **attention** to the **key signature** and **accidentals**.
Use the type of **accidentals** that the key signature uses or **natural signs** for notes not in the key.

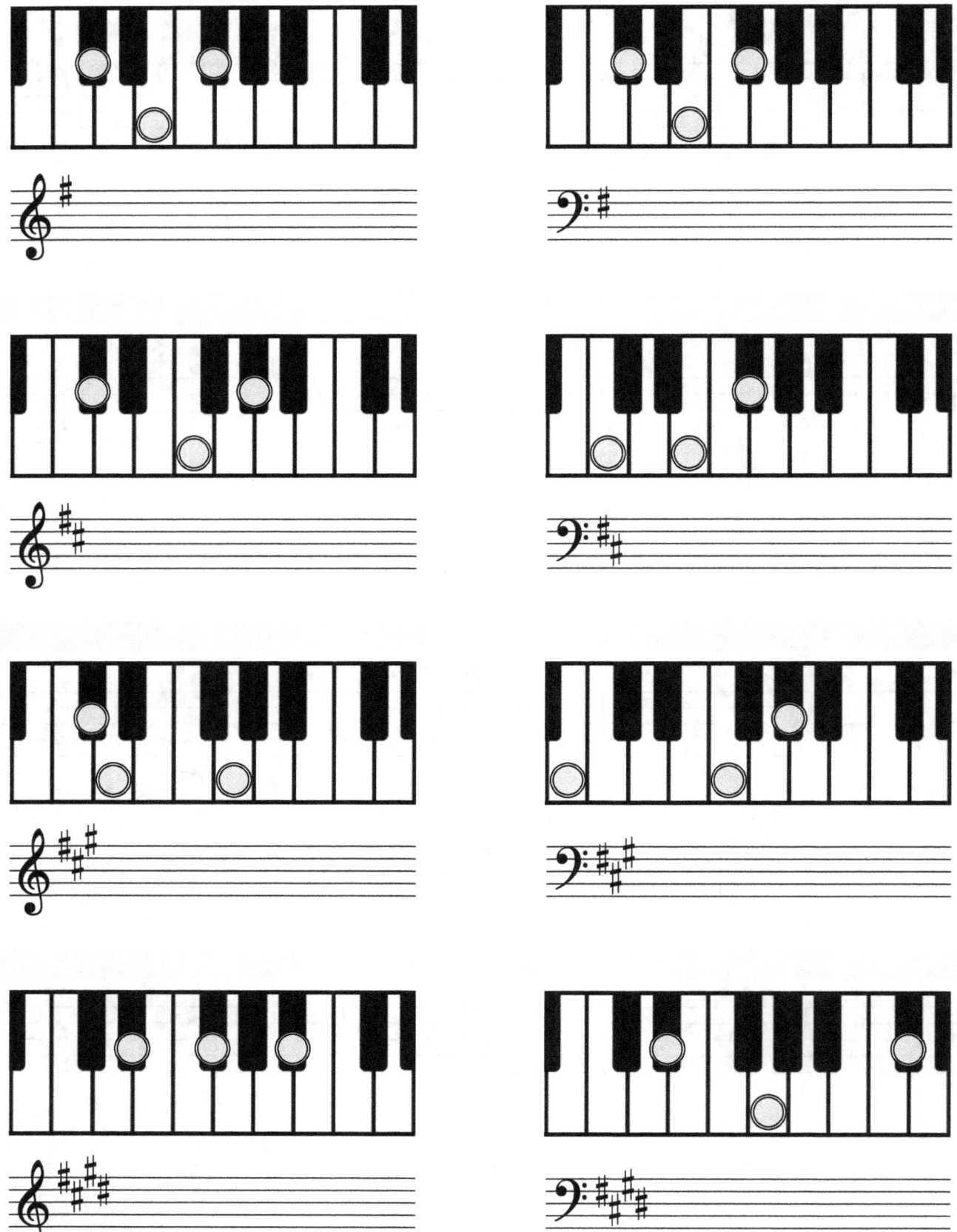

Draw the correct **notes** *(whole notes)* in the staves. Pay **attention** to the **key signature** and **accidentals**. Use the type of **accidentals** that the key signature uses or **natural signs** for notes not in the key.

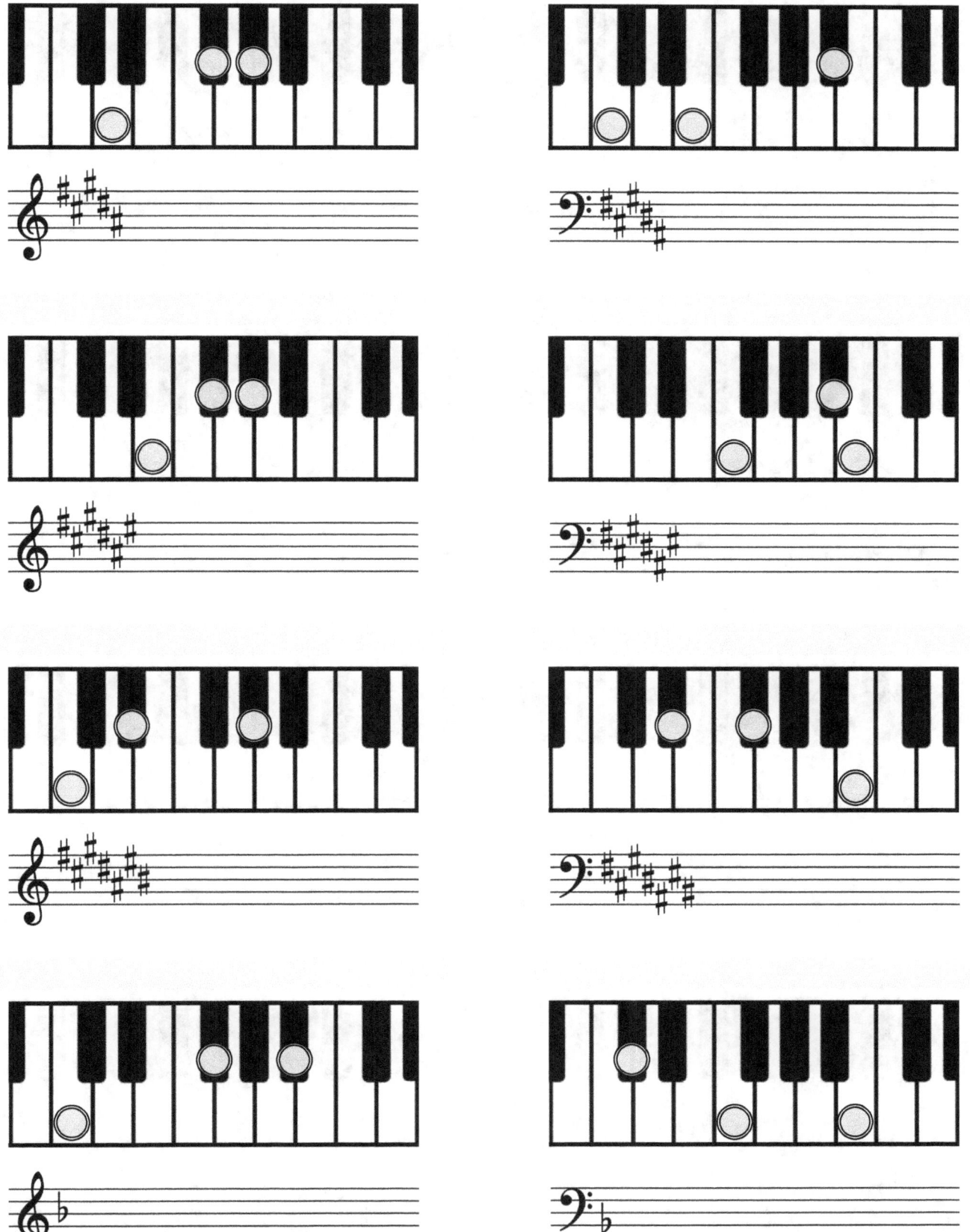

Draw the correct **notes** *(whole notes)* in the staves. Pay **attention** to the **key signature** and **accidentals**. Use the type of **accidentals** that the key signature uses or **natural signs** for notes not in the key.

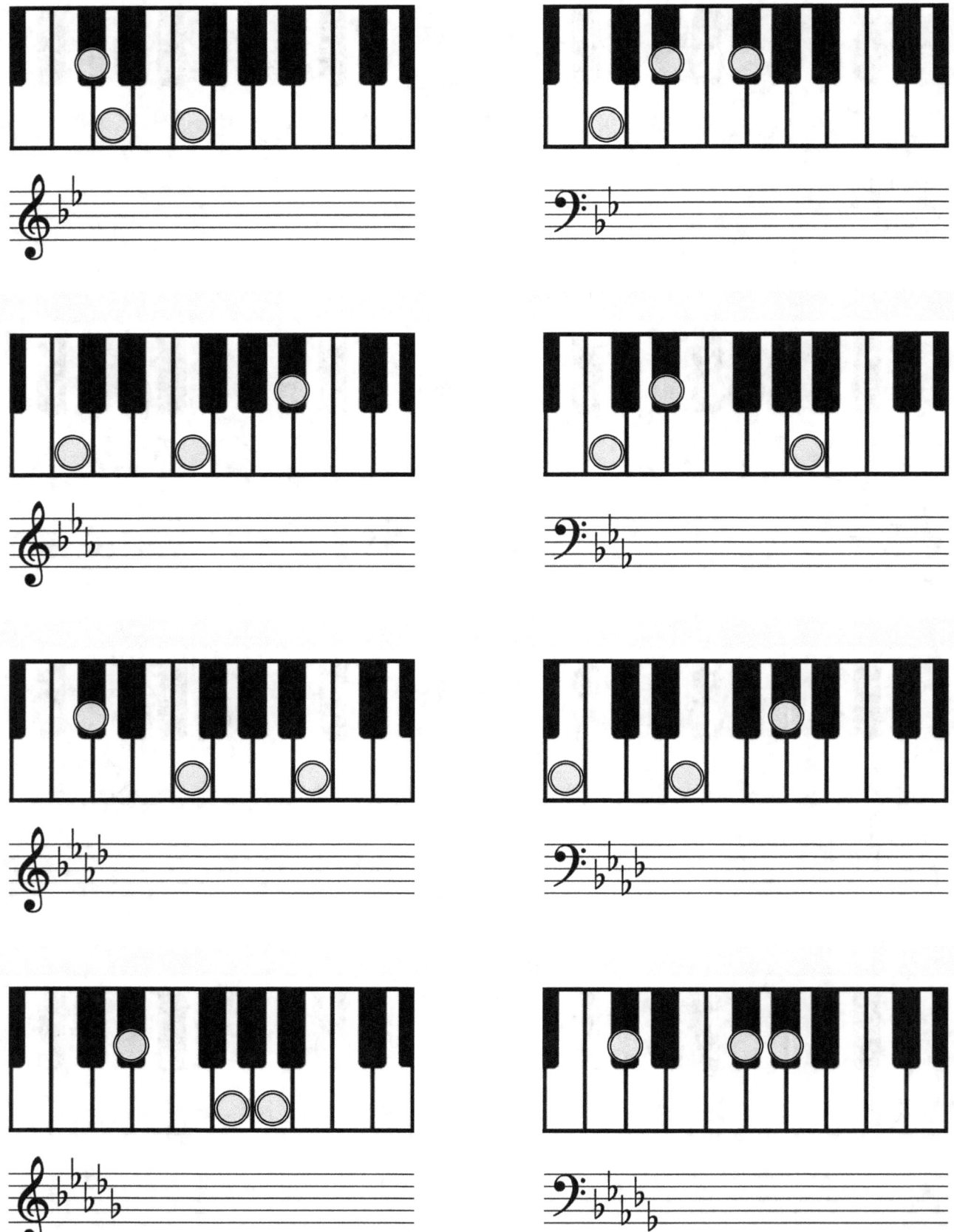

Draw the correct **notes** *(whole notes)* in the staves. Pay **attention** to the **key signature** and **accidentals**. Use the type of **accidentals** that the key signature uses or **natural signs** for notes not in the key.

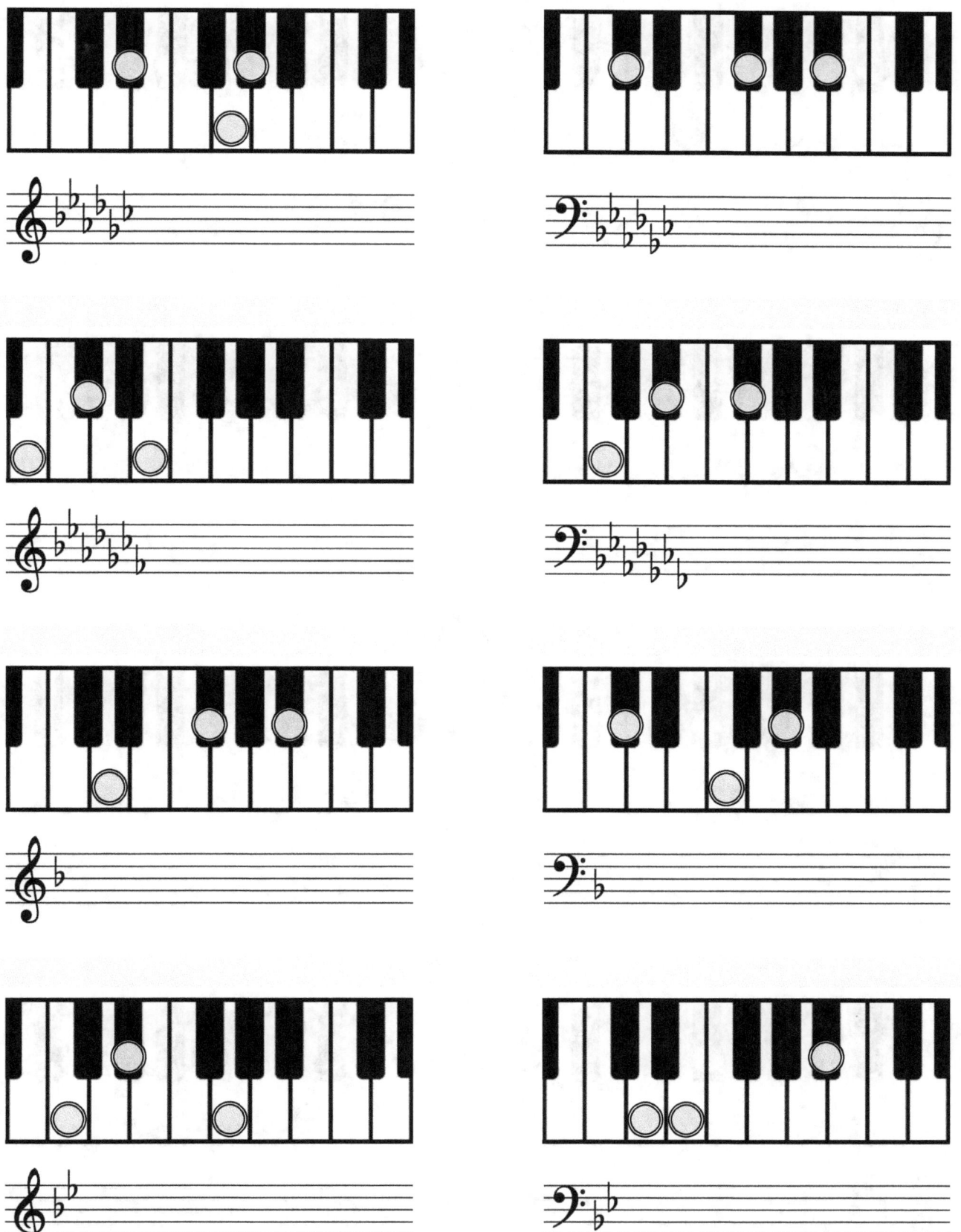

Draw the correct **notes** *(whole notes)* in the staves. Pay **attention** to the **key signature** and **accidentals**. Use the type of **accidentals** that the key signature uses or **natural signs** for notes not in the key.

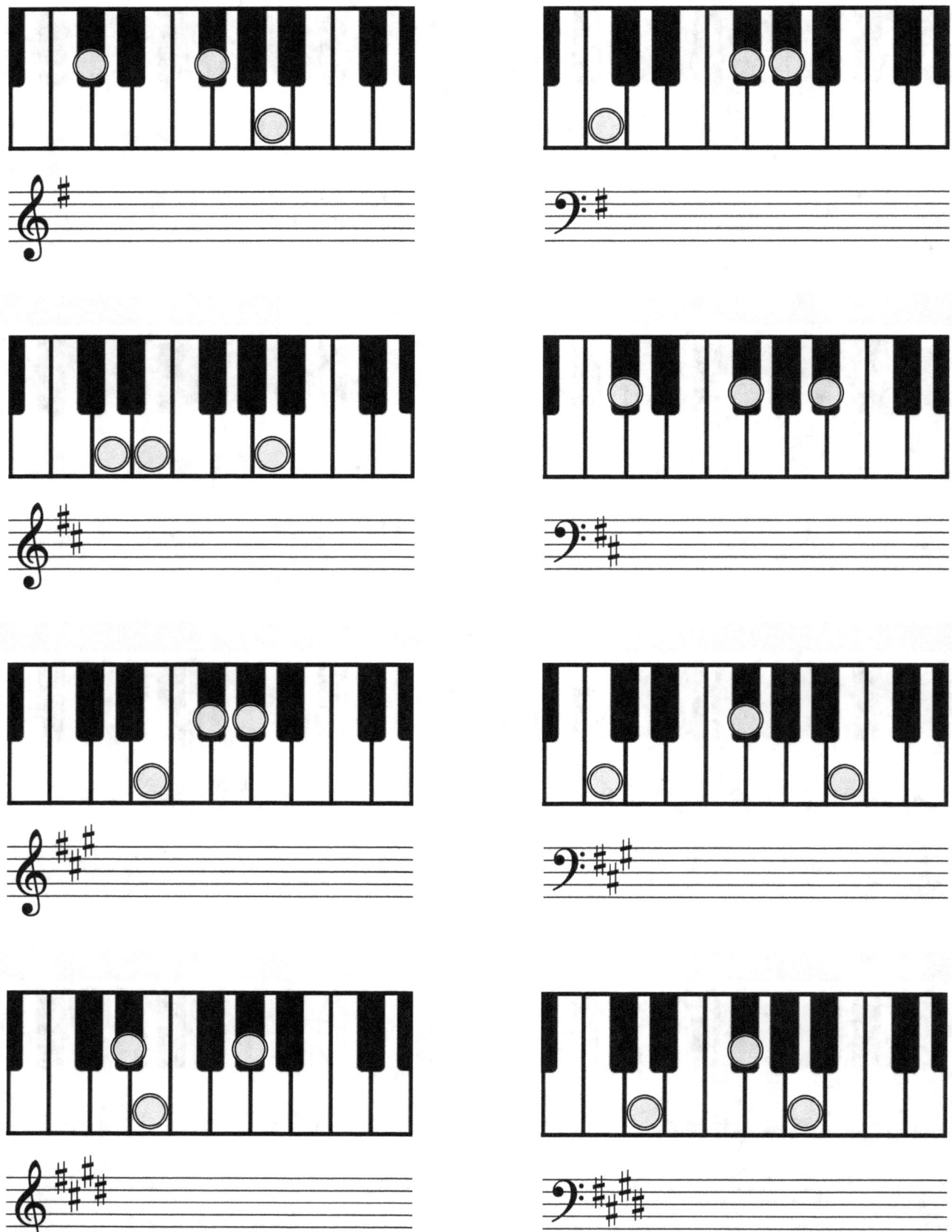

Draw the correct **notes** *(whole notes)* in the staves. Pay **attention** to the **key signature** and **accidentals**. Use the type of **accidentals** that the key signature uses or **natural signs** for notes not in the key.

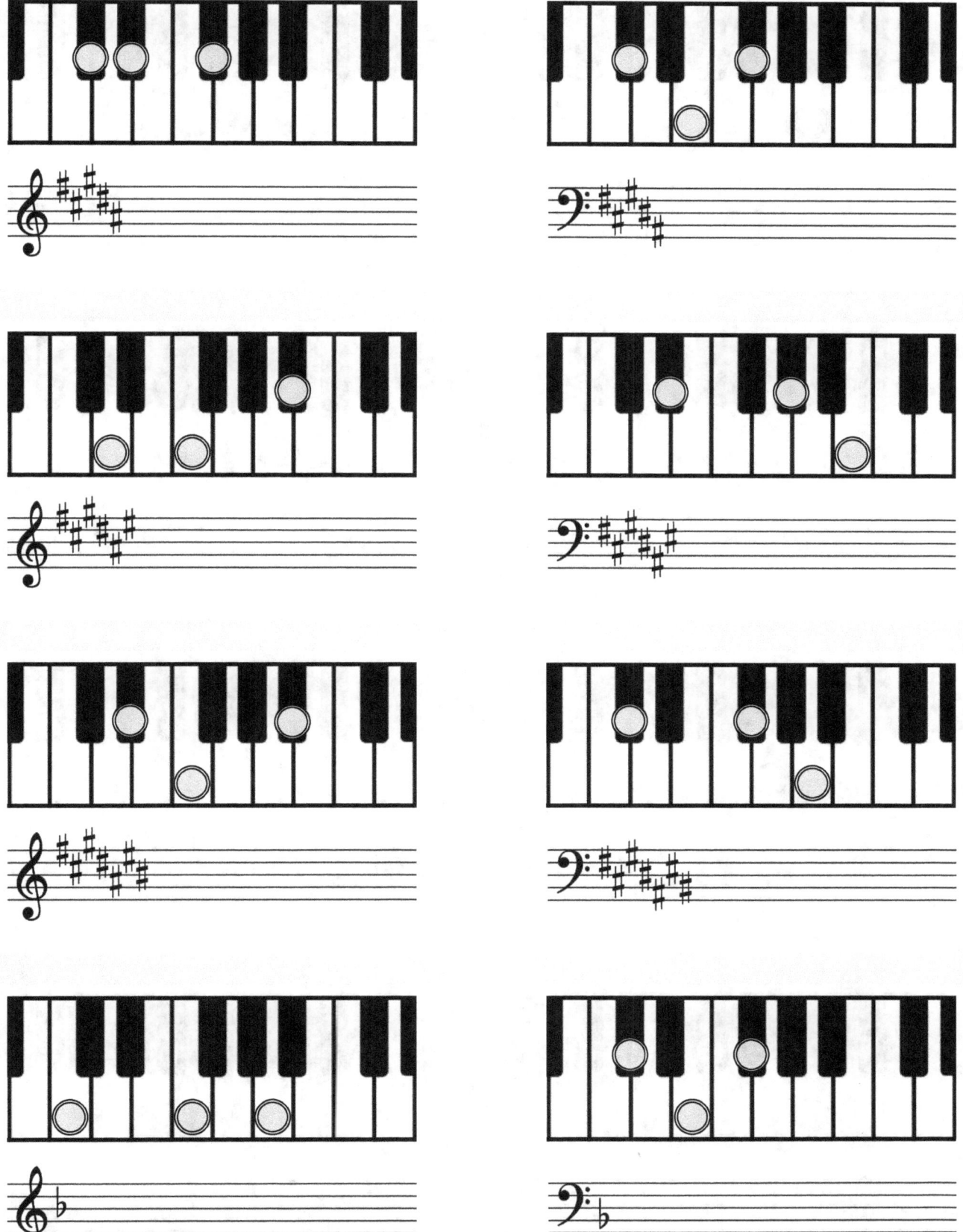

Draw the correct **notes** *(whole notes)* in the staves. Pay **attention** to the **key signature** and **accidentals**. Use the type of **accidentals** that the key signature uses or **natural signs** for notes not in the key.

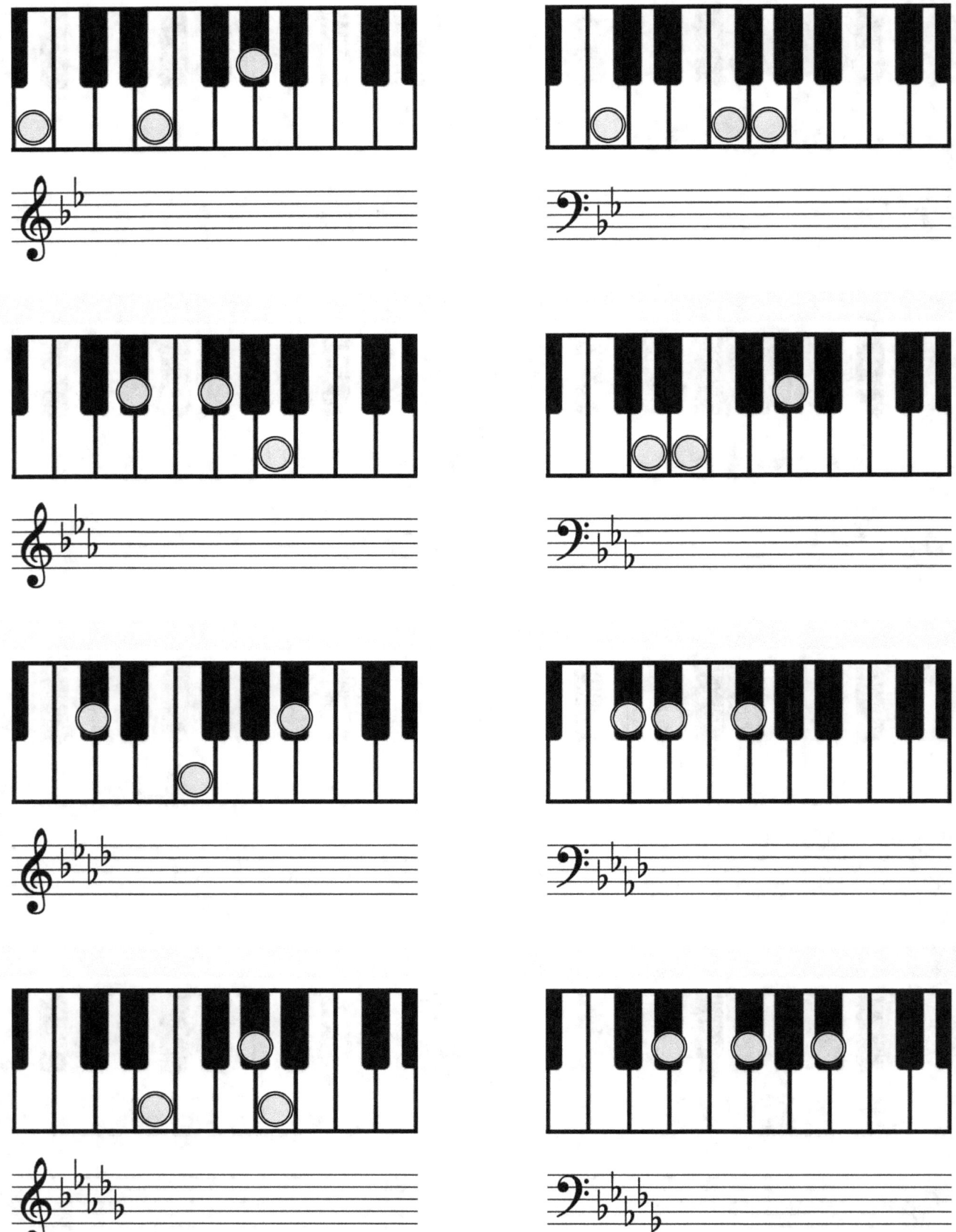

Draw the correct **notes** *(whole notes)* in the staves. Pay **attention** to the **key signature** and **accidentals**. Use the type of **accidentals** that the key signature uses or **natural signs** for notes not in the key.

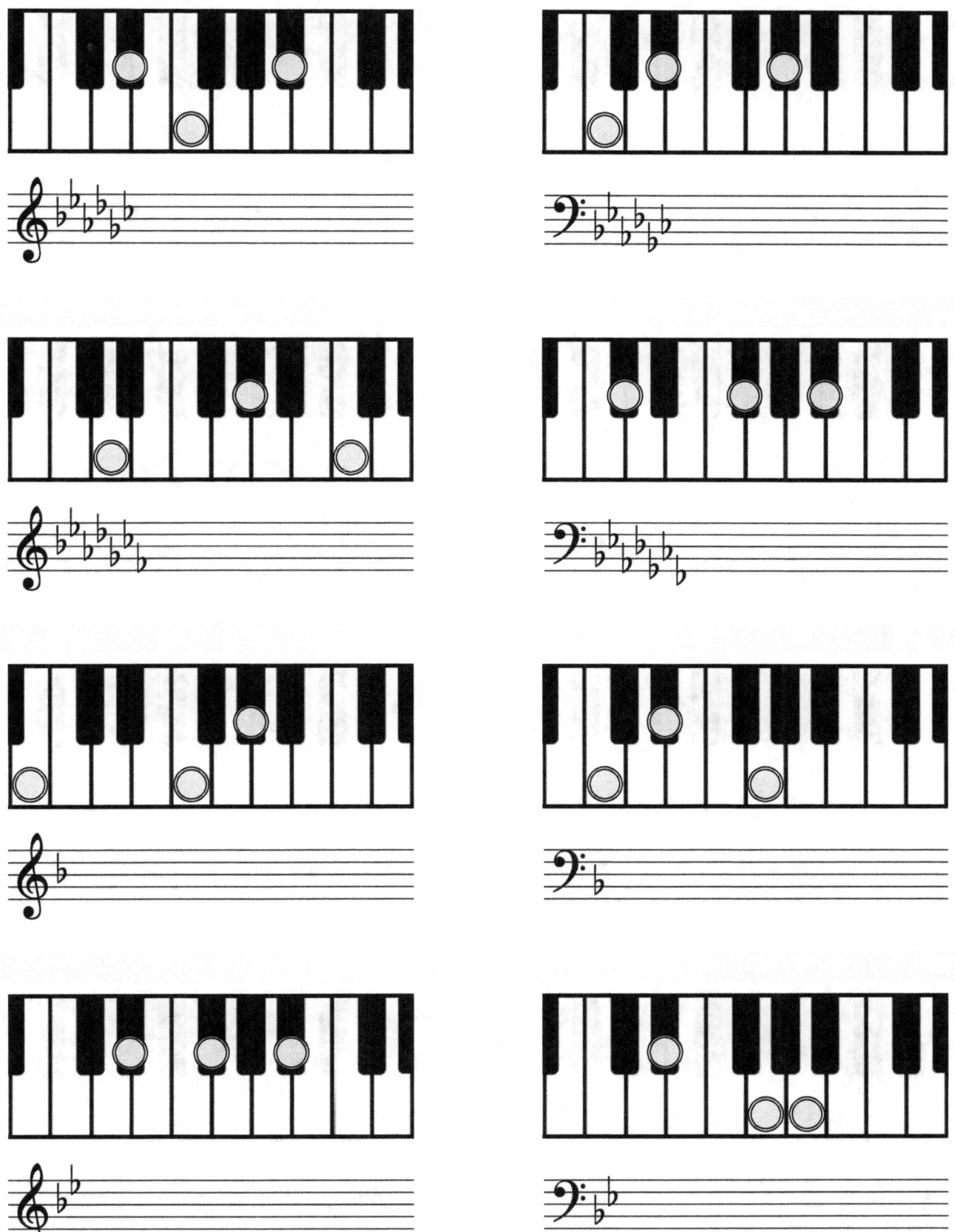

Circle the correct **keys** on the keyboard. Pay **attention** to the **key signature** and **accidentals**.

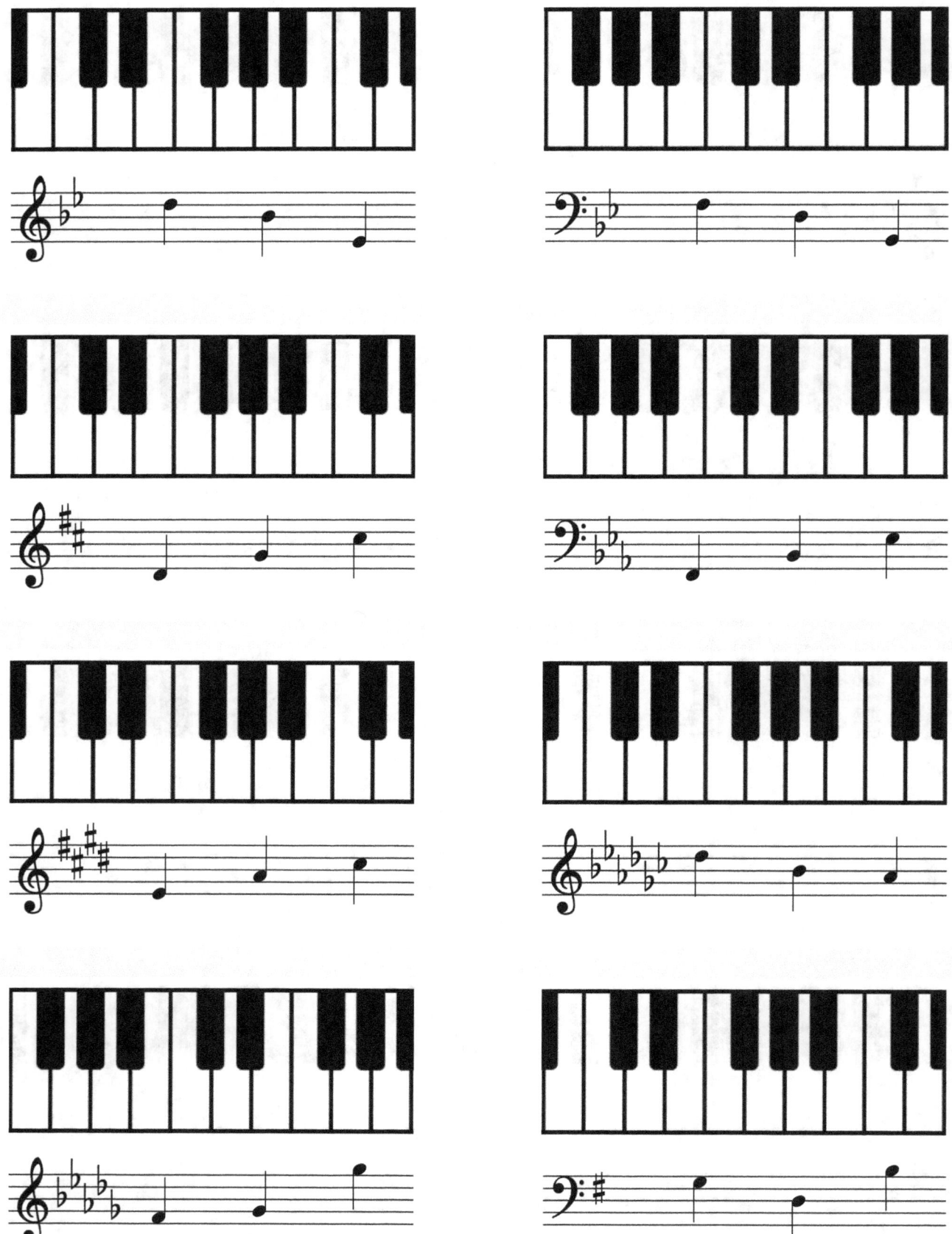

Circle the correct **keys** on the keyboard. Pay **attention** to the **key signature** and **accidentals**.

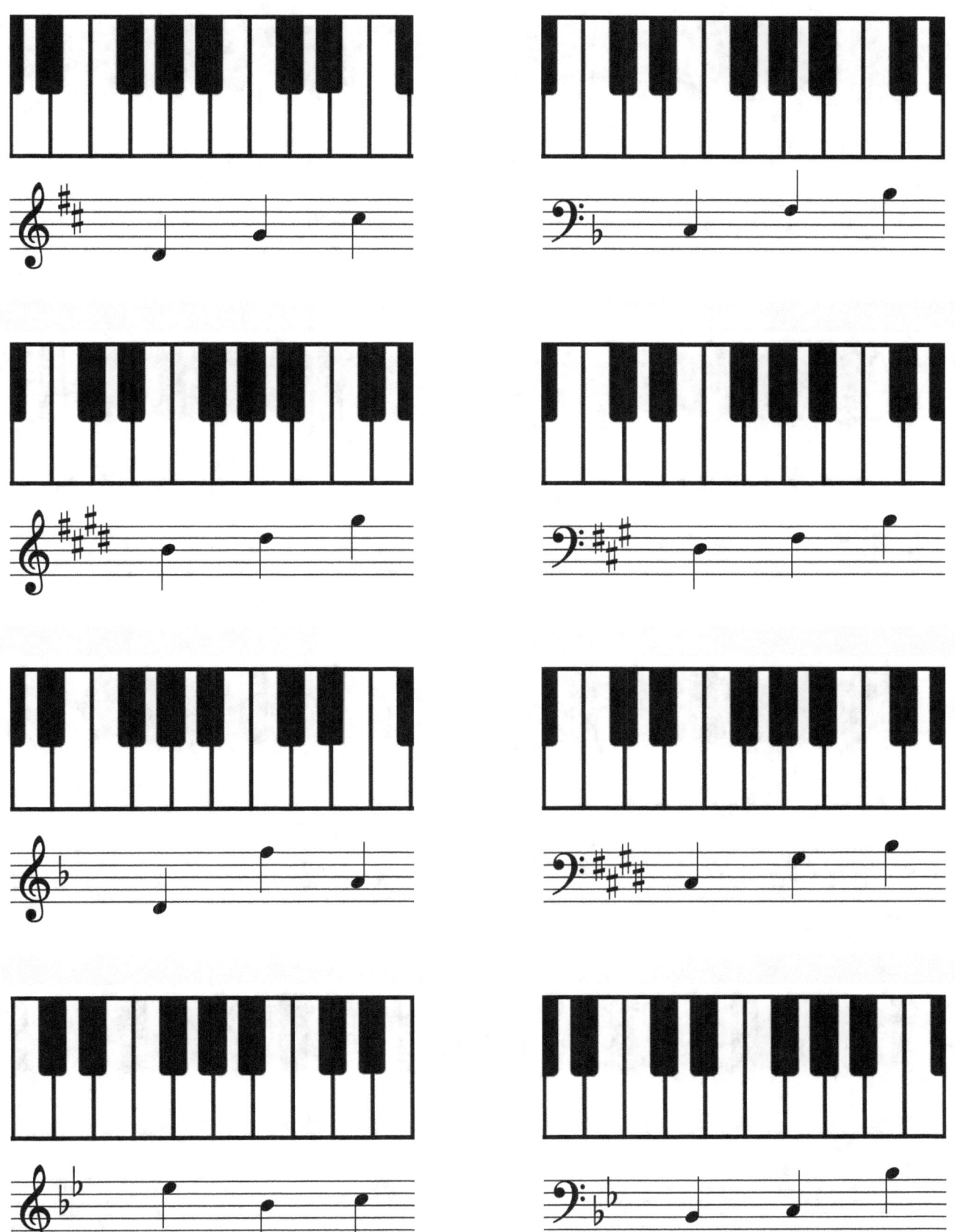

Circle the correct **keys** on the keyboard. Pay **attention** to the **key signature** and **accidentals**.

Circle the correct **keys** on the keyboard. Pay **attention** to the **key signature** and **accidentals**.

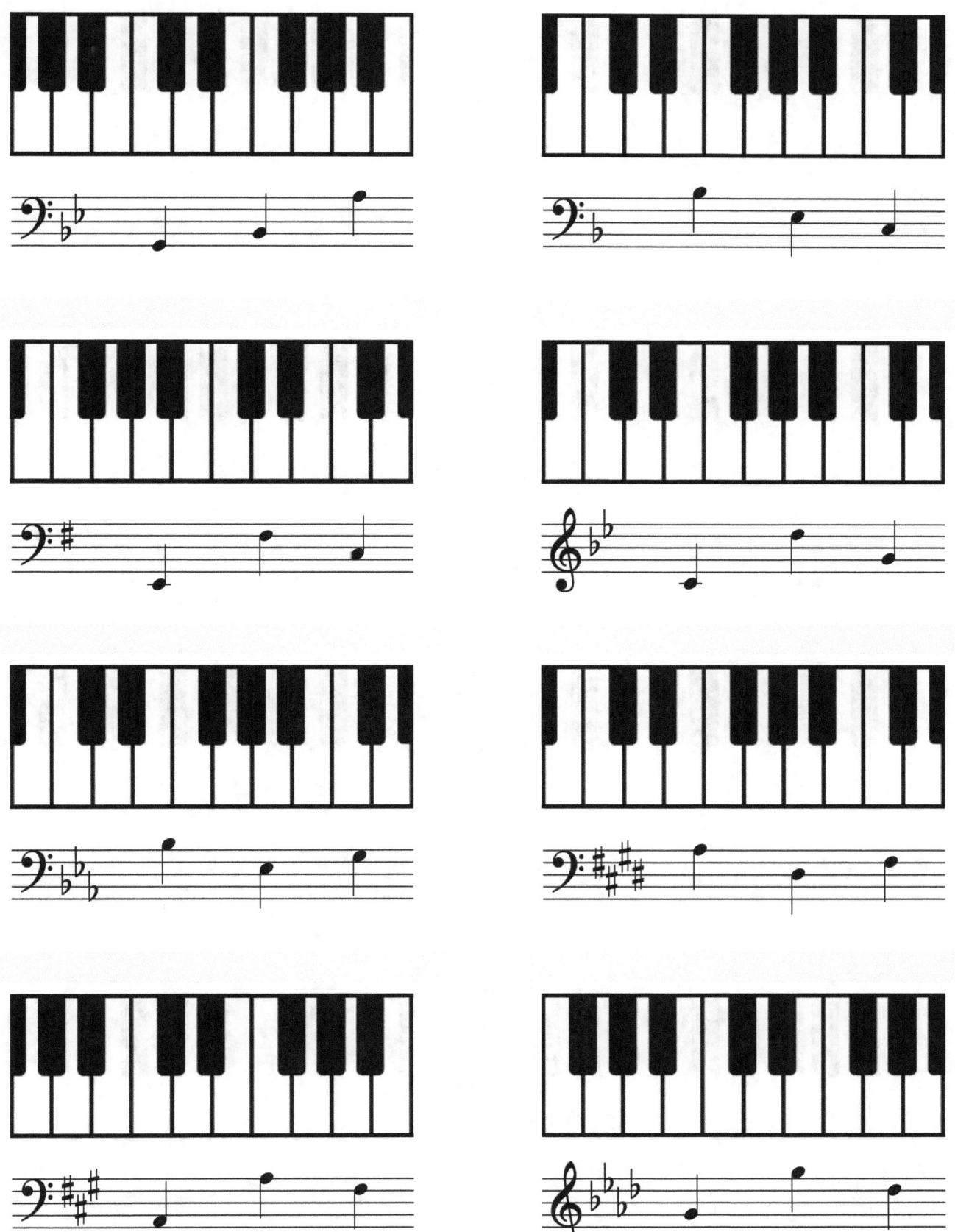

Circle the correct **keys** on the keyboard. Pay **attention** to the **key signature** and **accidentals**.

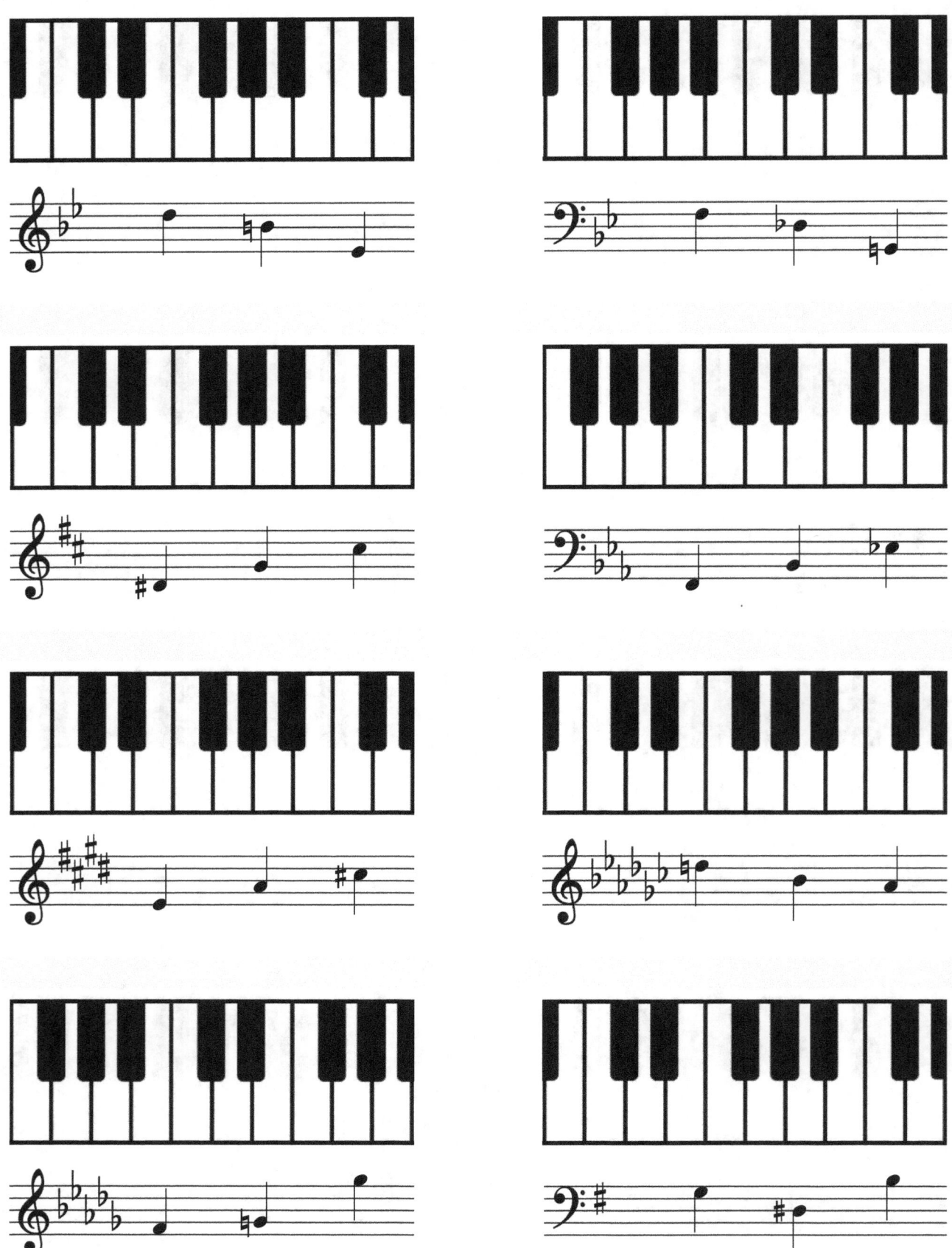

Circle the correct **keys** on the keyboard. Pay **attention** to the **key signature** and **accidentals**.

Draw / circle the correct **notes** (*quarter*) in the staves / keys. **Pay** attention to **accidentals**.
Use the type of **accidentals** that the key signature uses or **natural signs** for notes not in the key.

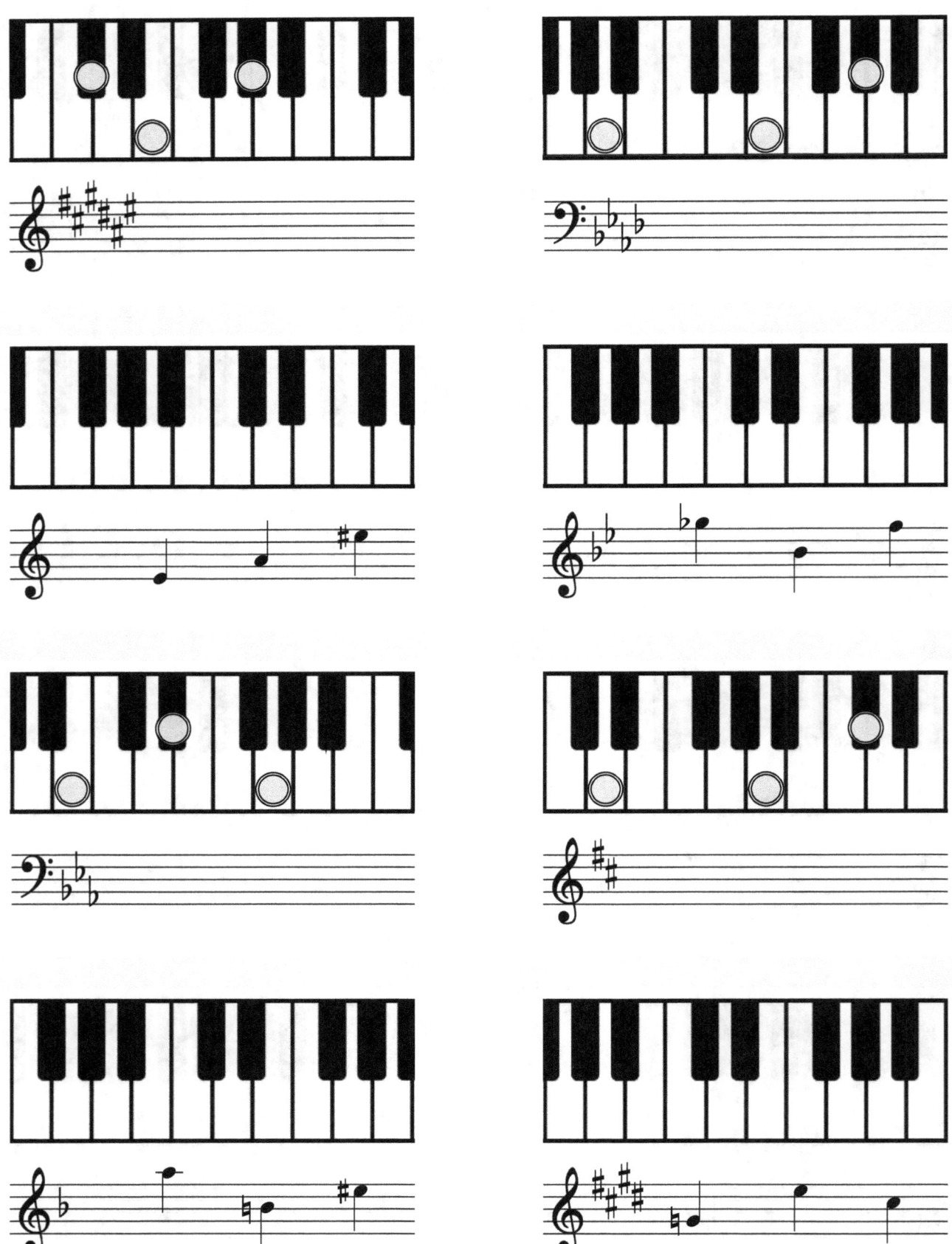

Draw / circle the correct **notes** *(quarter)* in the staves / keys. **Pay** attention to **accidentals**.
Use the type of **accidentals** that the key signature uses or **natural signs** for notes not in the key.

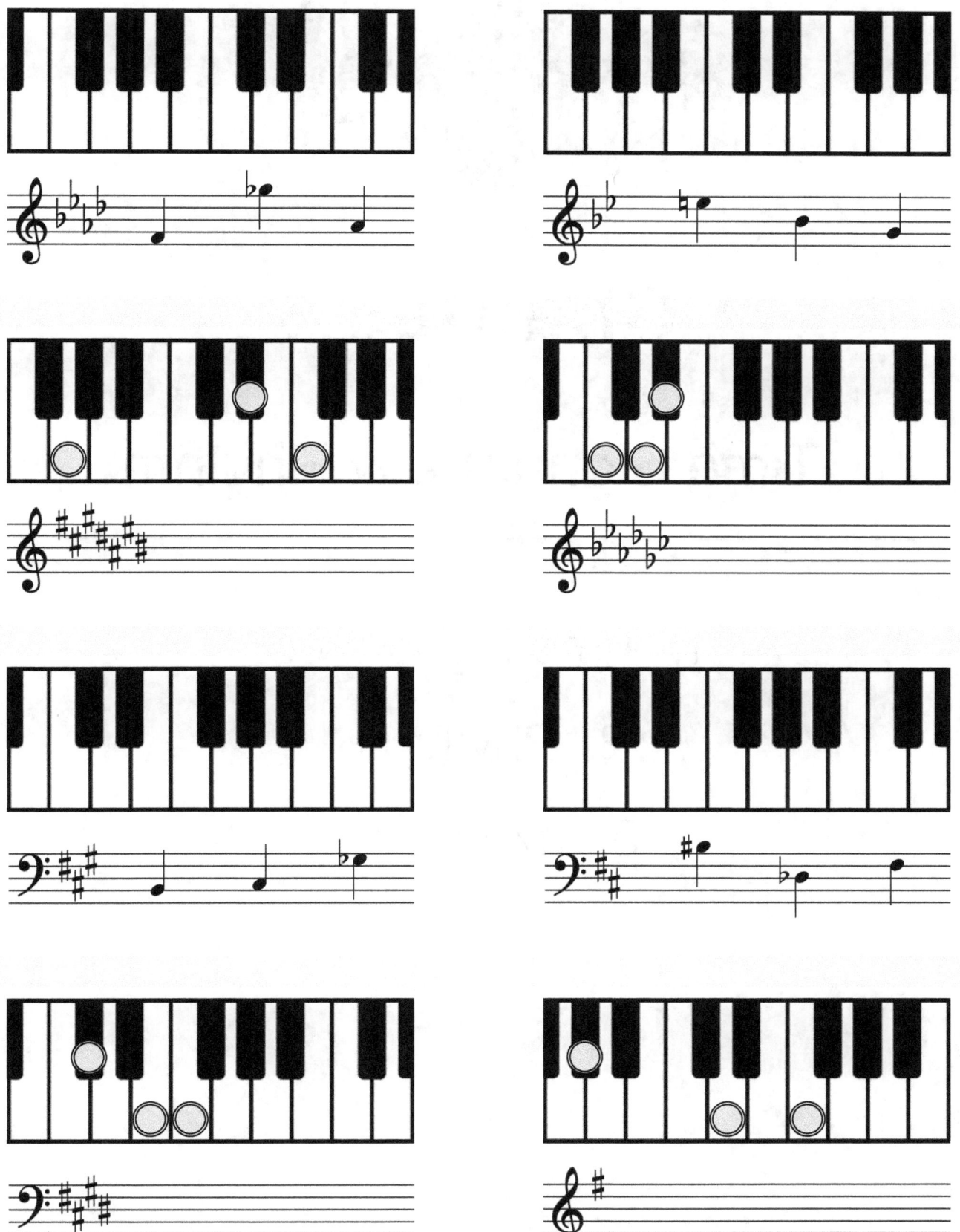

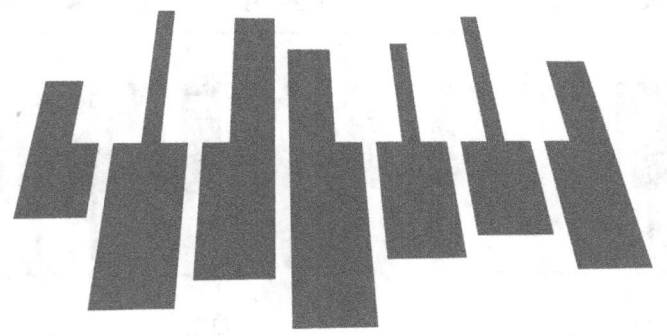

Chapter 4

Time Signature & Rhythm

1. Time Signatures

2. Rhythms

3. Exercises

Time Signature

The time signature appears at the beginning of a piece of music, right after the key signature. Unlike the key signature, which is written on every staff, the time signature does not reappear in the music unless the meter changes.

The meter of a piece represents its basic rhythm; the time signature is the symbol that shows you the meter of the music and how it is notated.

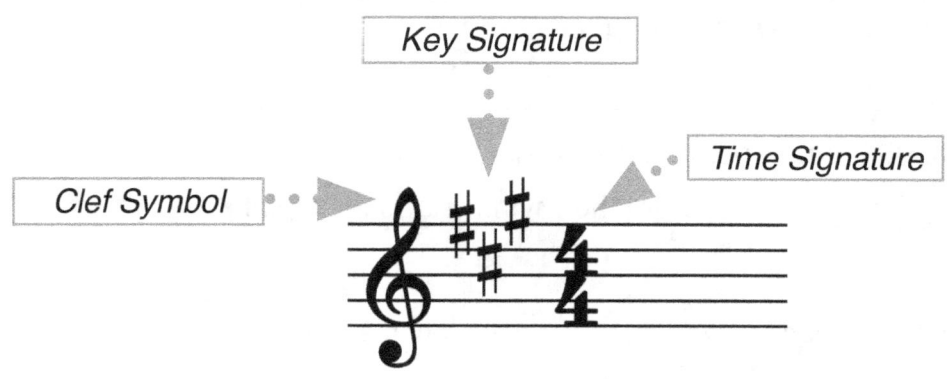

Most time signatures consist of two numbers:

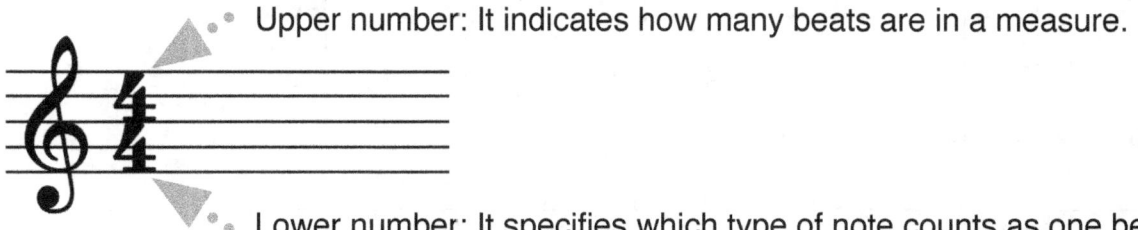

Upper number: It indicates how many beats are in a measure.

Lower number: It specifies which type of note counts as one beat.

In "four-four time" (4/4), there are four beats in a measure, and a quarter note counts as one beat. Any combination of notes that adds up to four quarters can be used to fill a measure.

You might notice that the time signature resembles a fraction in mathematics. Filling a measure is like finding equivalent fractions. For example, in 4/4 time, there are four beats in a measure, and a quarter note counts as one beat.

However, any other combination of notes that sums to four quarters would also work: one whole note, two half notes, a half note plus two-quarter notes, and so on.

Normally, all measures in a piece of music must contain exactly the number of beats specified by the time signature. The beats can be filled with any combination of notes or rests, as dictated by the time signature, but they must add up to the correct number of beats.

If a measure or a group of measures has more or fewer beats than specified, the time signature must be changed. Exceptions to this rule might include the first measure, known as an "anacrusis" or "pickup measure," and the final measure, known as the "closing measure."

Clapping exercises for rhythms

As music unfolds over time, it is primarily organized by dividing this time into short segments known as beats. In most pieces of music, something happens exactly at the start of each beat, making it easily audible and noticeable.

When you clap your hands, tap your toes, or dance, you are "moving to the beat." Your claps also sound at the beginning of the beat. This is often referred to as "being on the downbeat" because it represents the moment when the conductor's baton reaches its lowest point in motion and begins to rise again.

You can start without a metrnonome or begin slowly with one.

Counting "1, 2, 3, 4" as a lead-in before the rhythm starts is helpful.

Clap (Clap quarter notes; clap on every beat of the metronome.)

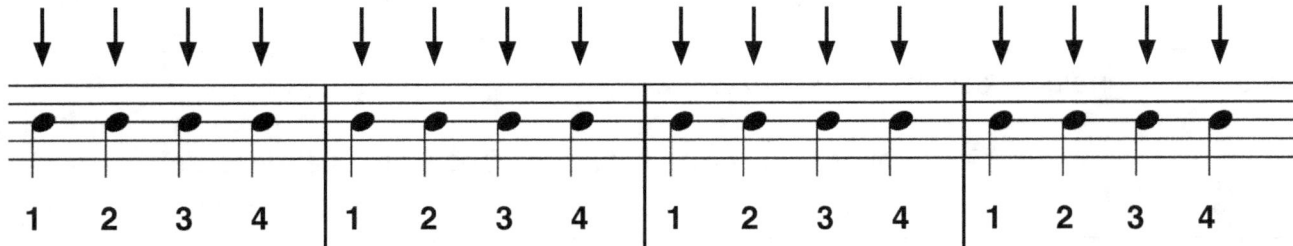

Count (Continue counting "1, 2, 3, 4" while you clap.)

Clap (Clap half notes; clap on beat 1, skip beat 2, clap on beat 3, etc.)

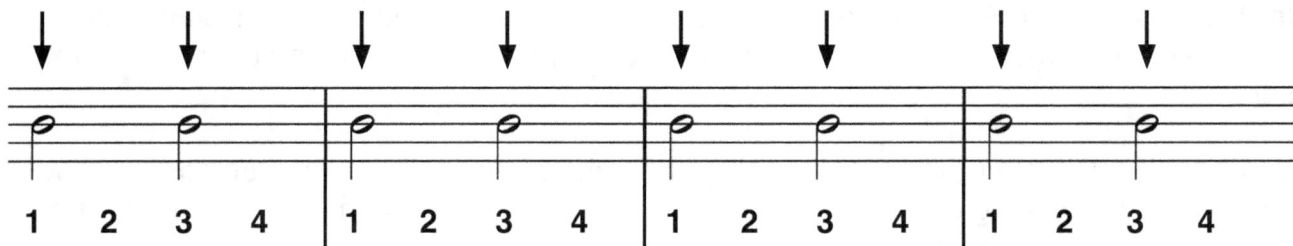

Count (Continue counting "1, 2, 3, 4" while you clap.)

Clap (Clap whole notes; clap on beat 1, skip beats 2-3-4, clap on beat 1, etc.)

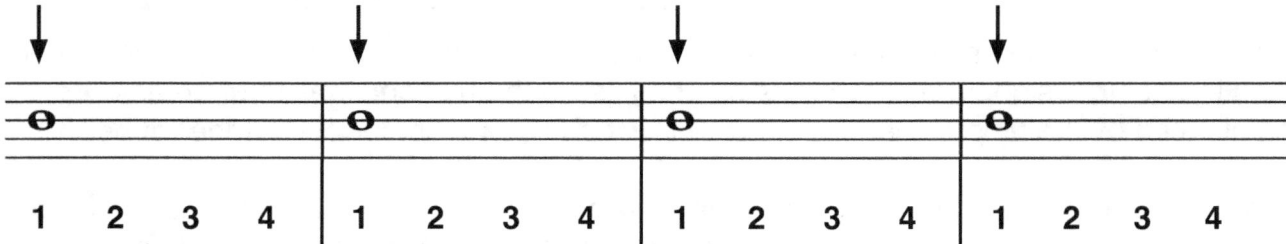

Count (Continue counting "1, 2, 3, 4" while you clap.)

Examples

In "three-four time" there are three beats in a measure, and a quarter note counts as one beat.

In "four-four time" there are four beats in a measure, and a quarter note counts as one beat.

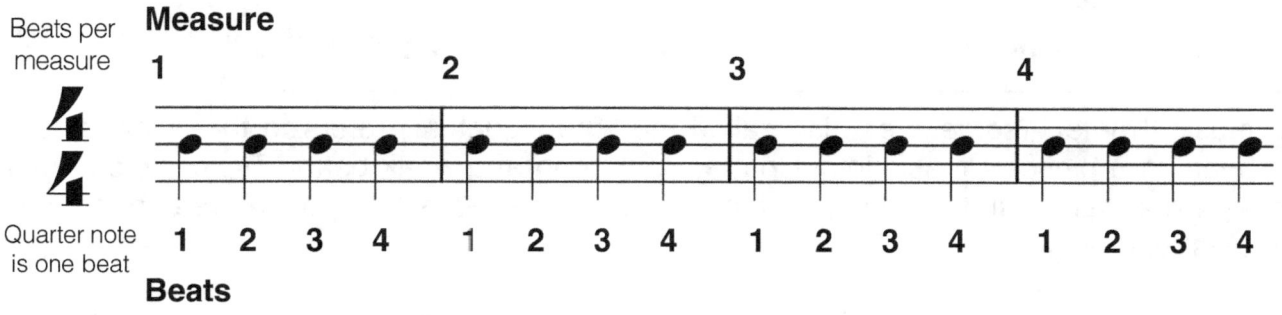

For example, in "four-four time," any combination of notes and rests that add up to four quarters can be used to fill a measure.

| 4 Quarter Notes | = | 2 Half Notes | = | 1 Whole Note | = | 2 Quarter Notes + 4 Eighth Notes | = and so on. |

In "three-eight time," any combination of notes and rests that add up to three eighth notes can be used to fill a measure. (As a reminder: A dot extends the value of a note by half its original value).

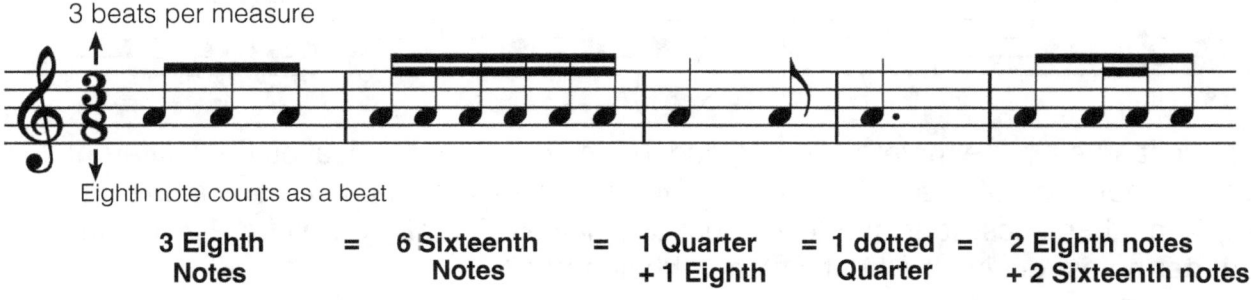

| 3 Eighth Notes | = | 6 Sixteenth Notes | = | 1 Quarter + 1 Eighth | = | 1 dotted Quarter | = | 2 Eighth notes + 2 Sixteenth notes |

Some time signatures do not have to be written as numbers. The four-four time is so commonly used that it is often referred to as "common time," represented by a bold "C" (standing for "common time"). When both fours are "halved" to twos, it results in "cut time," which is represented by a "C" crossed by a vertical line.

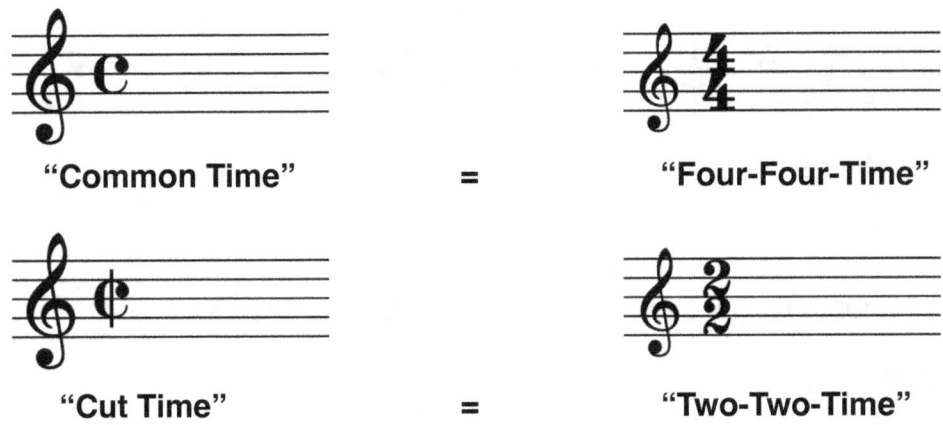

"Common Time" = **"Four-Four-Time"**

"Cut Time" = **"Two-Two-Time"**

In music, "meter" (sometimes also called the time signature) refers to the arrangement of beats in a piece of music into a pattern of strong and weak beats. Typically, one can recognize a pattern in the beats, such as strong-weak-weak-strong-weak-weak or strong-weak-strong-weak.

Therefore, beats are organized further by grouping them into measures. For example, a measure in a beat pattern of strong-weak-weak-weak-strong-weak-weak-weak or 1-2-3-4-1-2-3-4 would encompass four beats.

↓ **Downbeat** (The beat can be strong or weak, or heavy or light.)

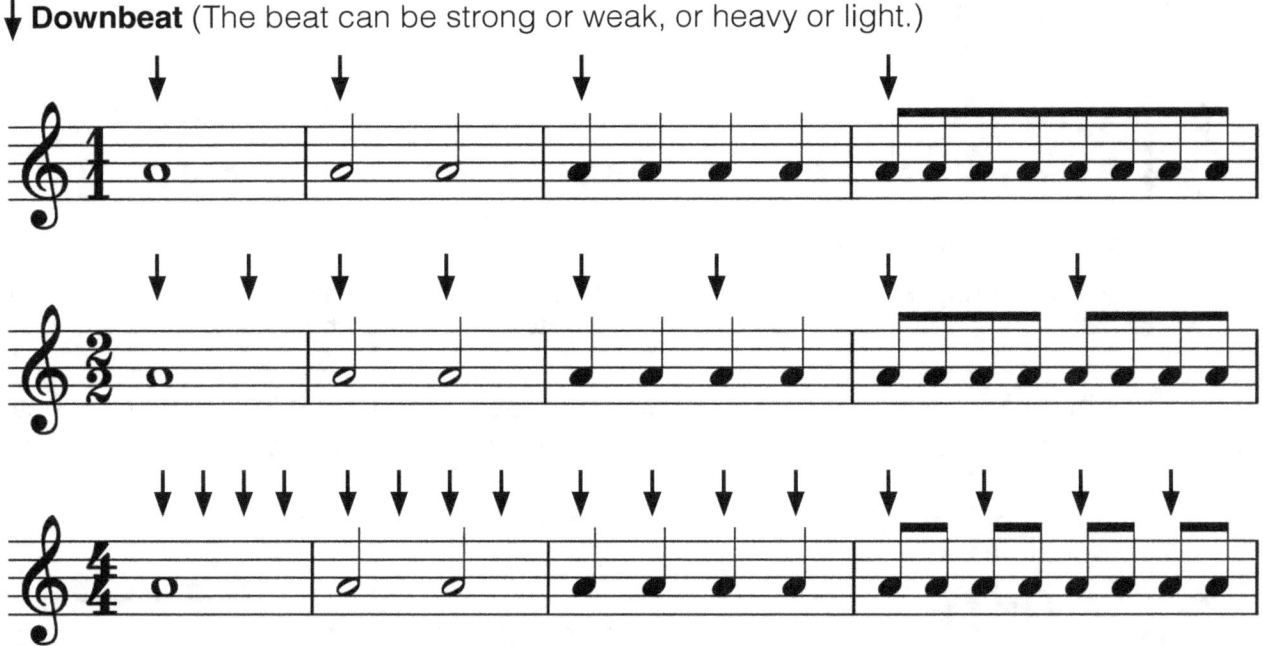

The measures in the meters 1/1, 2/2, and 4/4 may appear identical but feel different due to varying numbers of beats. A measure in 4/4 time looks the same as one in 2/2 time. After all, in mathematics, four quarters equal two halves. So why not write 2/2 as 4/4, where quarter notes receive the beat instead of half notes?

The music might appear quite different, but it would sound the same as long as the beats are at the same tempo. The composer typically selects a time signature that makes the music easy to read and count. Does the music feel like it has four beats per measure, or does it pass so quickly that you only have time to tap your foot twice in a measure?

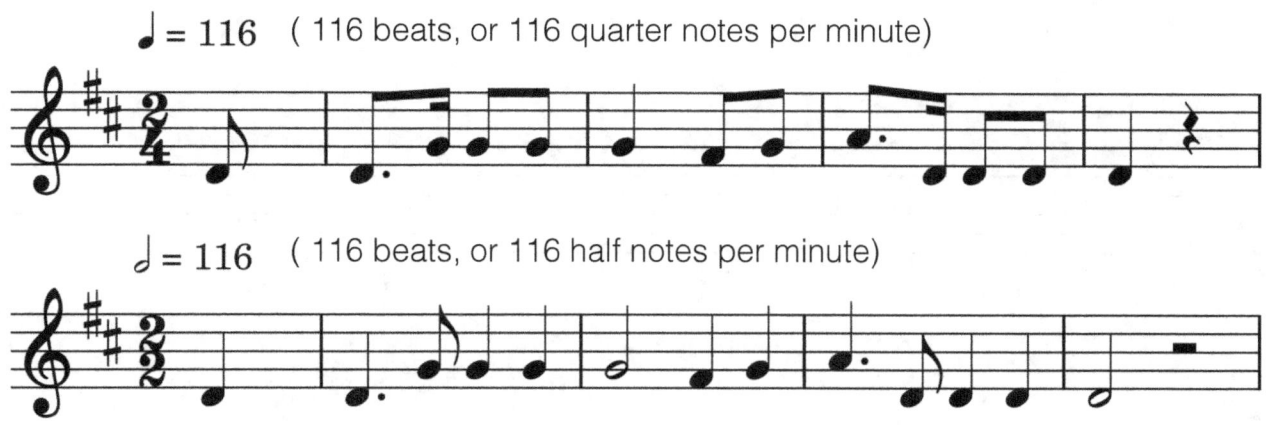

Compound Time Signatures

A piece in 6/8 time may have six beats per measure, with each eighth note counting as one beat. However, it is more common for a dotted quarter note (or three eighth notes) to represent one beat. Since beats are usually divided into halves and quarters, this is the simplest way for composers to notate beats that are divided into thirds. Similarly, 3/8 can have one beat per measure, 9/8 can have three beats per measure, and 12/8 can have four beats per measure.

Exercise *(solution on p.133)*

Write the following time signatures on the musical staves. Write each measure with different combinations of note lengths and include at least one dotted note in each staff.

1. **2/4** Time
2. **3/8** Time
3. **6/4** Time

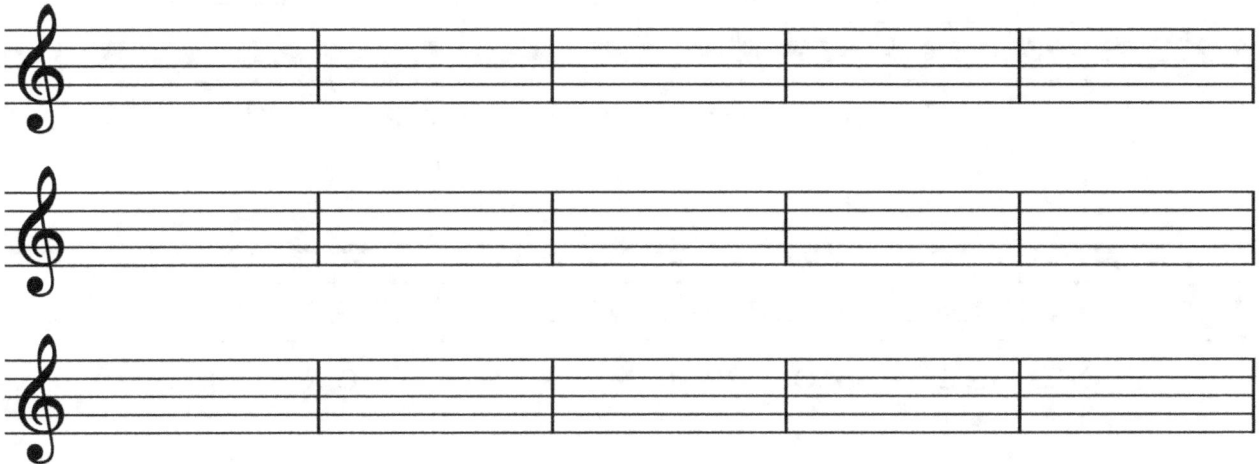

Counting Rhythm in 4/4-Time

Counting Rhythm in 3/4-Time

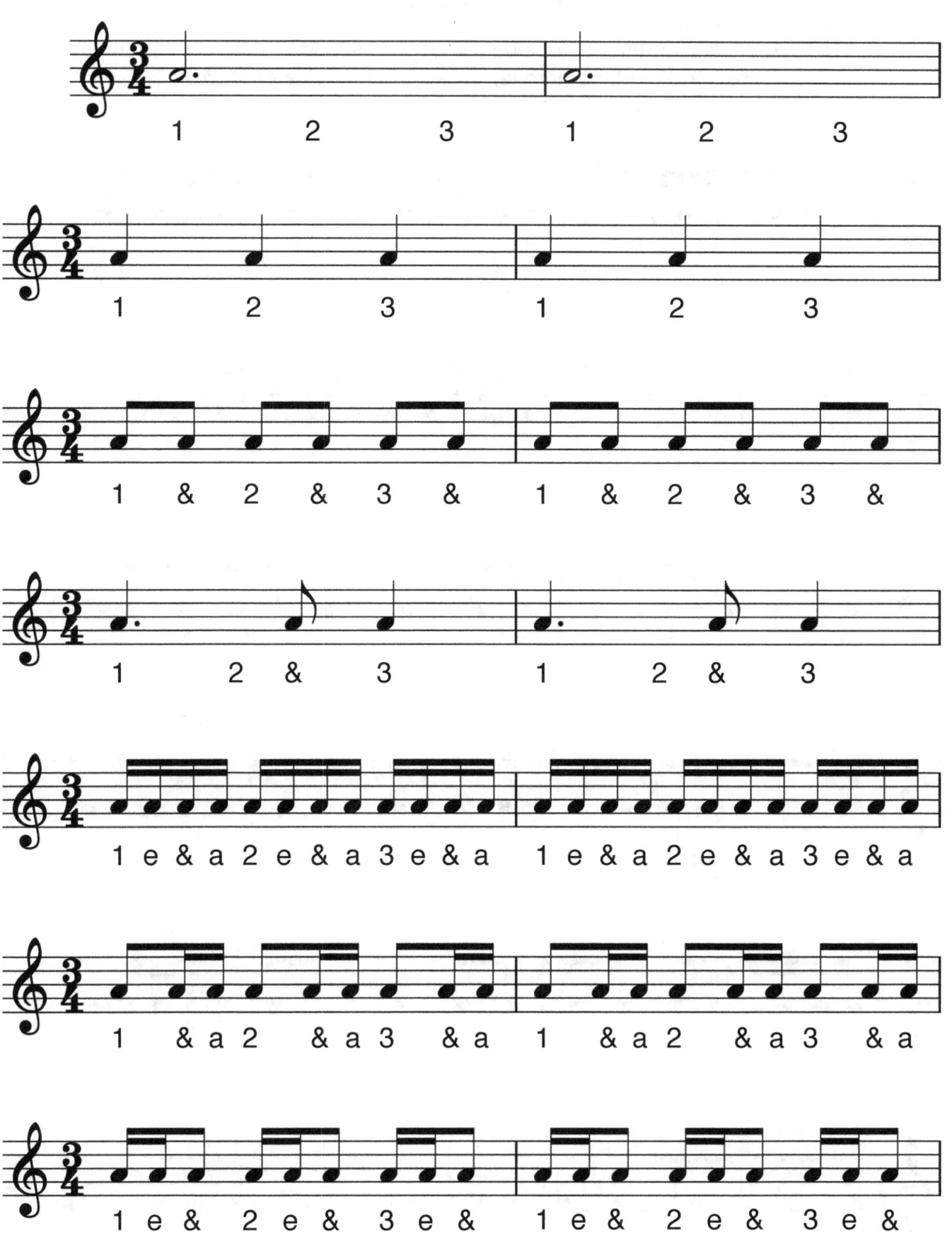

Rhythm Exercise - 1

Write the appropriate **rhythmic values** below the corresponding notes in each measure.
Be mindful of the **note lengths** and the **time signature**.

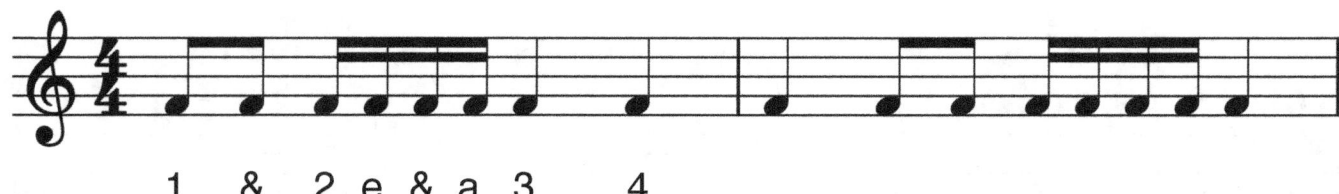

1 & 2 e & a 3 4

Rhythm Exercise - 2

Write the appropriate **rhythmic values** below the corresponding notes in each measure.
Be mindful of the **note lengths** and the **time signature**.

1 e & a 2 & 3 & a 4

Rhythm Exercise - 3

Write the appropriate **rhythmic values** below the corresponding notes in each measure.
Be mindful of the **note lengths** and the **time signature**.

1 & 2 & 3   4

1   2   3

Rhythm Exercise - 4

Write the appropriate **rhythmic values** below the corresponding notes in each measure.
Be mindful of the **note lengths** and the **time signature**.

1   2 & 3   4

1   2   3

Tips for Reading Music

1. Focus on the Sheet Music

When playing the piano or keyboard, develop the habit of not looking at your fingers while reading the sheet music. This practice will help you improve your skills and allow you to read music more effectively.

2. Pay Attention to Key Signatures and Patterns

Key signatures indicate which notes (if any) should be raised or lowered. Always consider the key while playing. Look for rhythmic and melodic patterns, as well as scales, arpeggios, and chords; these can act as guides.

3. Count Beats and Rhythms

The time signature, found after the key signature at the beginning, indicates how many beats you should count. To internalize the rhythm effectively, tap it slowly with both hands on the piano. Tap the upper staff with your right hand and the lower staff with your left while counting out loud as you do so.

4. Clap and Count

When practicing a new piece, clap the rhythm and count aloud. Writing the rhythm on the sheet music can be helpful. Always start by counting the rhythm to develop a good habit.

5. Practice Hands Separately

Whenever possible, practice each hand separately. Focus on one hand at a time. Once both hands have mastered their parts, you can move on to playing with both hands together.

6. Learn Short Sections One at a Time

Always practice small sections individually. Start with four measures. Remember the saying: How do you eat an elephant? One bite at a time. Practicing sections that are too large can lead to frustration.

7. Try Not to Stop

Avoid stopping or hesitating. Continue playing, even if you make mistakes—maintaining a steady pulse is more crucial than playing all the notes correctly.

8. Everything Takes Time

Relax and stay positive. It can be really frustrating when your hands don't follow what your mind tells them to do. Remember: practice makes perfect.

Solutions

In the solutions, note that there are often several ways to represent certain notes.

We aim to provide you with the simplest method by using as few ledger lines as possible and arranging the notes in the order they appear on the keyboard or in the staff.

Practice writing your treble clef symbol on this staff and write at least ten clef symbols.

Name the notes of the lines, spaces, and ledger lines in the treble clef.

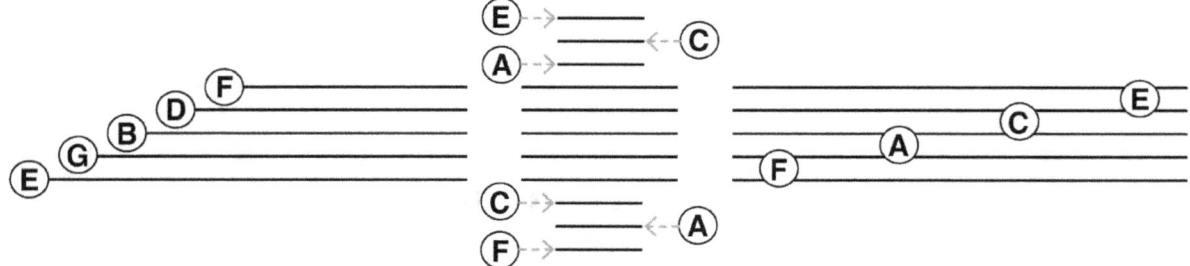

Exercise Bass Clef

Practice writing your bass clef symbol on this staff and write at least ten clef symbols.

Name the notes of the lines, spaces, and ledger lines in the bass clef.

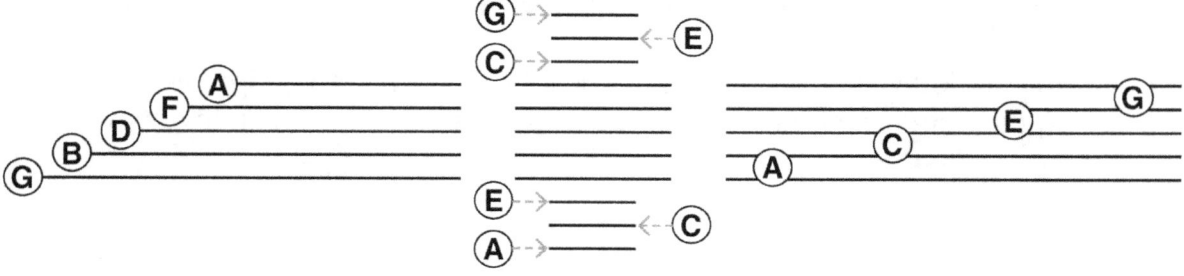

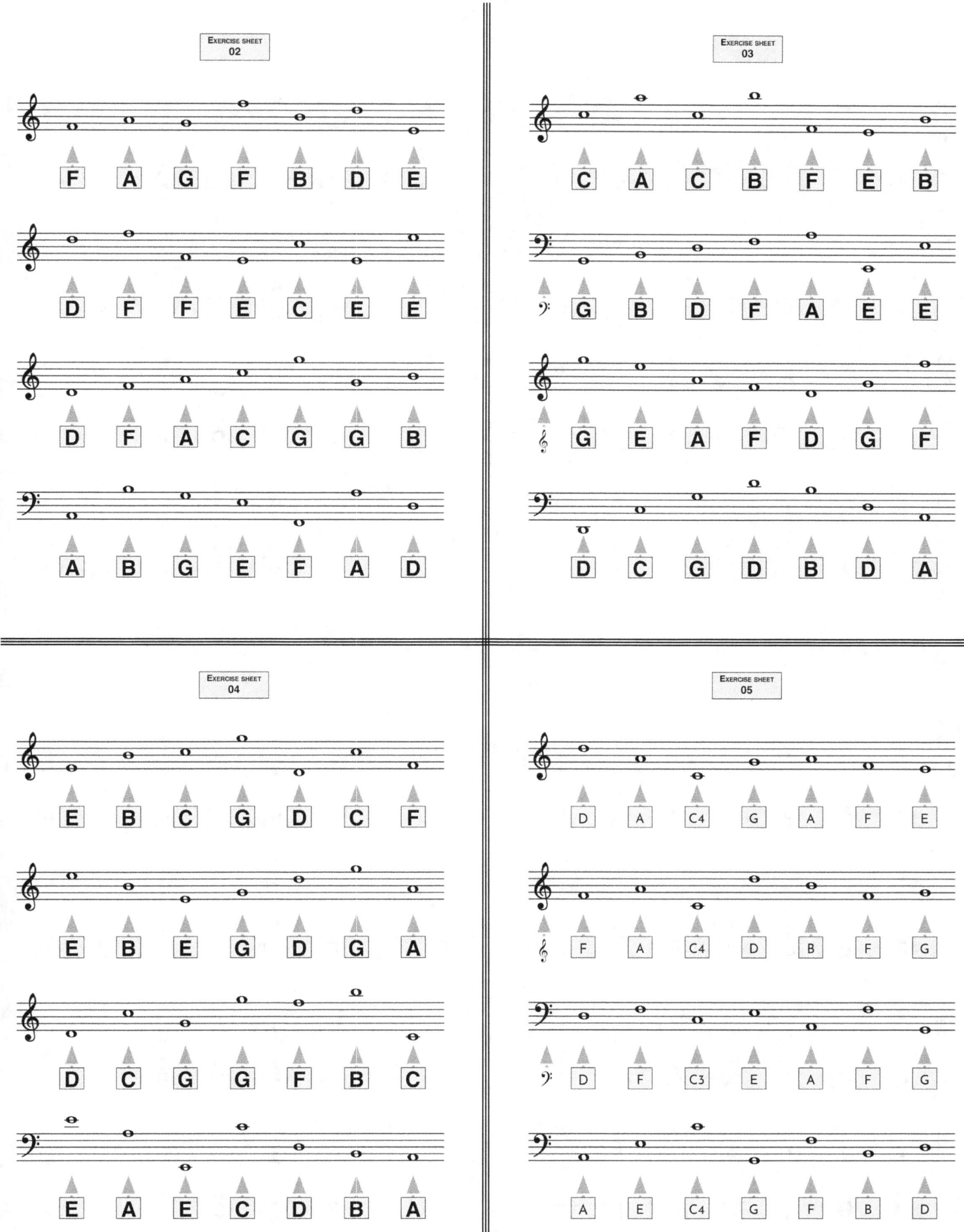

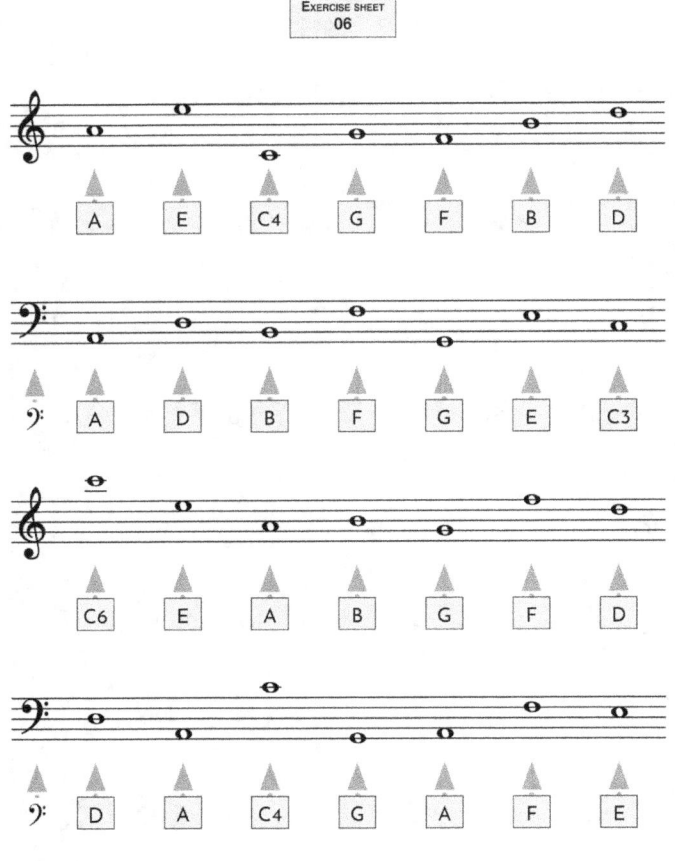

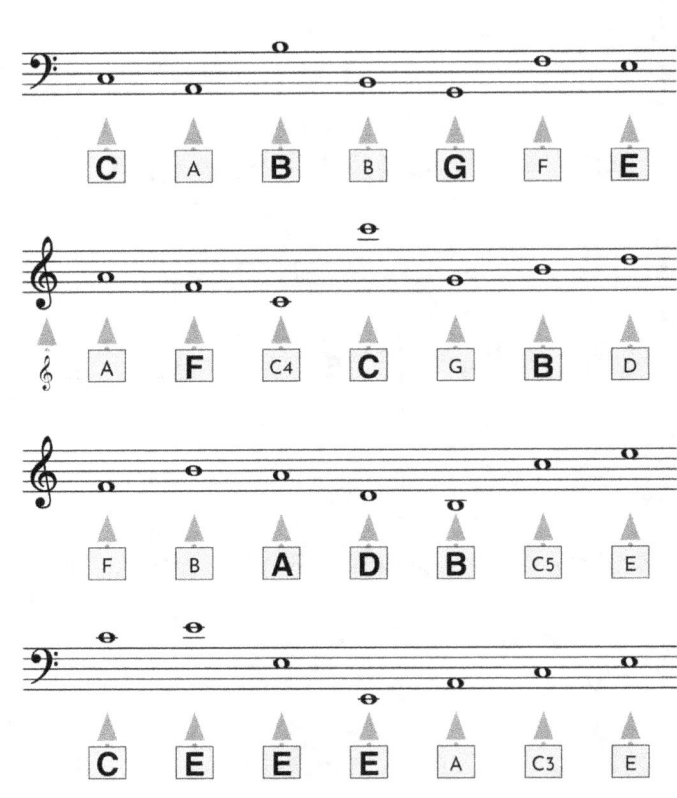

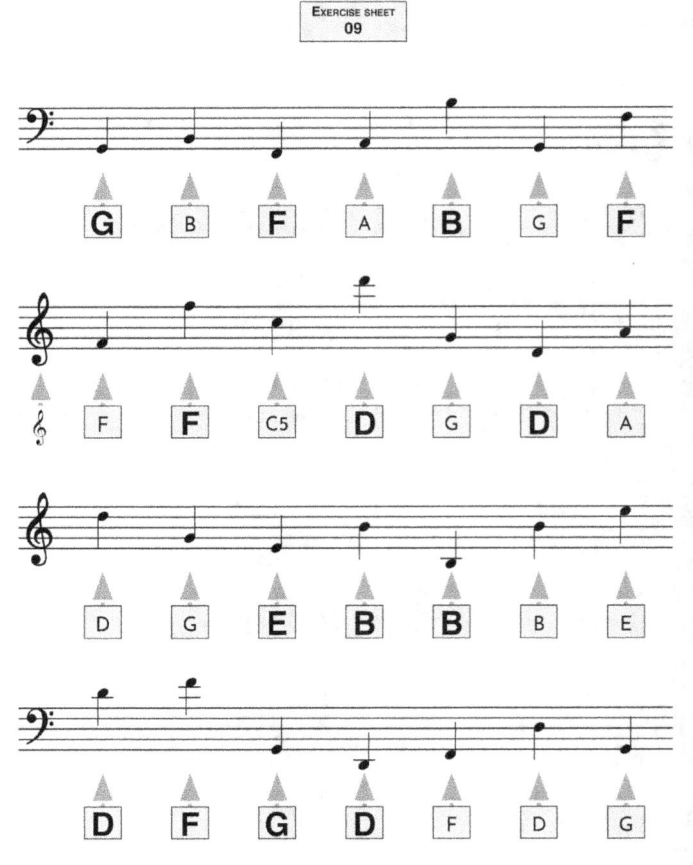

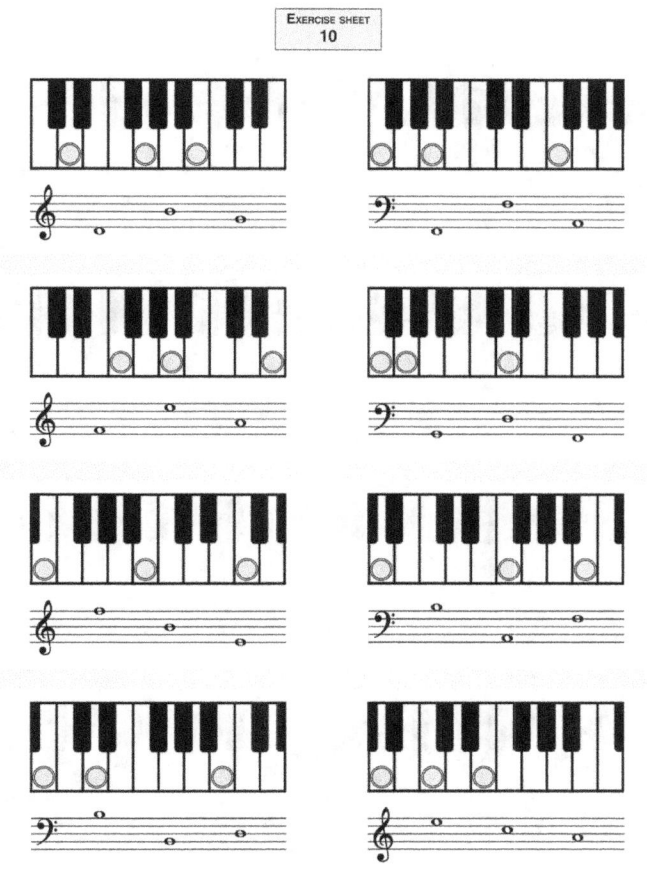

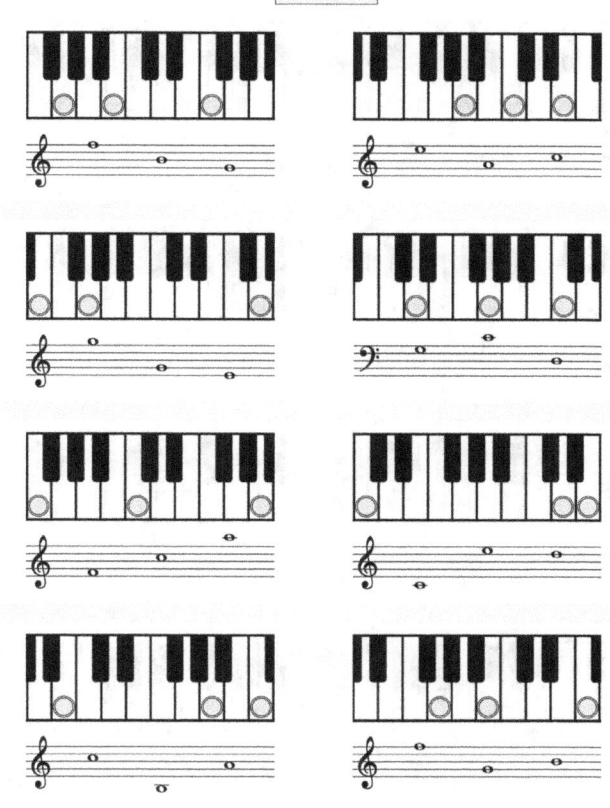

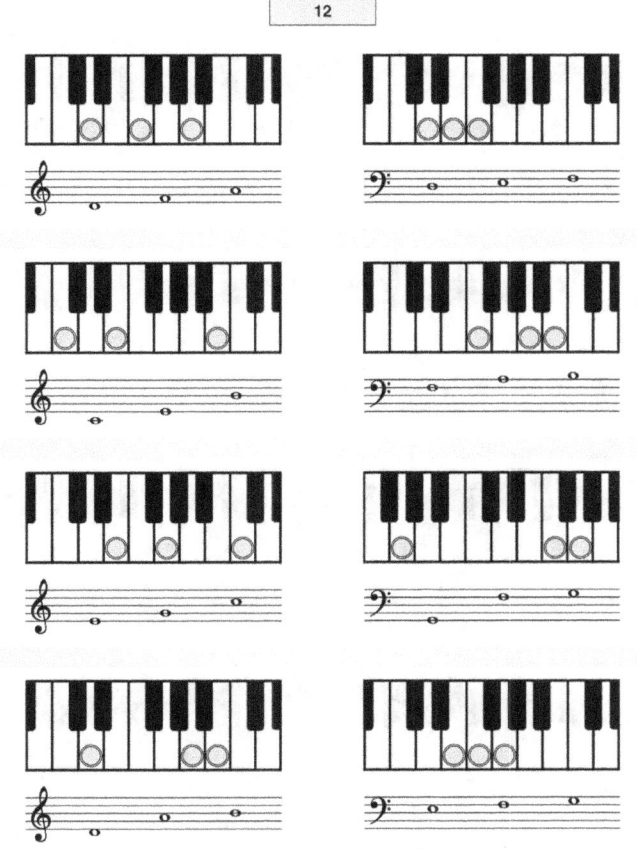

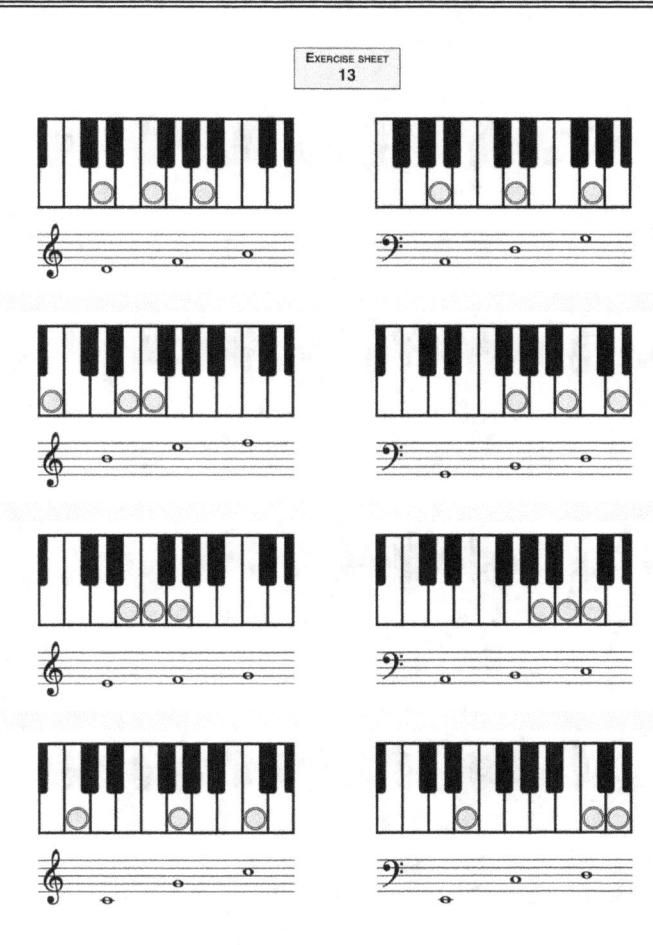

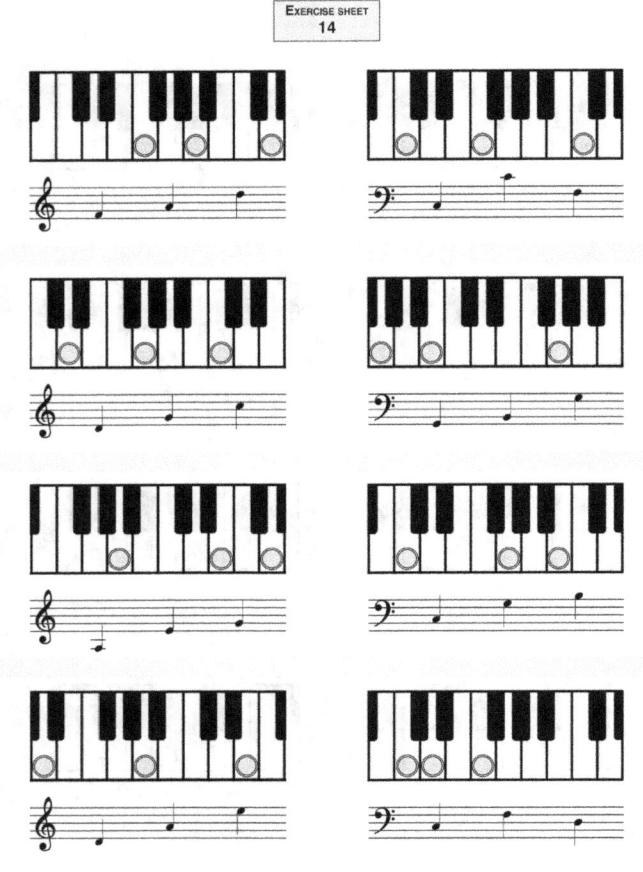

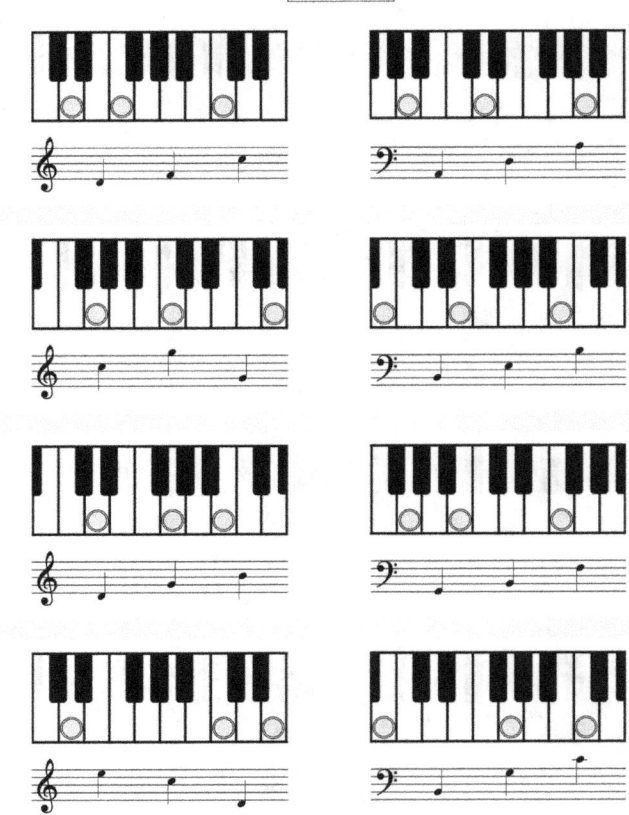

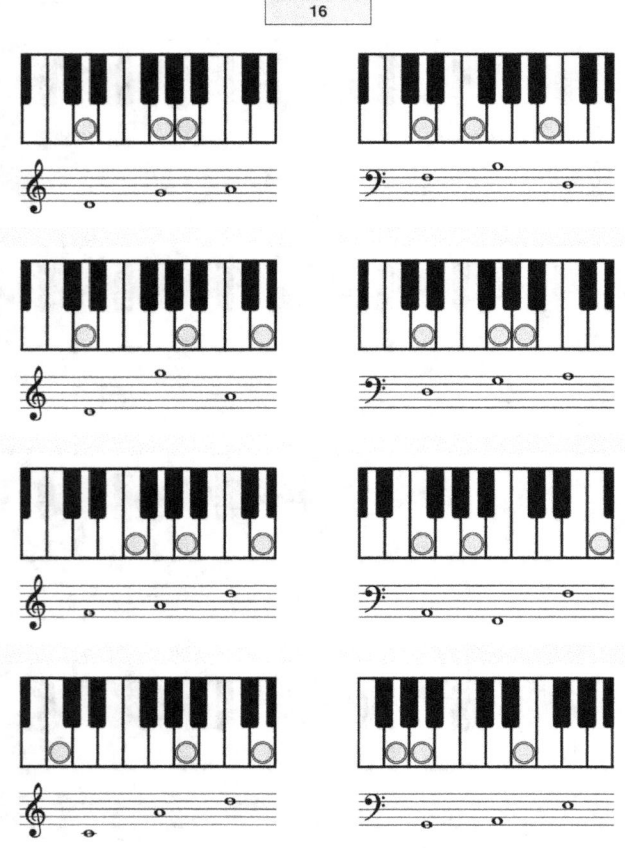

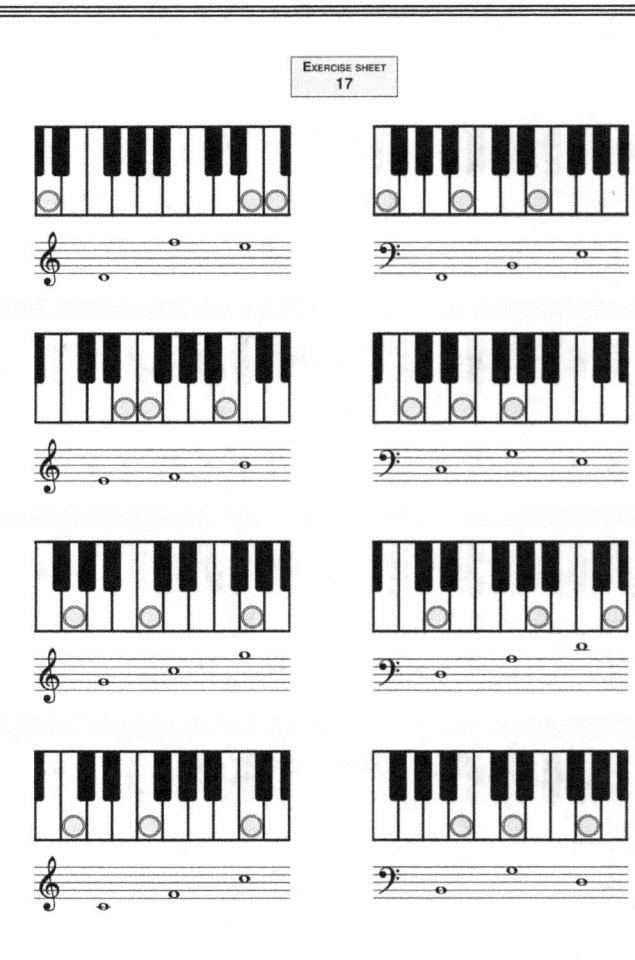

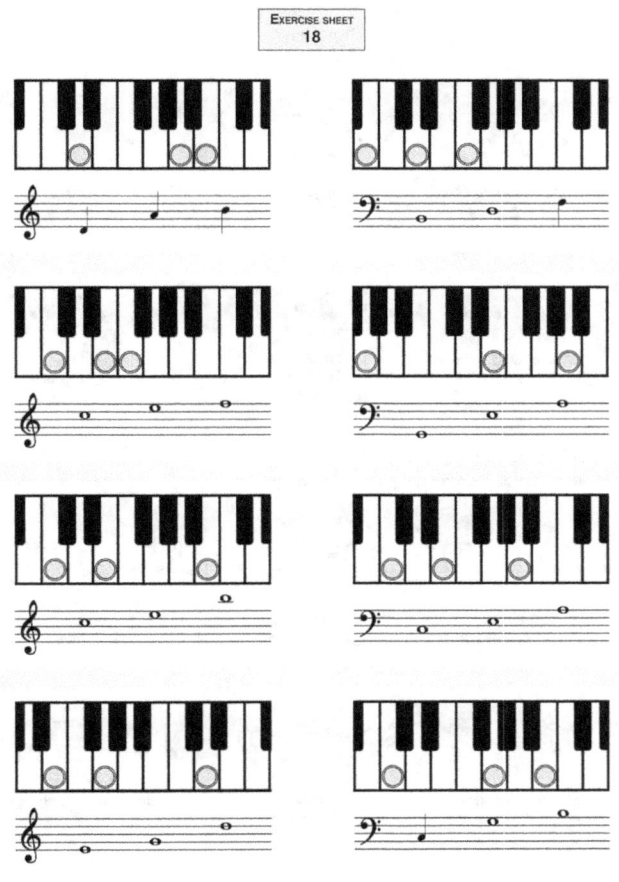

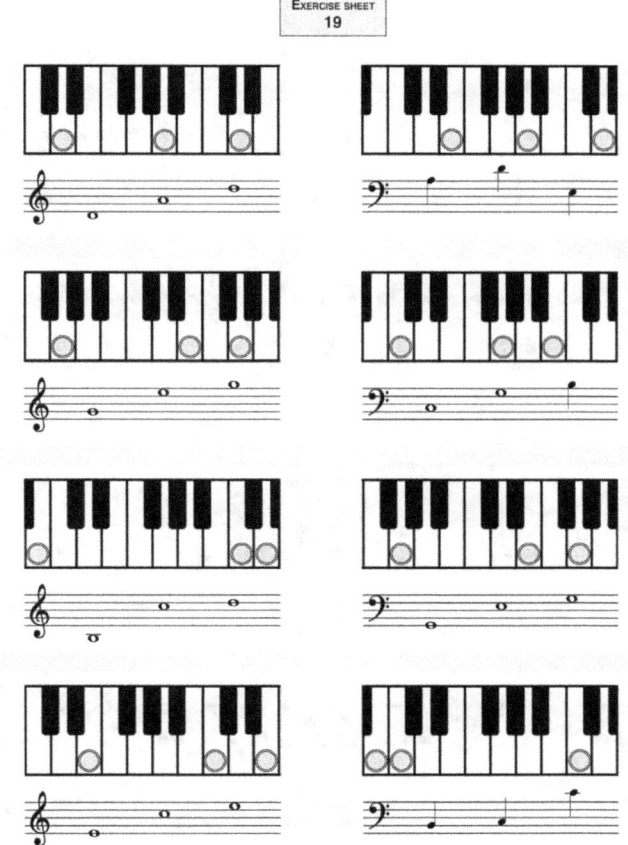

Example

Bar __1__   Bar __2__   Bar __3__

Bar __4__   Bar __5__   Bar __6__

Draw on the musical staff:
Eight **measures** / **Heavy bar line** in measure 8 / **Repeat sign** in measure 4 *(repeat first 4 measures)*

Example

Whole Rest   Half Rest   Quarter Rest

2 Eighth Rests   Start (Bar5)   End (Bar6)
                    Repeat Sign   Repeat Sign

Draw on the musical staff:
Six **Bars** / **A heavy double bar** in measure 6 / A **whole rest** in Bar 2,4,5

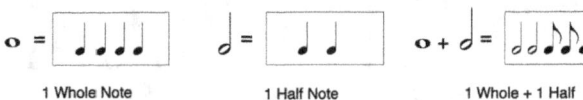

1 Whole Note	1 Half Note	1 Whole + 1 Half
= _4_ Quarter	= _2_ Quarter	= _2_ Half + _4_ Eighth

1 Whole Note	1 Half	2 Half
= _8_ Eighths	= 1 Quarter + _2_ Eighth	= 1 dotted Half + _1_ Quarter

Complete the diagrams:

Convert notes with beams into individual, **standalone notes**

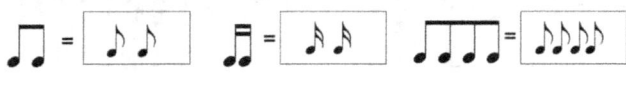

Beam	Beam	Beam
= _2_ Eighth Notes	= _2_ Sixteenth Notes	= _4_ Eighth Notes

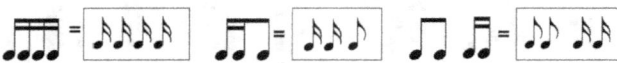

Beam	Beam	Beam
= _4_ Sixteenth Notes	= _2_ Sixteenth Notes + _1_ Eighth Note	= _2_ Eighth Notes + _2_ Sixteenth Notes

1 Quarter Note	1 dotted Half	1 dotted Whole
= _2_ Eighths	= _5_ Quarter	= _3_ Halfs

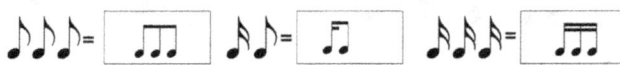

1 Whole with 2 dotts	1 Quarter with 2 dotts	1 Half + 1 Quarter
= _3_ Halfs + _1_ Quarter	= _3_ Eights + _1_ Sixteenth	= _6_ Eights

Complete the diagrams:

Connect the standalone notes into **beamed notes**

3 Eights	Sixteenth + Eighth	3 Sixteenth
= _1_ Beamed eight	= _2_ & _1_ beams	= _2_ beams

2 Eights + 1 Sixteenth	4 Thrity-second	2 Sixteenth + 1 Eighth
= _1_ & _2_ beams	= _3_ beams	= _2_ & _1_ & _2_ beams

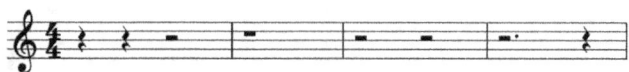

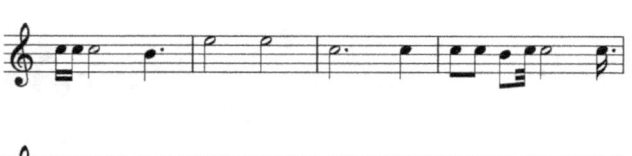

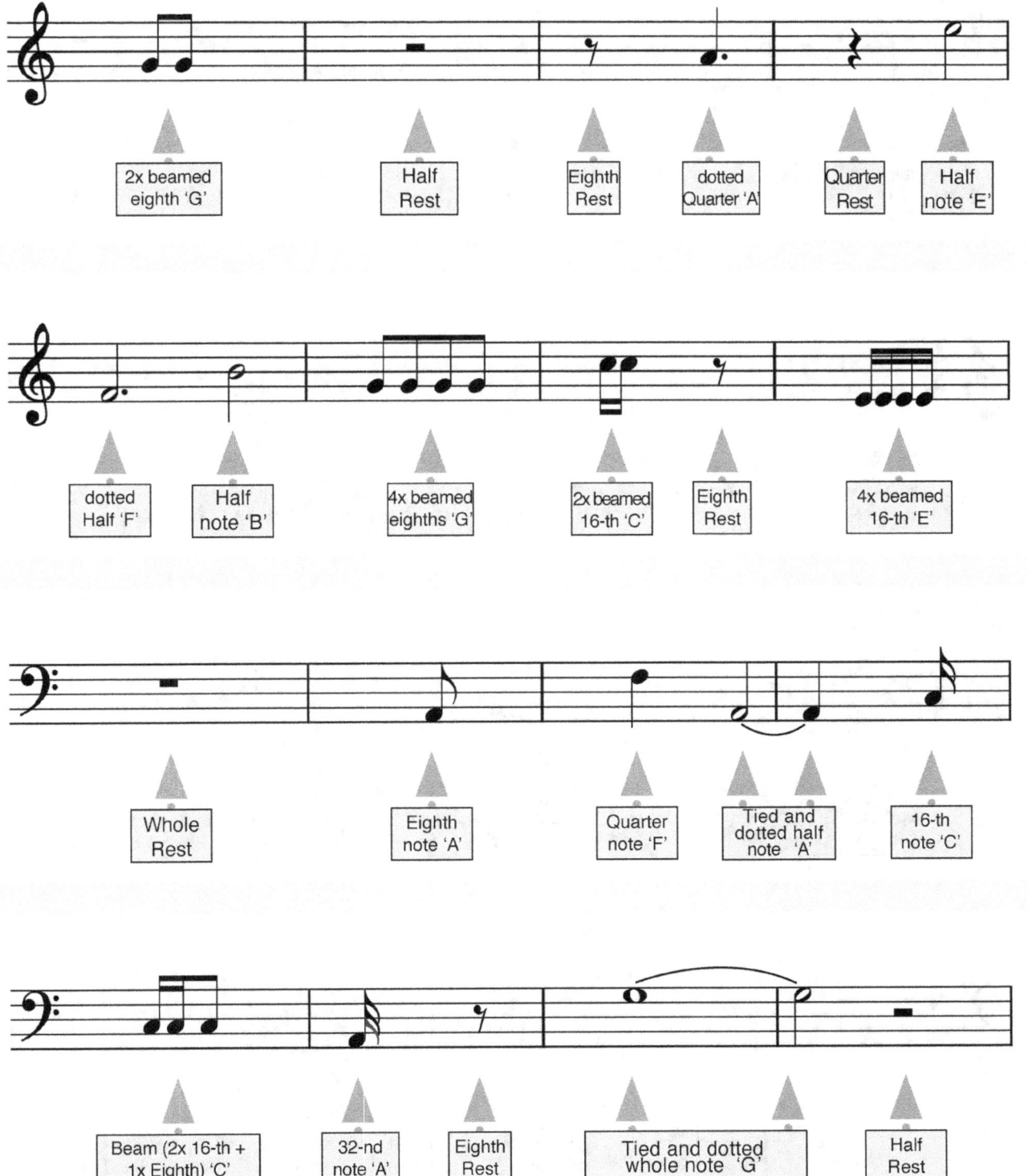

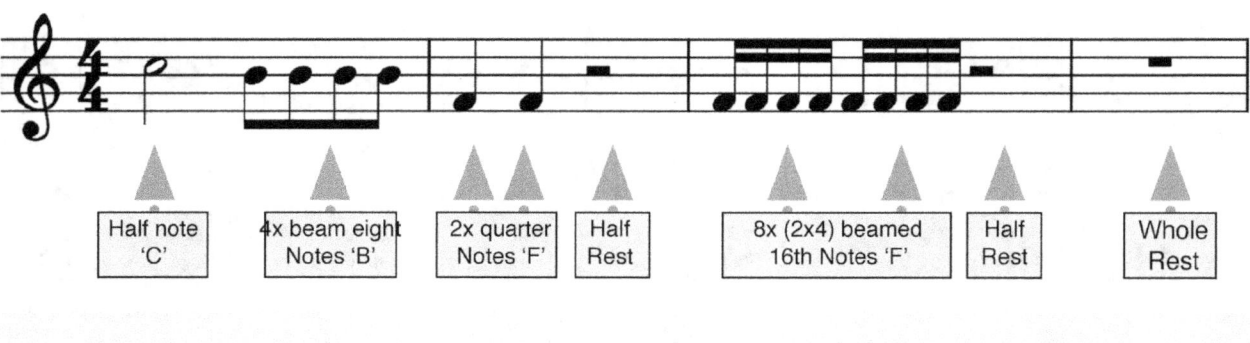

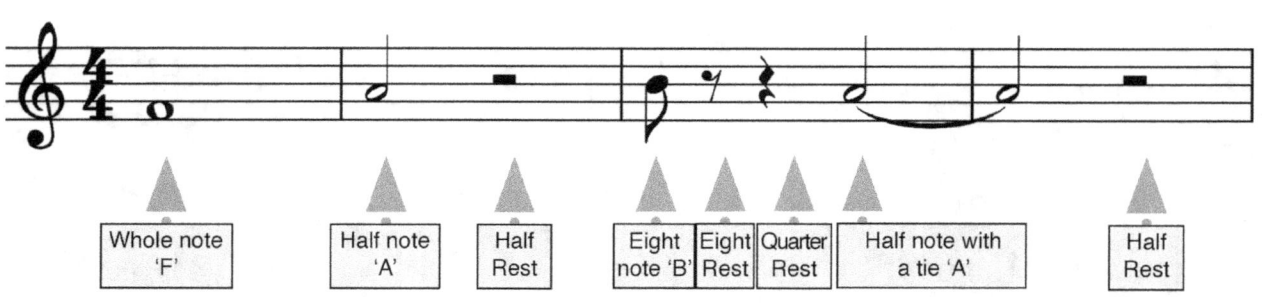

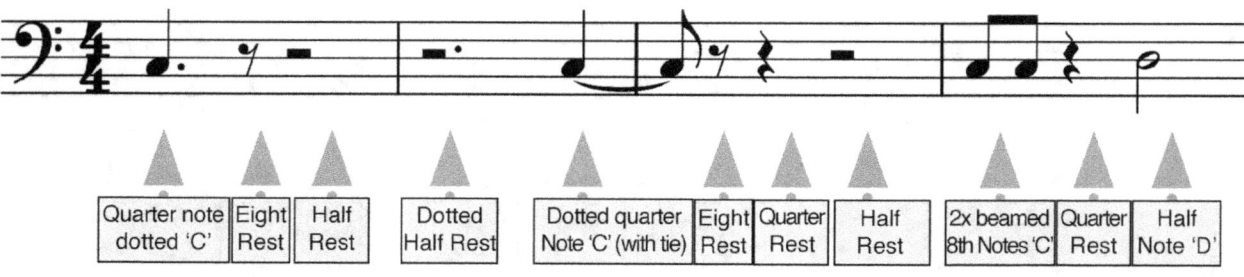

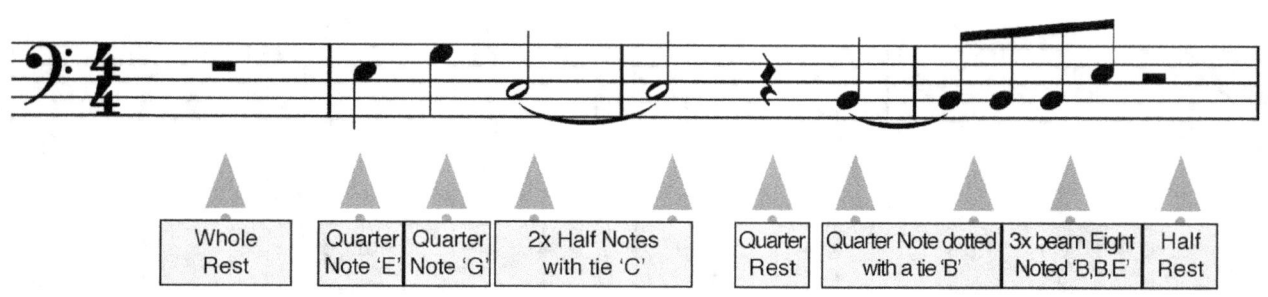

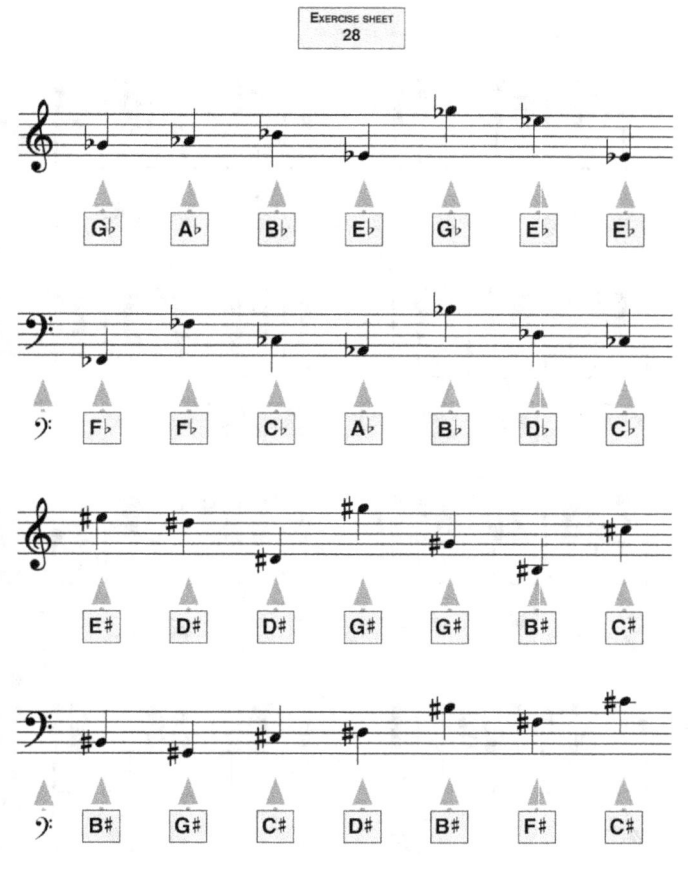

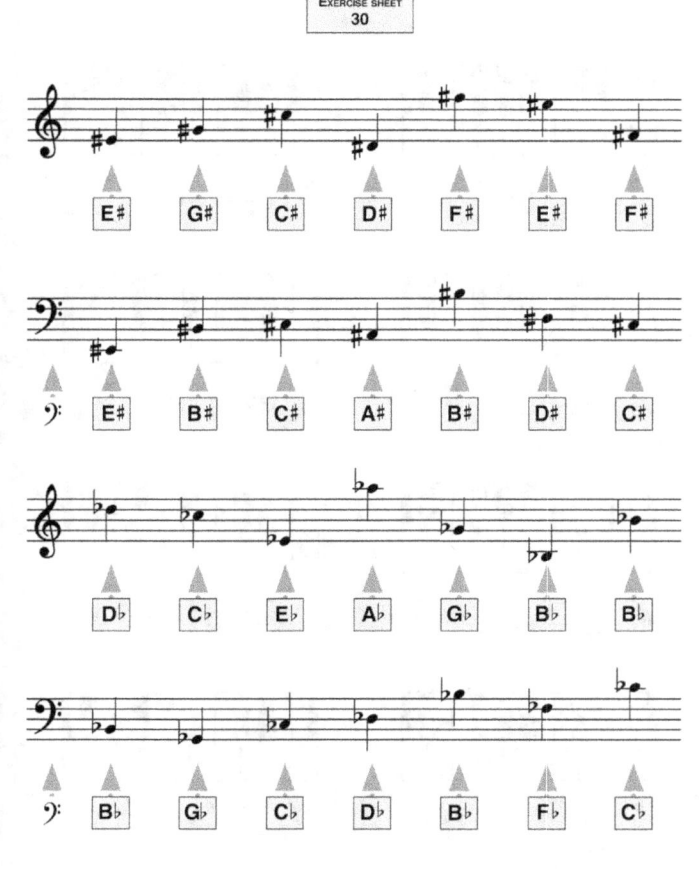

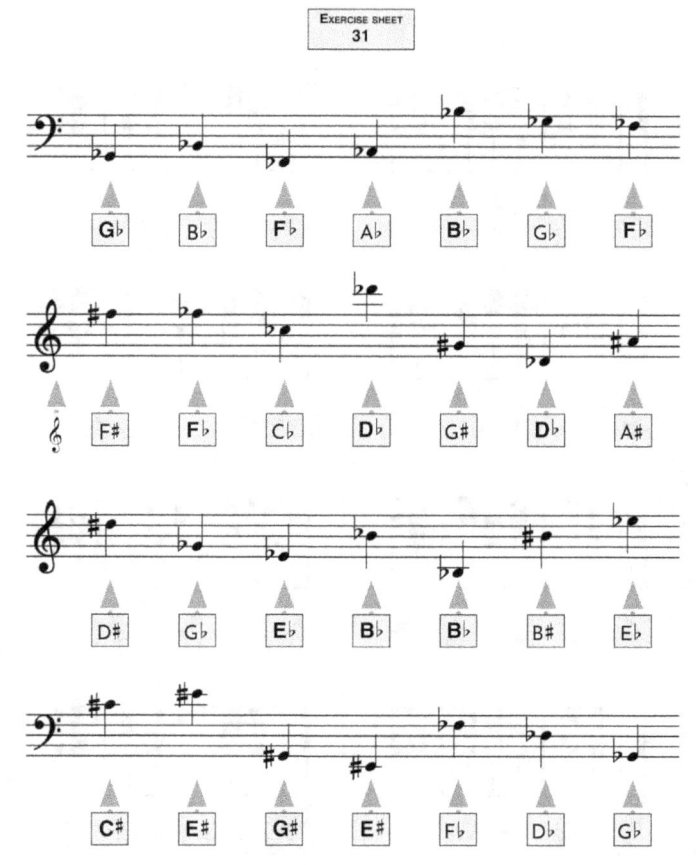

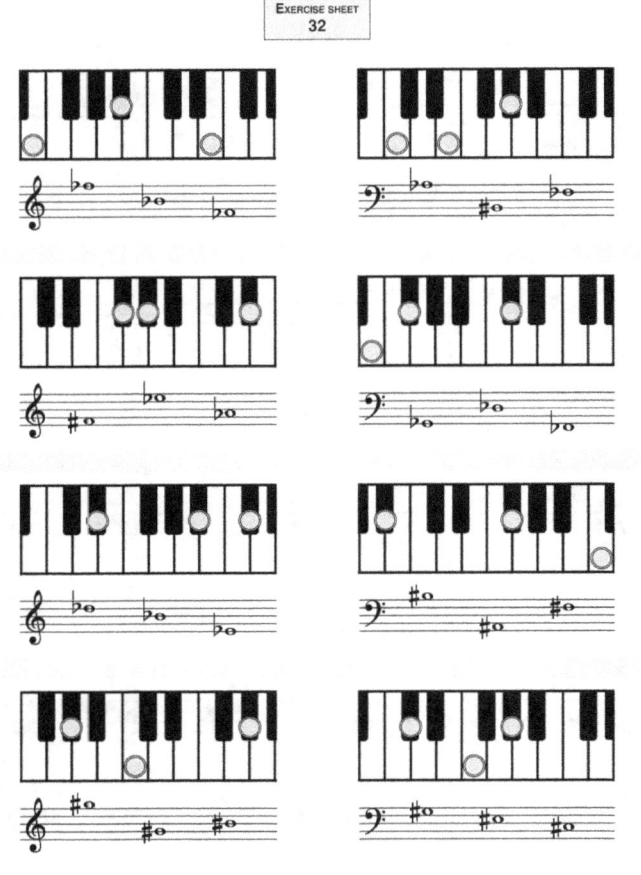

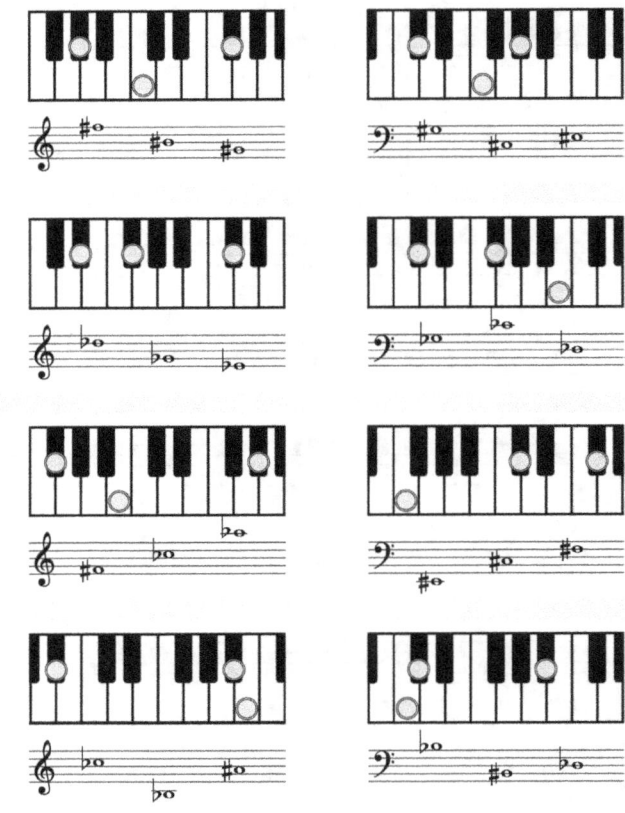

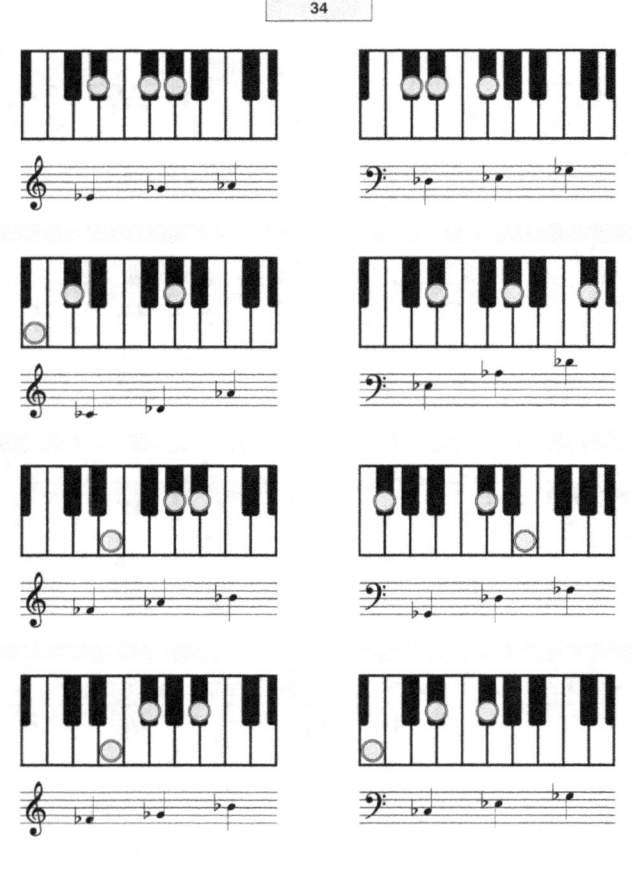

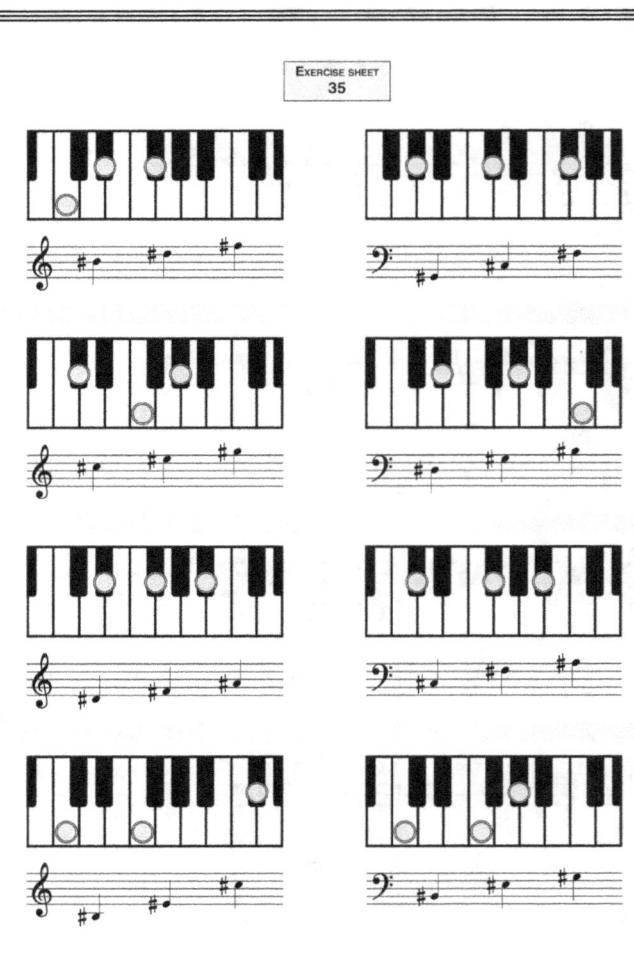

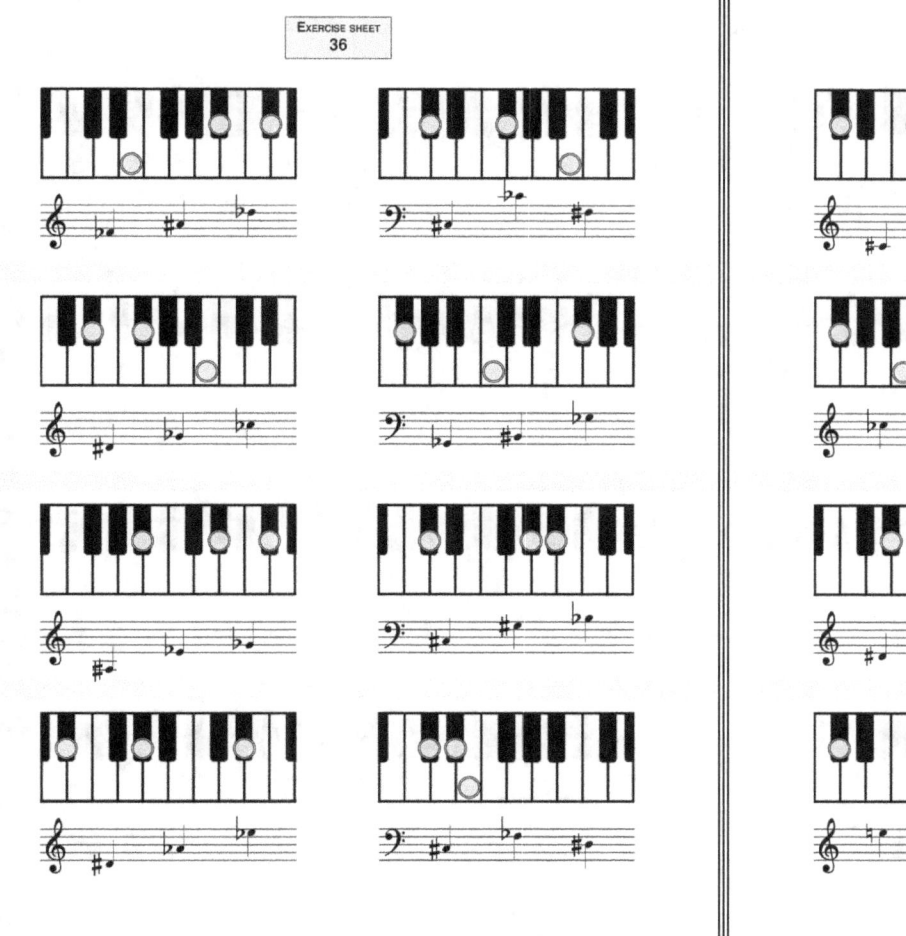

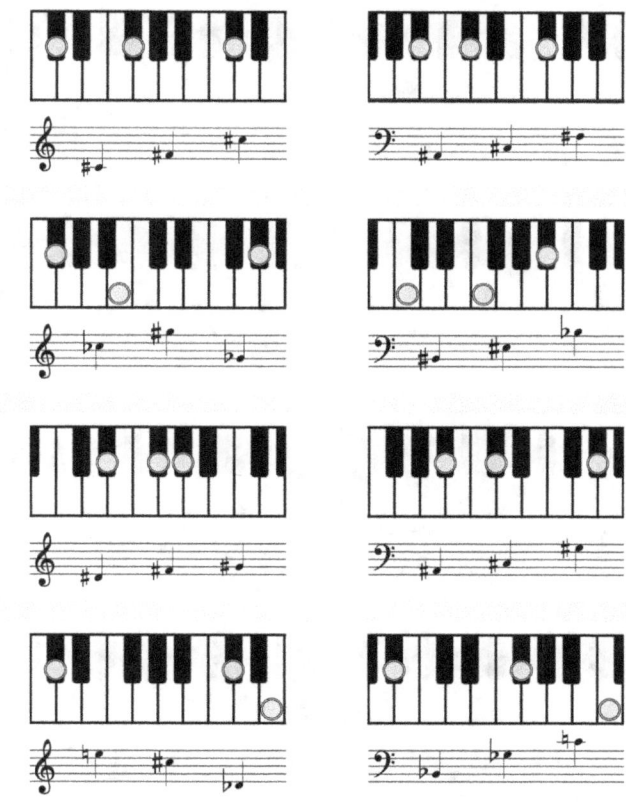

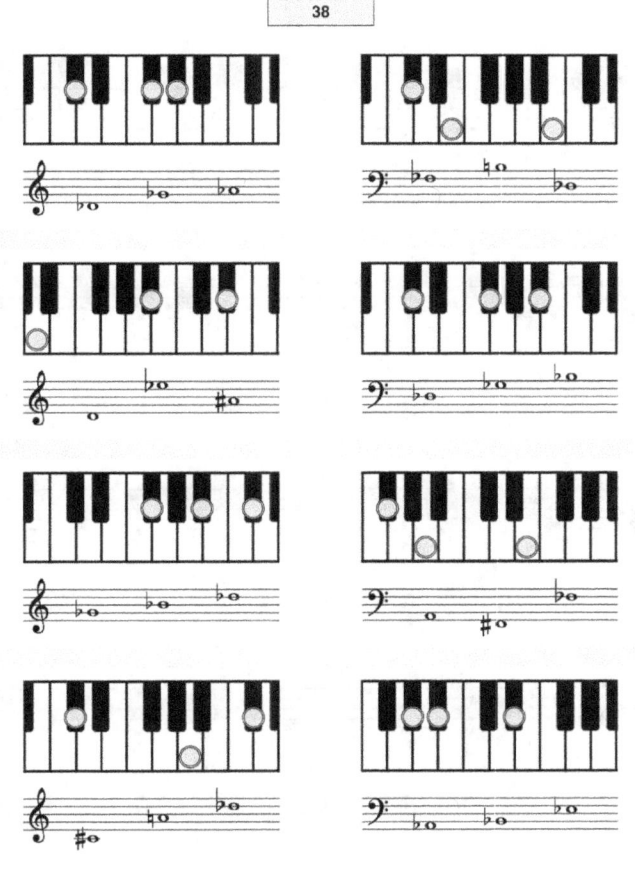

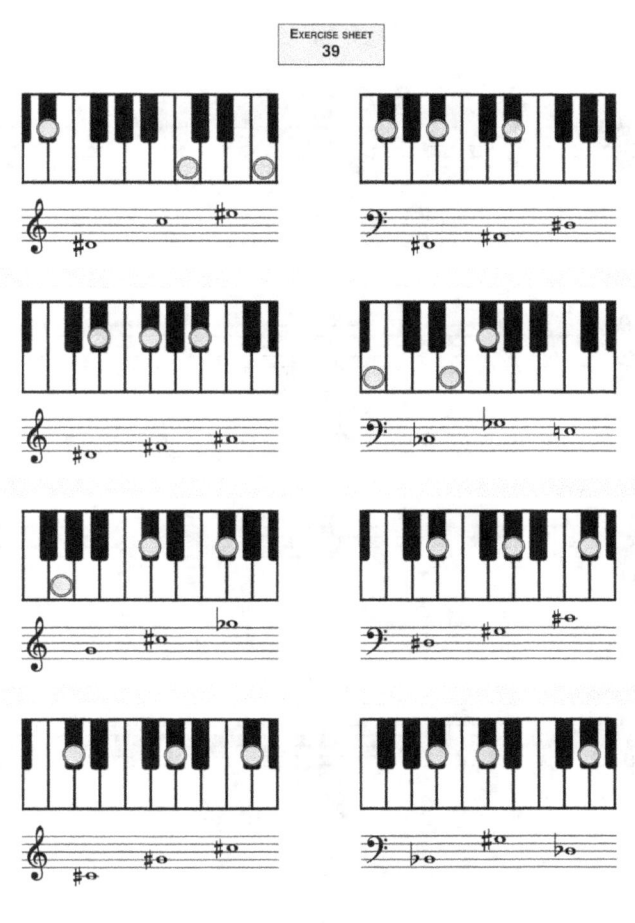

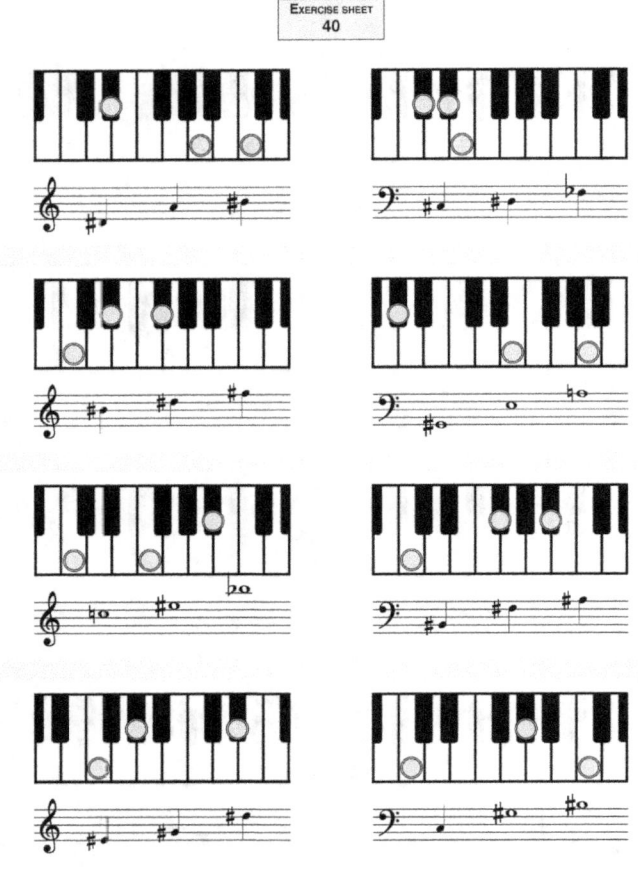

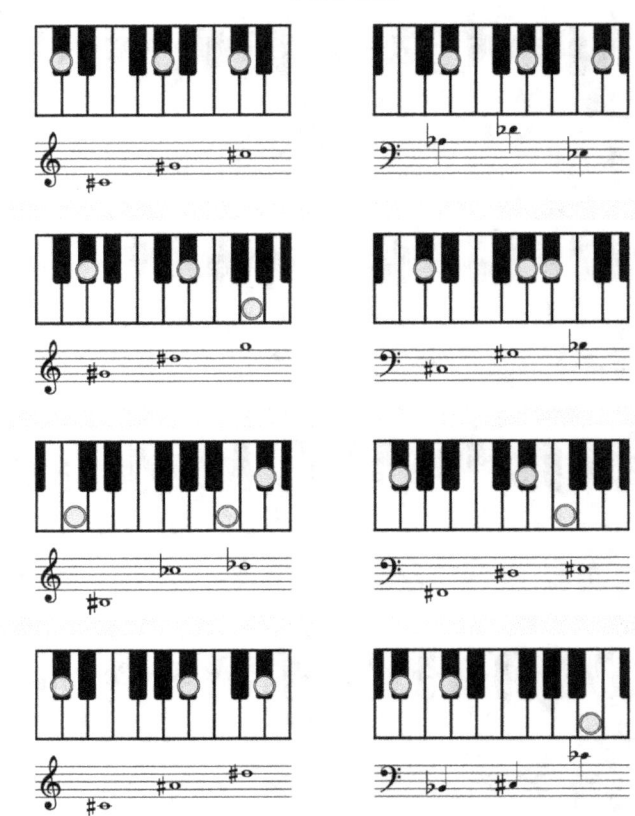

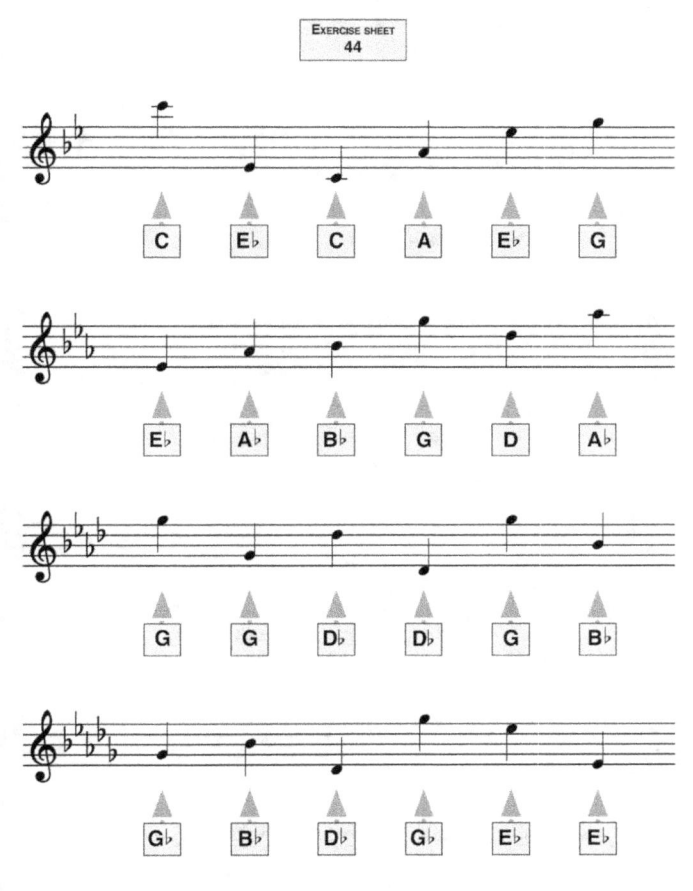

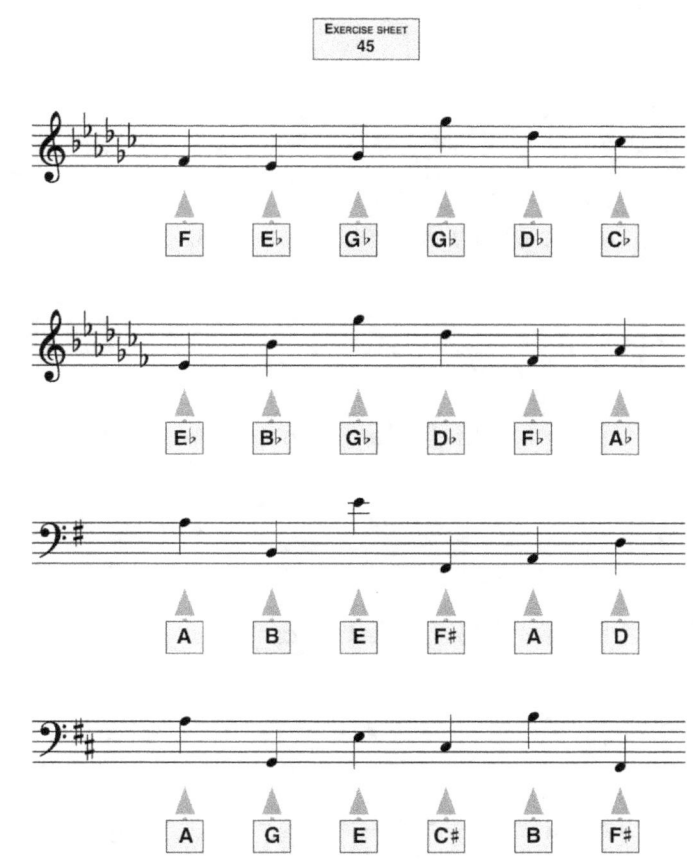

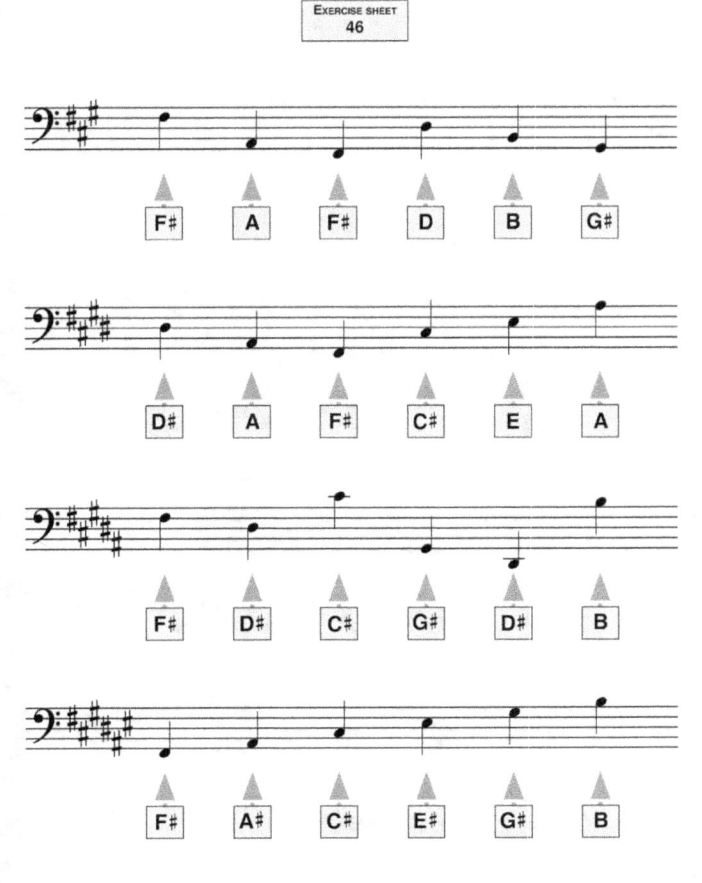

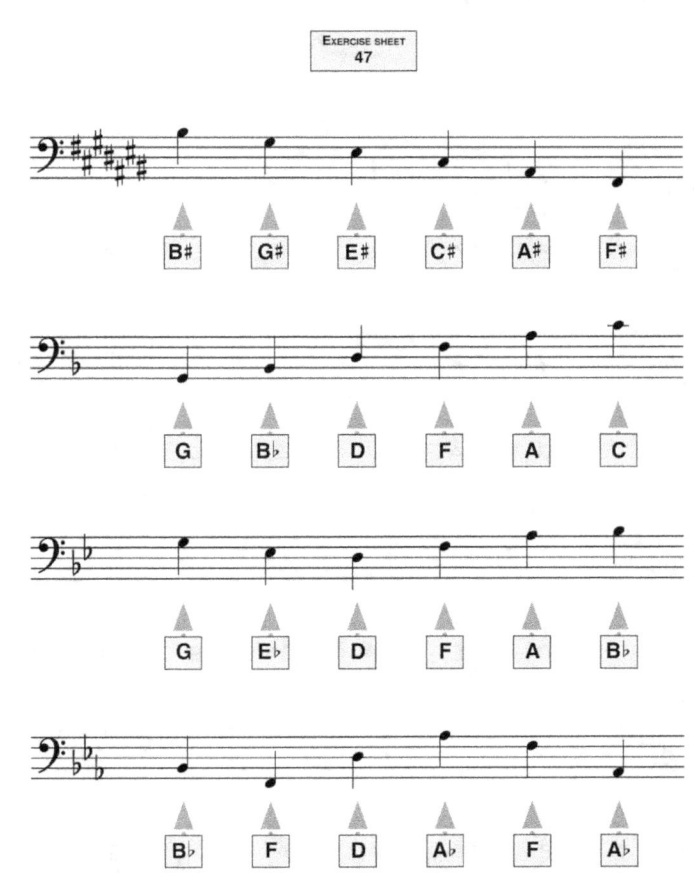

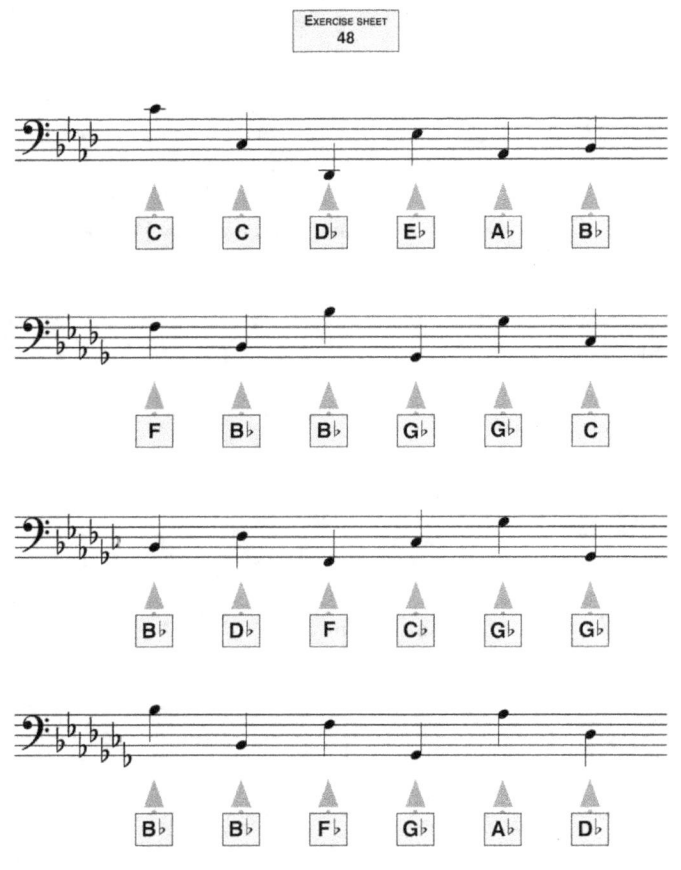

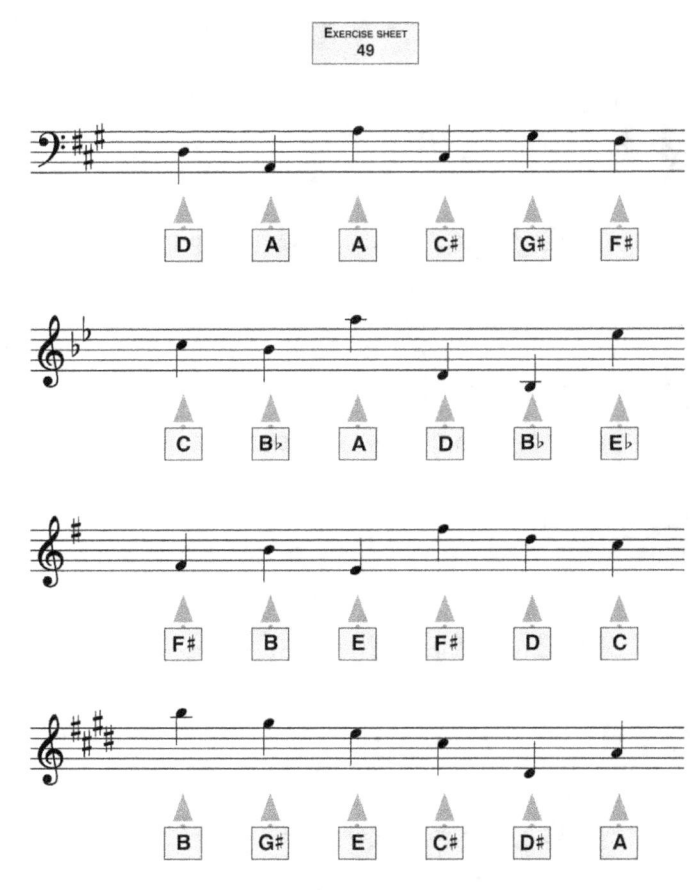

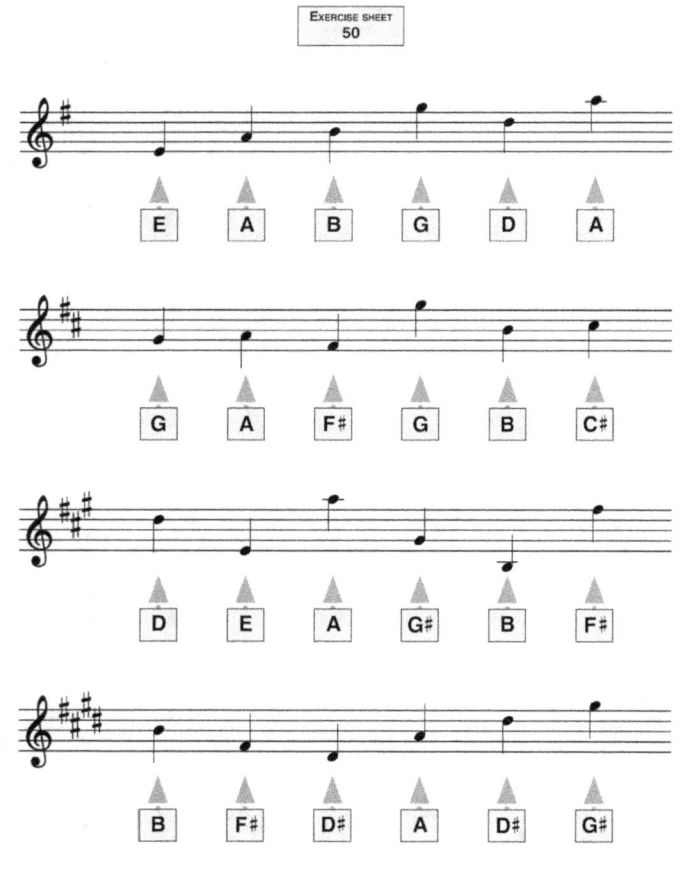

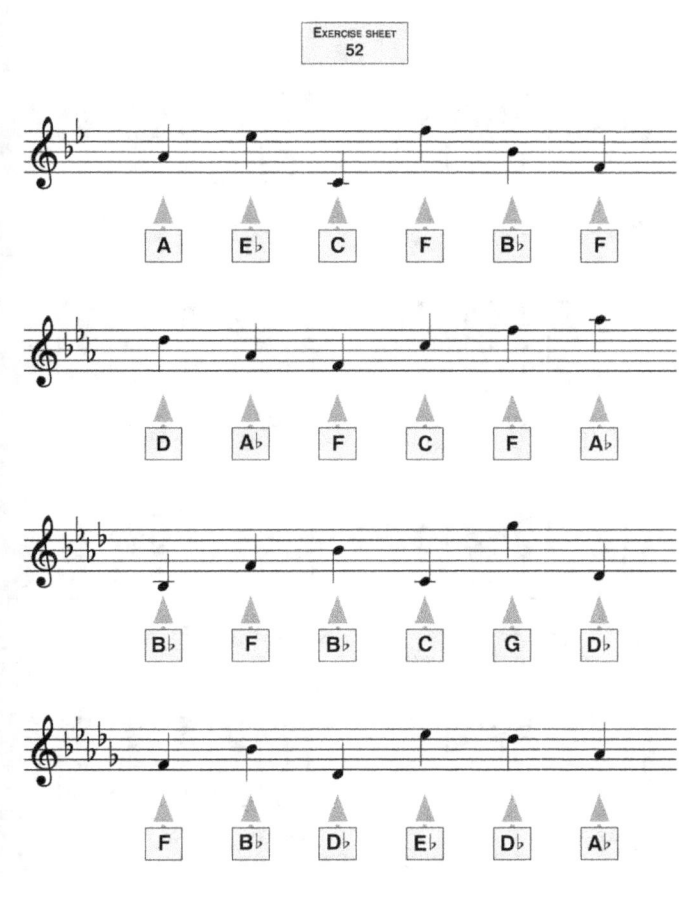

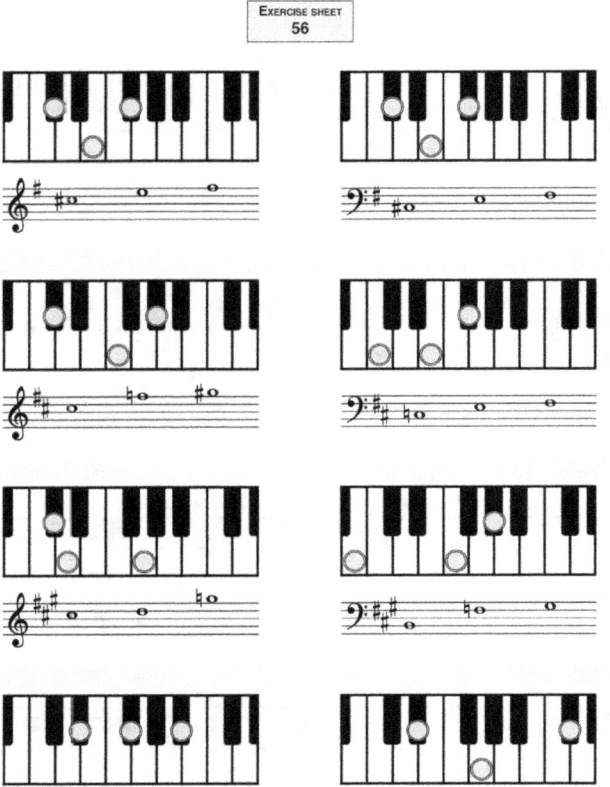

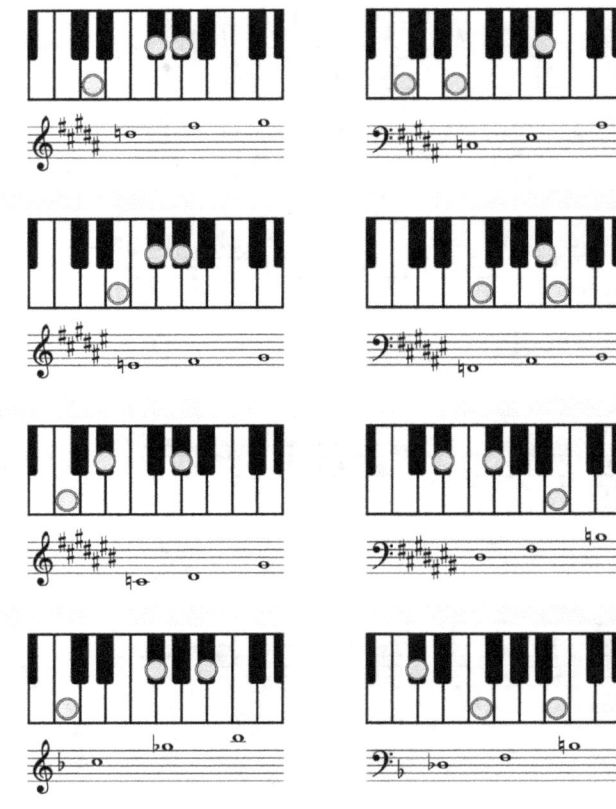

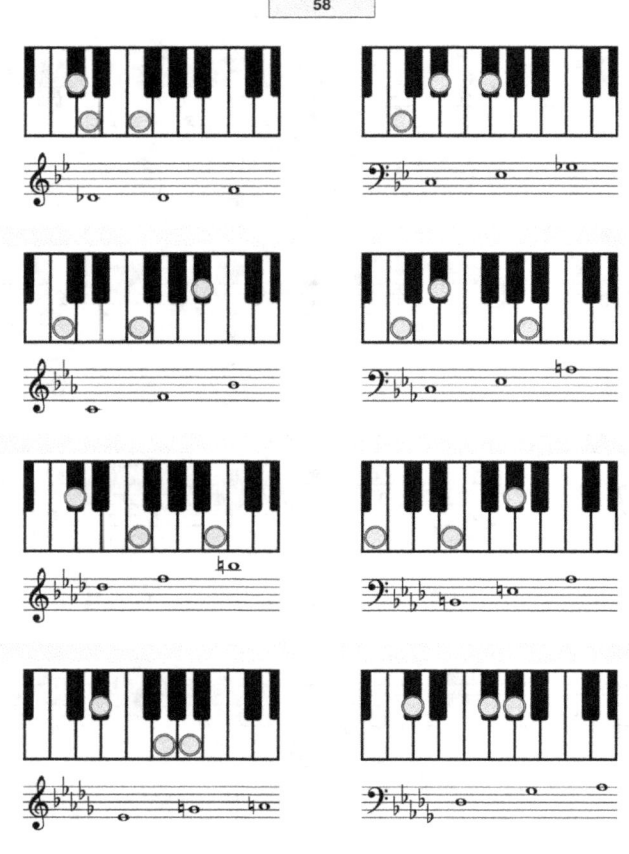

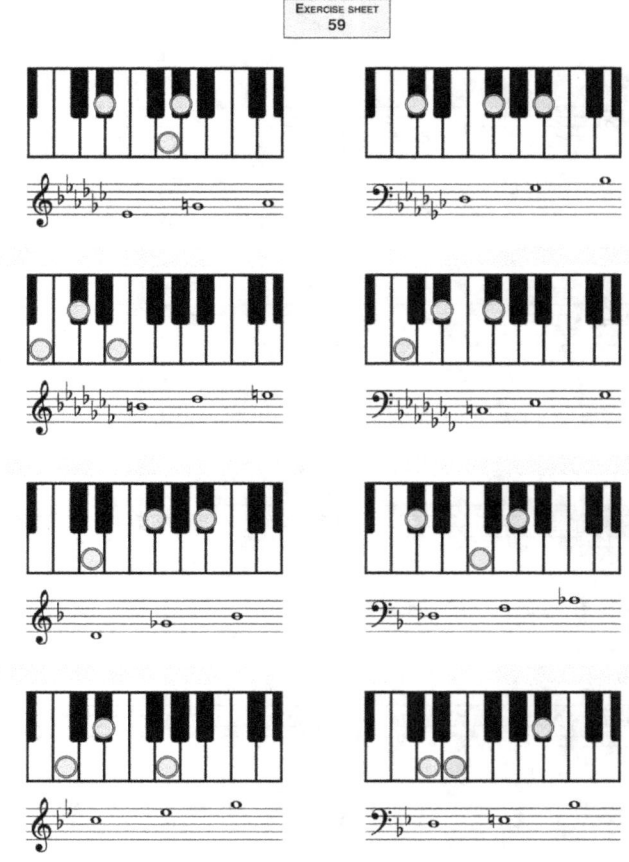

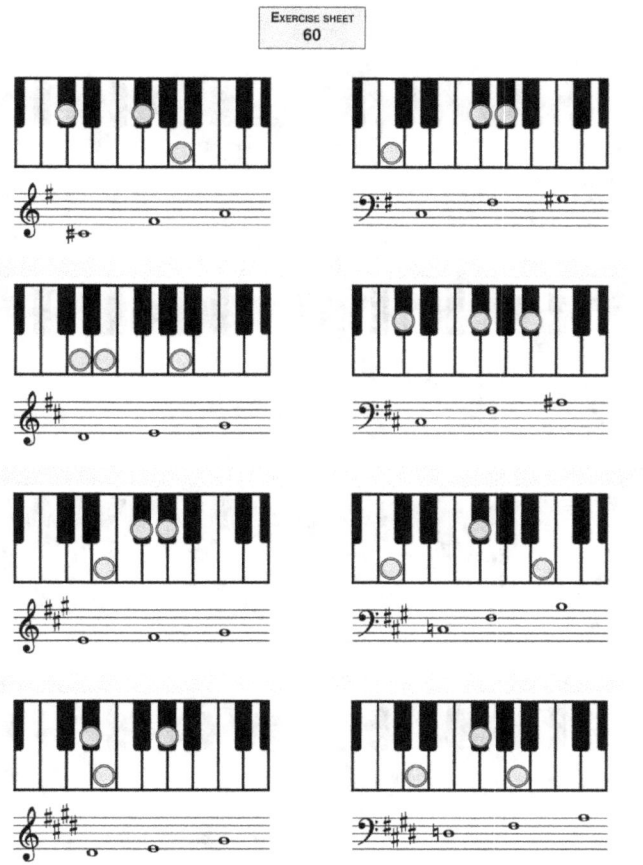

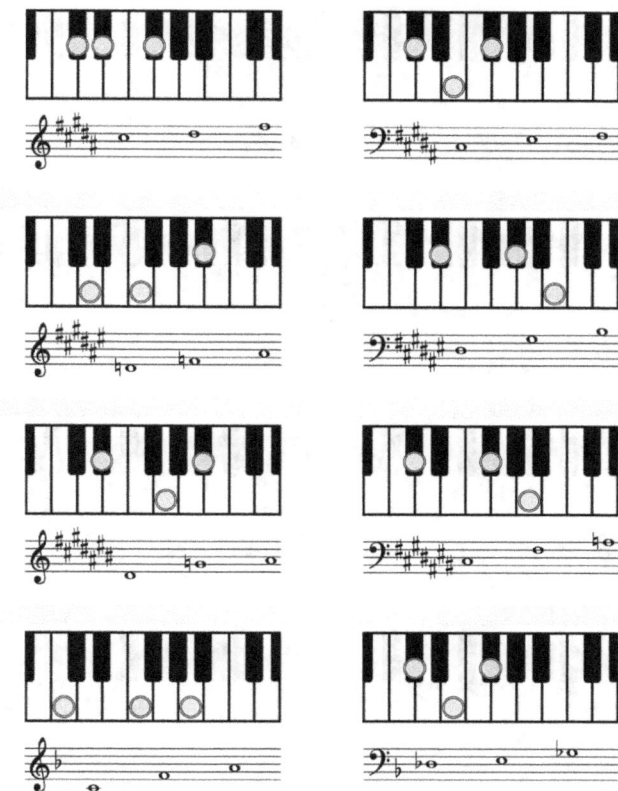

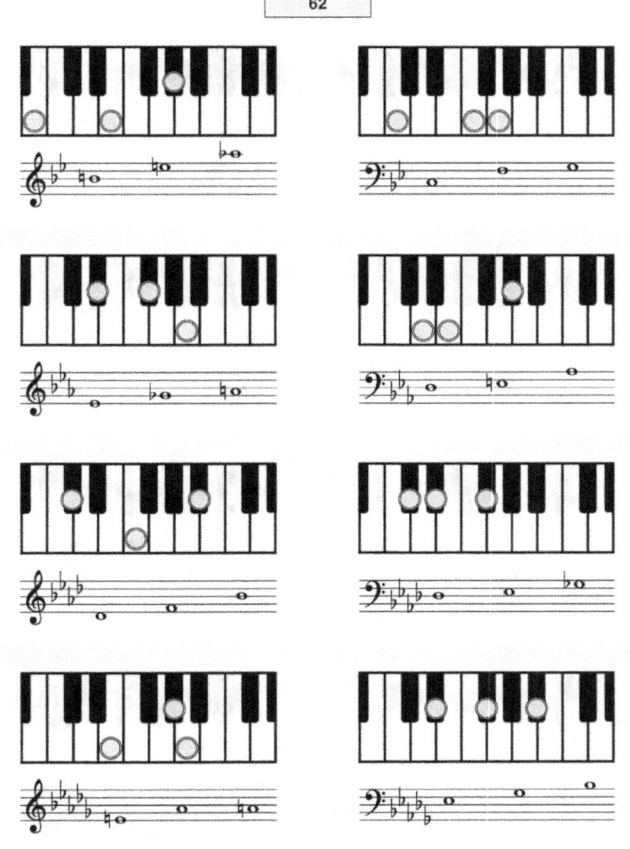

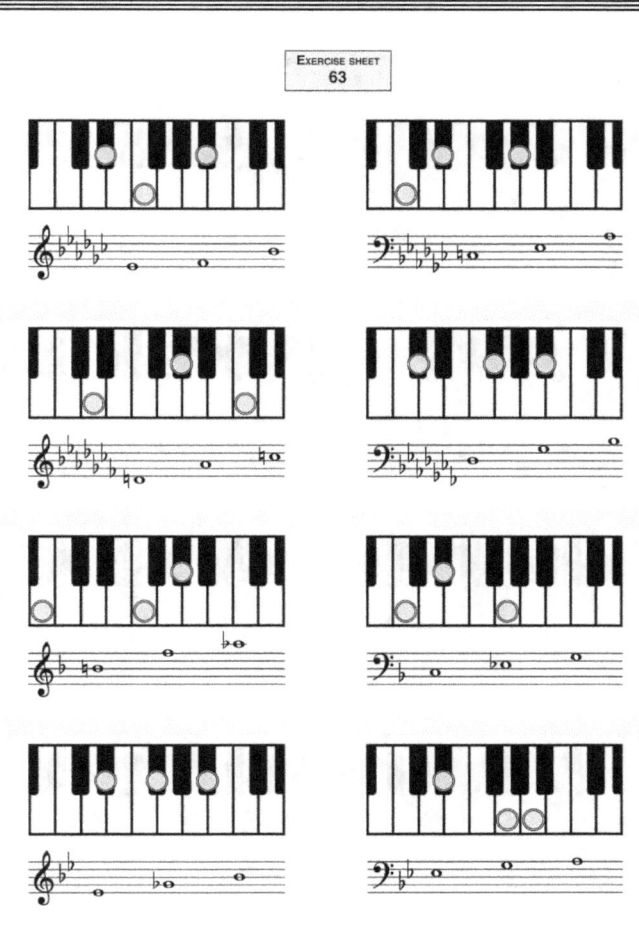

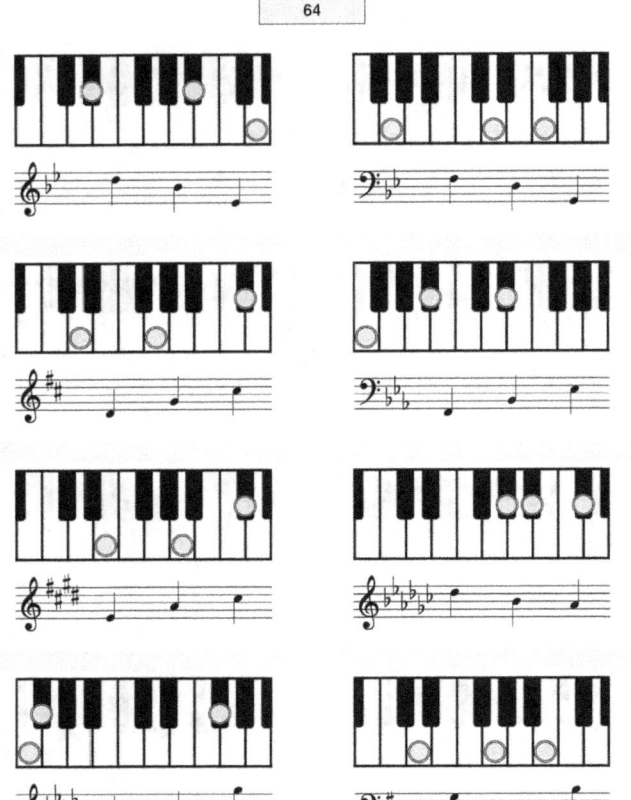

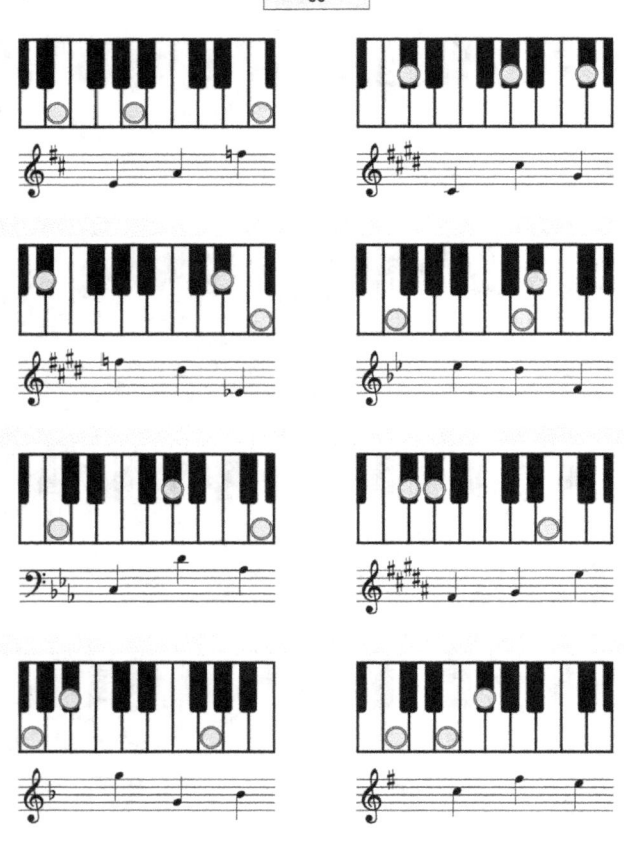

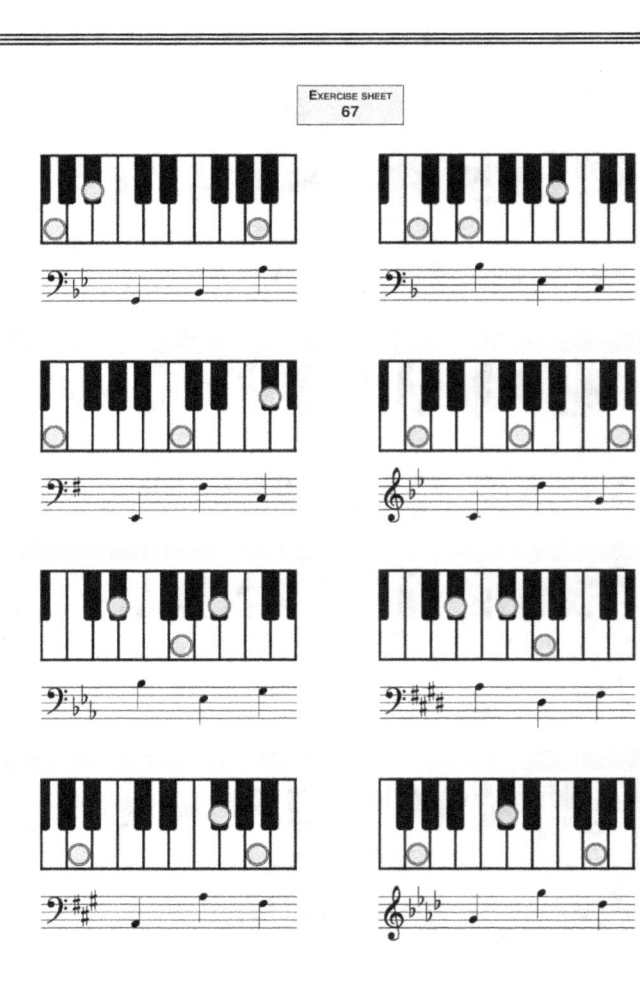

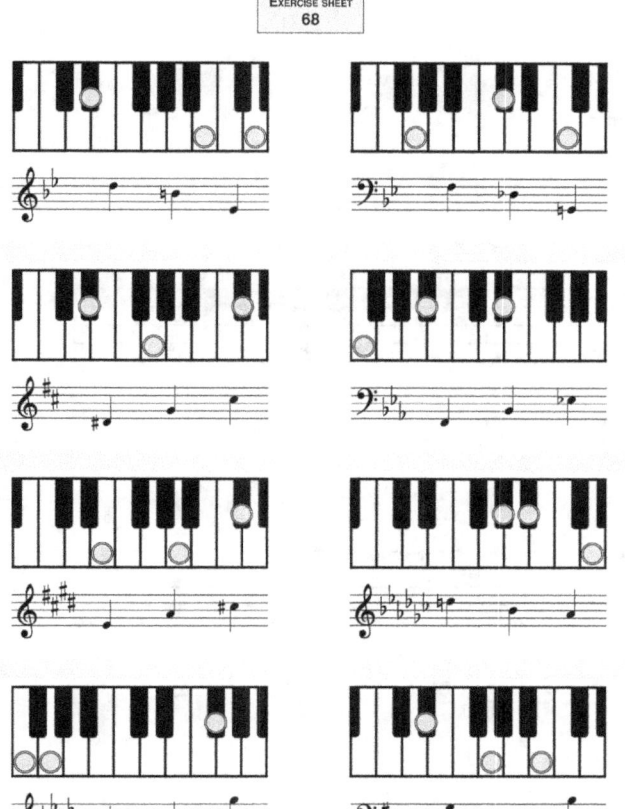

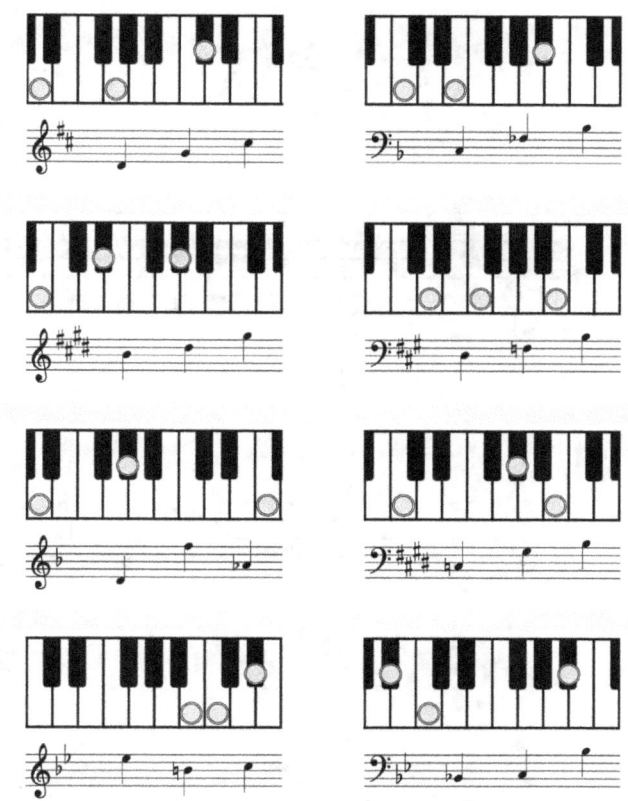

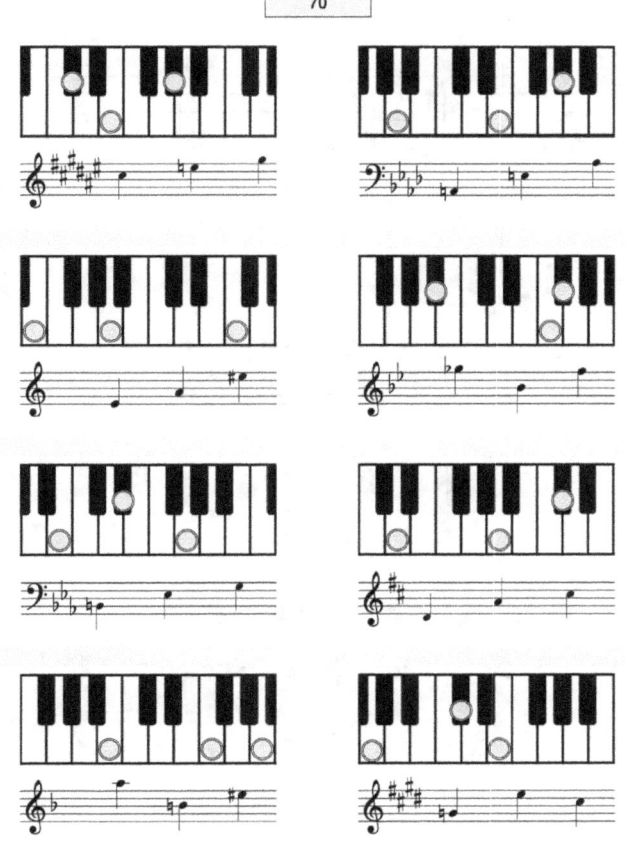

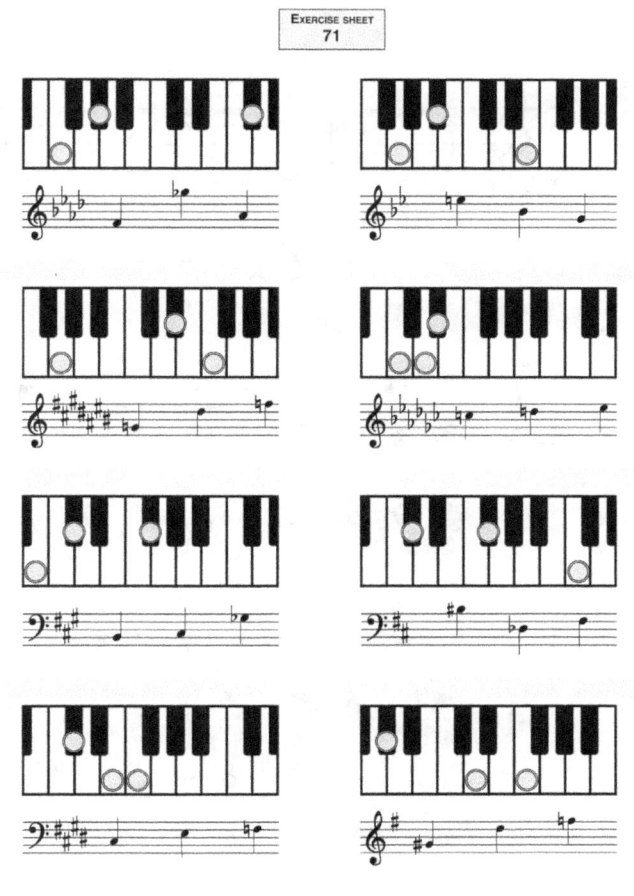

There are countless possible note combinations for any time signature. This is one of the aspects that makes music beautiful. Below are some examples. If you're unsure about your combinations, consult your music instructor for guidance.

Grand Staff

Congratulations!

I hope you have learned as much as possible and would greatly appreciate it if you could recommend this book to others.

Feedback on Amazon would also be very helpful. We use this to continuously improve our offerings and bring the world of music closer to you in the best possible way. Thank you!

To Download:

https://hermannpress.kit.com/944594f1fd

Thank you for using our educational materials!

At *Hermann Press*, we are committed to providing you with even more free learning aids and exercises.

Visit the link above or simply scan the QR code with your mobile phone to download your **free musical staves**. You can use the staves for your practice or print them out conveniently. Additionally, you will receive more helpful materials and exciting news directly to your inbox in the future.

If you have questions, suggestions for improvement, or any other concerns, please feel free to contact us at **hello@hermannpress.com**.

www.HermannPress.com

HERMANN
—PRESS—

www.ingramcontent.com/pod-product-compliance
Lightning Source LLC
Chambersburg PA
CBHW080752120626
46557CB00005B/1232